# AS I LAY PONDERING

### daily invitations to live

### *a transformed life*

## KAYCE STEVENS HUGHLETT

Virginia

*As I Lay Pondering*
© 2019 Kayce Stevens Hughlett. All rights reserved.

No part of this book may be reproduced in any form or by any means, electronic, mechanical, or digital (including photocopying and recording) except for the inclusion in a review, without written permission from the publisher.

First published in 2012 by Abeja Press
Seattle, WA 98107

Republished in 2019 by
WriteLife Publishing
(an imprint of Boutique of Quality Books Publishing, Inc.)

Printed in the United States of America
978-1-60808-216-2 (p)
978-1-60808-217-9 (e)
Library of Congress Control Number: 2019945971

Book design by Robin Krauss, www.bookformatters.com
Cover Design: Rebecca Lown, www.rebeccalowndesign.com
Editor: Olivia Swenson

*To follow your internal spark,*
*you must first acknowledge it is there.*

Kayce Stevens Hughlett

# An Invitation to Ponder

Capturing a spark and holding it in one's hand is virtually impossible from a logical point of view. However, if you choose to believe in a world that drifts spontaneously between vision and hope, it becomes not only possible, but also richly inevitable. For me, the publication of this book is the manifestation of my ultimate spark. It is witness to an innate tenacity to follow what began as a glimmer and grow it into something tangible and potentially heartwarming.

To pause and ponder is to consider something—anything—deeply, often through meditation and always with the possibility of bringing greater meaning. This book arose during a time of personal strife and grew to serve as witness to a life transformed. It honors the moments, great and small, I've experienced along the way. What originated as a series of journal entries has morphed into this daybook of poetry, prose, and personal musings. Have you ever known deep within your soul that you had to do something or your life would not be complete? The knowing is your spark communicating. The doing is your acknowledgment of the spark. *As I Lay Pondering* arose from that place of deep knowing. Compelled to write this volume as a witness to my ever-growing body of reflections, I offer it to you with the hope that it will add richness and awareness to your life.

At the point in my journey where I began writing, I had two choices: one, to let overwhelming events swallow me whole and conceal my spark forever, or two, to find my authentic voice by beginning to write. Writing chose me. Yes, you read that correctly, writing chose me.

While trying to find stable ground during this perplexing

period, I was given an assignment by a sagacious teacher. At his request, I was invited to find a quiet spot, be still, listen attentively, and simply record anything of note. Within moments of receiving this initial task, I found a quiet corner and the words began to inexplicably pour through me and out of me onto the paper. They flowed clear and strong like a torrent released when a dam breaks. I wrote and wrote as if guided by another force until I ultimately cried, "Enough!" while simultaneously witnessing my pen run out of ink. I had just recorded my first miracle. It was not to be the last.

What you hold in your hands is a culmination of this journey. I was compelled to write this book as acknowledgement of the internal spark I believe each of us carries. My hope is that the words shared in *As I Lay Pondering* will provide essential kindling to ignite the flame of your life. May you know the joy of following your own spark. May you be present to the life you have in order to experience the one you desire. May you pause and ponder thoughtfully and often.

— Kayce

Dedicated to my faithful four-legged companions,
Curry and Aslan

# Gentle Tips on How to Ponder

My hope is that *As I Lay Pondering* will become a trusted friend in your personal journey. Whether you're seeking a simple dose of daily inspiration, riding a crest of fulfillment, or floundering in a dark sea, it is designed to meet you where you are.

*As I Lay Pondering* isn't a chronological story. Each entry is a complete lesson, so you can begin reading at any point within the year. Since original publication in 2012, I've discovered there are several types of readers. There is the sequential reader who must begin on January 1 and read straight through the year. The intuitive reader likes to start by opening to a random page to see what shows up. The what-about-me reader starts with major event dates in his or her life (birthday, anniversary, etc.). Bottom line, *As I Lay Pondering* is flexible and meant to be used as you like! Read it once. Read it one hundred times. New awareness will show up each time you invite inspiration to join you.

Every entry has a brief story from the author's perspective and is followed by an invitation to step into your own experience. You may find deep resonance or disagree with different passages. Either understanding is great as long as you are thinking about what is meaningful for you. Activities at the end of each entry vary in length and are loosely categorized for frame of reference (e.g., Meditation, Journal Meditation, Visualization, and Action).

There is no right or wrong way to engage with this book. The thoughts shared come from this author's perspective with the invitation to ponder how the words apply to your life (or don't). *As I Lay Pondering* is a companion you can turn to anytime you need a dose of inspiration or motivation. It's the perfect alternative to scanning social media and my hope is that you'll feel inspired after spending ten minutes each day pondering. It's a small investment to make in living a better life.

# January 1

# Bienvenue. Hola. Welcome.

As a sojourner in life, I have traveled far and returned home time and again. Along the way, I have tamed dragons, met enchanting people, crossed moats and mountains, dipped my toes in foreign seas, traversed mazes of language and maps, dined on exquisite foods and wine, and been greeted by exotic beings and many mortal creatures. I have stepped into worlds of fantasy and been mesmerized and moved by simplicity and silence. My path has wound through limitless alleyways. My feet have blistered and burned. I have sipped champagne, nibbled on market food, been toasted by locals, and eaten alone. I have strolled along the Seine, hiked the peaks of Mt. Sinai, and logged countless miles through my local Seattle streets.

My body has been cramped into a coach compartment seat, as well as wrapped beneath a cozy first-class blanket. I have stayed in five-star hotels, slept in mosquito-infested crannies, and luxuriated under the magnificence of stars. My body has rocked and rolled in a train sleeper while crossing borders through the night. My passport has acquired new stamps and more than a few languages have been exquisitely mangled by my earnest efforts.

As we enter a new year, I acknowledge my life is rich and full, tender and tempestuous, miraculous and mundane. There is no magic spell and no destination other than *now*. At the risk of being trite, I firmly attest that home is where the heart is, and every twinkling in life deserves its due acknowledgement.

*Visualization and Meditation*

Close your eyes and imagine the coming year as a hero's journey. What challenges, dreams, and adventures lie on your path? Breathe deeply and envision yourself as the conquering hero(ine). Allow the feeling of triumph and freedom to permeate your body. Make a conviction to carry that feeling with you daily.

# BE LIKE WATER FLOWING

For several years, at the dawn of the new year, I've chosen a word to accompany me for the months ahead. In 2010, the word was water. The year began with solo winter walks along the shore not far from my house and drew to a close while I nestled into a friend's seaside cabin with my beloved husband. Water greeted me with her fluid mystery and manifested in ways I could never have imagined. A winter vacation included first-time surfing lessons and a mesmerizing encounter with a sea turtle. I learned throughout the year to "go with the flow," and as the year sailed to a close, having rushed by like a flash flood, I found myself grateful for the seas I had traveled.

There is an old tale of a man who has the choice between a map and a boat to accompany him on his journey. Choosing the boat, the man's wise teacher offers these words: "You are the boat. Life is the sea." I've always loved those words, because wherever we find our center (our boat), we have the ability to go with the flow, weather the storms, and enjoy the immensity of life. My boat carried me well during the year of water. I patched it when necessary and provided a new coat of paint or two to spiff things up, always remembering the importance of caring for my vessel and appreciating the sailor's life.

*Visualization*

Picture yourself as a boat. Breathing fully, allow yourself to move with water's flow. Immerse yourself in the imagery as you imagine being held and carried by the sea.

# Pondering

Waking up at the beginning of the new year, we shake our heads and wonder how we got here. Time flies by and we forget how to slow down and listen. Holiday excitement pushes aside daily contemplation and restoration.

Somewhere after the first of the year, I begin to look for that small window where rest comes more easily and attention turns toward inner and outer murmurs. I look for the space where I am drawn to sunlight dancing across the winter landscape. I tune into the wind rustling through barren branches. I hear the whir of the heater alongside the call of a lone crow. I find myself in sync with the voices of my loved ones, and life becomes a veritable symphony in creation. Blank pages of my journal await my thoughts and musings. Ponderings of what lies ahead await their place on the blank canvas. Many motions or metaphorical strokes may feel repetitive, but each day will be fresh. There can be no other exactly like it. Every moment is its own the instant it happens.

*Journal Meditation*

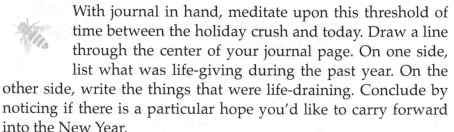

With journal in hand, meditate upon this threshold of time between the holiday crush and today. Draw a line through the center of your journal page. On one side, list what was life-giving during the past year. On the other side, write the things that were life-draining. Conclude by noticing if there is a particular hope you'd like to carry forward into the New Year.

# Thirty Spokes

> "Thirty spokes join one hub."
> —*Tao Te Ching*

Today I must write gently, lovingly, and with ease. Allure wants to flow across the page. The wings of a thousand angels float through the sky disguised as clouds of cotton and the majestic olive-colored mountain beckons to be seen. I desire to capture this space and hold it gently without must's or should's. There is only now.

Loveliness and lightness of being flow through me and around me, raising eyes toward the sky and lifting arms and hearts to heaven. Resounding heartbeats pound as one. Moving bodies choreograph a dance for this perfect moment, never done before and never to be repeated. Thirty spokes create a wheel filled with love and light, the air in between as important as the container of friendship and solidity.

Today I must write about love, loveliness, hope, and ease. Moving toward tomorrow. Living only for today.

*Artistic Meditation*

 Draw a simple bicycle wheel on a piece of paper. Name each spoke after something you see or feel right now. Express gratitude for each of these spokes.

# JANUARY 5

# TRAILHEAD

"Sought through prayer and meditation to improve our
conscious contact with God as we understood Him, praying
only for knowledge of His will for us and the power
to carry that out."
—*Alcoholics Anonymous, Eleventh Step*

Pondering often leads me down a trail marked, "When did this all begin?" "This" can be anything. Life. Creation. Relationship. Career. Anything. When people ask me how long I've been writing, one trailhead always comes to mind: the day I got out of my own way and acknowledged listening to the Universe. Unbeknownst to me, my true calling had started aligning and coming into focus.

Participating in an introduction course to Twelve Step work, our instructor essentially asked us to meditate on command when we got to the Eleventh Step. "Yeah, right," my internal cynic grumbled. I couldn't imagine solemnly quieting in such a brief period of time. But being the obedient student, I decided to at least go through the motions of jotting down any thoughts that came forward during this quiet time.

From the moment I sat down, the words began to flow onto the page in near prophetic style. I wrote and listened and listened and cried. My heart quaked and I followed. The tumblers began to click into place as I wrote and wrote until finally my pen ran out of ink. I tried to ignore what was happening, and then the internal prompt came again.

*Share this. Share it with the group.*

"No way," my scared self shuddered. The next thing I knew, I was standing in front of a group of near strangers in a shabby hotel in Mexico, reading what I had penned. People listened with rapt attention as I passionately choked out the words that brought tears and connection throughout the room. I imagine this is what some might call an out-of-body experience.

When I finished, a new friend (who is now an old friend) inquired, "How long have you been a writer?" Never having considered myself in this light, my instinctual response was, "I don't write." Little did I know I was standing at the trailhead of a wondrous new adventure.

*Journal Meditation*

 With journal nearby, quietly center yourself and begin to follow your breath. As thoughts arise, jot them down as the trail leads. If you have difficulty free flowing, begin with a prompt such as "This all began when . . ."

## JANUARY 6

# DON'T SHY DOWN

Stepping out of old patterns begins from the inside. Early in my life, someone other than myself declared me shy. It's taken years to know and believe that I always have everything I need to be fully me. All I have to do is acknowledge it, first to myself, and then to others (if that's what's necessary). I need to speak. To be heard. To be witnessed. I must listen to myself and ask moment by moment, what is it I need? And if the answer comes out demanding a bigger audience, a louder voice, or more space in the room, I have the choice to make it happen. I get to decide when my desire has been met. Then, and only then, can I declare myself satisfied. Only I can discern what "satisfaction" is for me, and if I shy away and remain silent, then no one (especially me) will ever know what I need.

Standing alone one still dark night, I practiced listening and turning my insides out. On this evening, my rising desire was to have my written word spoken and heard. With tentative boldness, I asked one friend if she would listen, and she asked another, and soon the gathering burgeoned to an audience of a dozen. The miracle swelled as I cleared a young girl's throat and stepped into a grown woman's voice. I read. They witnessed. Together we laughed, cried, and applauded. They met me where I was as I offered them a map toward my deepest desires.

One crystal night, I stood on the edge and tenderly listened. I offered my voice within and without. I didn't shy down and tears transformed to joy. The night danced with magic. The shy girl healed a misplaced wound as she risked stepping from the inside out.

*Journal Meditation*

With journal close, consider these two questions: 1) What would it look like to turn your insides out? 2) What does your heart demand yet you keep hidden?

Begin by writing these dreams and demands in your own private journal. Name them for yourself, then pick one item off this list and share it with another person today.

# CLEAR THE WINDSHIELD

Under ideal circumstances, my morning meditation leads to setting an intention for the day. During one sitting, the words "clean and clear" popped into my mind. As I pondered this meaning, I recalled the previous morning when I arrived at my car only to find a hard frost covering the windshield. Being in a hurry to get to an appointment, I was frustrated and didn't have time to properly scrape the windows. Using my museum membership card as a not-very-effective tool, I managed to clear just enough space to peek out through the windshield. It was still dark outside and the space was narrow, so I was on high alert with my body hunkered down the entire way to my destination. Anxiety was my companion because I didn't know when a bike, car, or pedestrian might cross my dimly lit path. It was quite uncomfortable, yet I pressed on because I was in a rush. I managed to arrive at my endpoint without incident, but the way there certainly wasn't clean and clear.

Isn't this just like life? When we're not clean and clear with ourselves (i.e., when we ignore our feelings or circumstances), we jump or startle when something comes out of the dark and/or we live life curled up inside ourselves. How much better would it be to have a clear windshield and less obstructed vision? Doesn't clean and clear sound more satisfying than crouched and constricted? The obstacles don't necessarily go away, but with clean space we have increased opportunity to see clearly.

*Artistic Meditation*

 Take a blank piece of notebook paper and poke a small hole in the center. Bring the paper to your eye and look through the hole. Check in with your body. Is this experience satisfying? Pause. Enlarge the opening and look again. Continue this process and notice how your vision and responses change.

# LISTENING TO THE TWO-YEAR-OLD

"Jesus said, Let the little children come to me, and do not hinder
them, for the kingdom of heaven belongs to such as these."
—*Matthew 19:14*

Have you ever witnessed the power of a two-year-old? Or perhaps you remember being that age yourself? Can you recall having the audacity to say "No!" or "Mine!" without apology? Are you able to call on that energy today (in a slightly more adult fashion, of course)?

Saying no has been a very odd thing for me to consider since I really don't view myself as a yes-girl, especially when unreasonable demands come my way. Still, I'm aware of certain places where I naturally revert to patterns of hanging on. Transition arrives slowly when it comes to letting go of people, places, or things I consider an integral part of my growth and development. There are times, however, when it's essential to take hold of something different. The letting go often requires the tenacity of a two-year-old.

So, what do you think? Do you have an inner two-year-old begging to come out and scream, "No!" or "No more!" or "Not yet!"? Where do you desire to be empowered to let go of the familiar and claim something new? To solidly declare, "Mine"? Perhaps the power sits in the voice of a little person within you.

*Active Meditation*

 Flip through a magazine or photo book and find an image of a child about two years old. Explore through the eyes of this child as you ask the question, "What do you desire?" With your non-dominant hand, record the child's response. Notice the quality of the emotions that arise. What feels like "yes" in your body? What feels like "no"?

## January 9

# Lists

Every now and then I wake up with incessant lists running through my mind. Why lists? Why not poetry or even prose? Our culture has taught us to live by lists. *Do this. Do that.* You aren't successful if you don't get things done. It's easy to get caught up in everyone else's should do's.

Whose standards do you use for productivity or success? Personally, I've tried to develop ways to redefine success by coming back to the present moment and asking what needs to happen right now. Through gentle mindfulness, I'm able to shift my train of thought from traditional should do's toward life-giving must do's. These involve things like watching a beautiful sunset. Listening to my dog breathe. Taking time for me to breathe. Stopping to smell the roses. Moving my body freely without prohibitive intention or purpose. Listening. Prayer. Simply being.

To pursue contentment, it's important to open up internal space and allow it to find us. And so, we write our lists and mark them off—not to be successful in the worldly sense, not to show how much we have accomplished, but to make space for joy and content living.

Don't get me wrong—I love the simple joy of completing a task, a pat on the back, or a line drawn through a to-do list item. It feels even more sublime when I know I'm making space for things I treasure most.

*Meditation*

Consider what's on your list today. Why is it there? What will you feel when you've marked it off? Before you move on with your day, make sure there's at least one great, feel-good item on the list. Create space for that item.

# THE WORDS WILL NOT COME

the words will not come. they do not flow like water.

they drip in my mind interrupting solace like a leaky faucet.
they come in ragged, jagged fits and bursts and then they resist—
stop—refuse to congeal and thus
leave me wanting—yearning—aching and unsure of what needs
or wants to be said or heard or read.

my words are insufficient. cards held close to my vest.
"thank you but your words are not right for us." "have you tried
this or that?"
words of advice slip through the air and hang like graffiti on a wall.

needing words to communicate—to feel complete. finding words
get in the way.
interpretation. collision.
mood and mystery.
is there meaning in this text? mine or yours?

the inner (and sometimes outer) critic speaks. softly.
loudly.
in fits and spurts.
in screams and sighs. the words will not come. and they will not stop.

*Journal Meditation*

 With pen and paper, spend ten minutes writing
whatever comes to mind. Set a timer and keep your
pen moving for the allotted time. If the words will
not come, then write that: "the words will not come."
Express gratitude to yourself for this simple offering of
words.

# TALKING HEADS

There's a great scene from a campy movie of the nineties where two characters have their heads severed and then reattached to the bodies of small dogs. It's an amusing vision and one that sticks in my mind as I think about how often we, as human beings, try to sever our heads and disengage from our bodies. We begin to believe our mind is the only valuable tool we possess. We fail to notice our bodies screaming for attention as we numb them through work, addiction, television, food, and busy-ness.

The only thing I might change in the movie scene would be to attach a head to a cat's body and see what happens. Many times I've sat writing while my cat pushes his body into my lap and nudges my hand and arm with his nose. He maneuvers his feline curves until my fingers begin to knead the fur on his back and his motor begins to purr with contentment. I wonder if he thinks about what he's doing. Or does he simply inhabit his whole self and move with the full expression of it?

Learning to trust your body and to listen to it brings compassion and integration to yourself and thus to the greater world. Body, mind, and spirit listen, trust, and move together—not as a disembodied head, not as something to fight or numb. The pieces become whole and begin to purr with contentment.

*Body Practice*

 Place both feet evenly on the floor and begin to balance your body. Follow your breath for a few cycles and relax where you are. Scan your body and notice if there is one place that calls for attention—perhaps a tight muscle, an achy joint, a queasy stomach. For the next few moments, direct your breath to that area and listen to what your body might have to say.

# WHEN PIGS FLY

Pedrita gazed upward into the night sky, pondering the question: When will I ever learn to fly? Her nights were dream-filled while her days were spent in the barnyard surrounded by other swine. The others passed their hours trudging back and forth between feed trough and mud pit. They slogged through the days mimicking perfect barnyard behavior infused with virtually no enthusiasm.

Pedrita, however, knew she was destined for more. Instead of scarfing down her slop, she would pause and be curious about where her meal had been before. Whose leftovers was she sharing? Did the grains come from the field visible beyond the fence? Could her mother's crankiness be explained by a gluten intolerance? Pedrita spent her waking hours pondering and pondering. Even though the other animals made fun of her and called her wacky, she offered them kindness and gentleness rather than match their derision.

Every night she would gaze into the heavens and imagine herself floating among the stars. She could see herself reflected in the constellations and knew she was special and shiny. She tried to tell her friends about the magic night sky, but they were more concerned about the next meal and what everyone else was doing. Pedrita would not be dissuaded. She continued to dream her dreams and wish upon the glowing stars. She saw beauty in everything and offered compassion unceasingly, even to the piglets who laughed at her wistfulness. Nothing could deter her from reaching for the stars.

Each evening while standing under the moonlit sky, she offered compassion to the whole world—especially the parts she didn't understand. She sincerely believed we are all made of stars, and as she nurtured this belief, something gradually changed within her. Her heart sprouted wings and under the winds of generous compassion, one night she defied gravity and rose to join the twinkling lights of the sky.

She quit trying to convince others to change and saw her mates perfect as they were with their slogging and slopping. By day, she was a simple swine reaching out to others through curiosity and kindness. Little did they know, however, that through these daily actions she nurtured the incredible lightness of being that carried her, Pedrita the pig, soaring through the starlit night.

*Ponder and Apply*

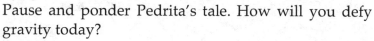

Pause and ponder Pedrita's tale. How will you defy gravity today?

# RETREAT IS A VERB

*Retreat: to withdraw, retire or draw back,*
*especially for shelter or seclusion.*

The lexicon of our modern day insists that one must leave home, go away, and/or spend lots of money to officially be on retreat. This perception is bothersome to me because what happens to people without accrued vacation time or resources to afford an expensive spa? It's time to change our thinking. In my experience, daily life is totally accessible as an ongoing retreat center. It's a place where at any moment in time we have the ability to take a pause and seek shelter from our thoughts or seclusion from our surroundings. If we can change our thinking, we can change our mood. When we allow ourselves to separate from narrow definitions and expand our notion of "retreat," life becomes a playground.

In this current moment, I sit in my neighborhood café and take a break from writing at home. As the pull of distractions, like laundry and Internet, became too great, I chose to create a new space of shelter, seclusion, and inspiration. The smell of espresso now fills my nostrils as a fresh breeze floats through open windows. Smooth jazz music and the patter of quiet conversation soothe my clanging thoughts. Local artwork flanks my sides and a soft leather chair cushions my body. I begin to imagine the laughter that will come this evening when I gather with family and it makes me smile. Pausing, I take in all that surrounds me and gratefully declare, "Here and now, I am on retreat."

*Meditation*

Set aside time today for your own retreat. Make space to intentionally draw back from the tensions that clamor for your attention. Begin with several deep breaths and the declaration, "Here and now, I am on retreat."

# OLD BRAIN

There is a voice inside our heads that comes from the places of old and is reptilian in nature. Karen Armstrong simply calls it "old brain." Seth Godin, Martha Beck, and others name it our "lizard." It also goes by such pseudonyms as the inner critic, a devil on your shoulder, or possibly some persistent family member like Aunt Edith or your mother. It is the voice that keeps us in check and goes back to primordial times when all we needed was to be safe, fed, and able to procreate. Since there are no saber-toothed tigers stalking us today, our brain has a tendency to make up stuff that emulates danger.

As it is an old brain, it is both sophisticated and naive in a very primitive way. My inner critic says things like, *Who do you think you are? No one will read this drivel! Stop while you're ahead, fool.* It doesn't sound very helpful, does it? I want to shout back and name call, too, in a display of my own unevolved self. Experience, however, demonstrates that what we resist persists. Fighting, pushing, ignoring, and shouting back all feel like resistance to me. Perhaps a new tactic is in order. Pause. Breathe. Listen a little more closely.

Hey, Lizard, what do you really want? Like a sultry teenager or a petulant child, she pouts and whines and calls me more names. By engaging in the name-calling, the drama escalates and no one wins, so I choose to listen more deeply. What she really wants is to simply keep me safe. By convincing me to back off from my goals—which entail taking risk—she thinks she's performing her job successfully. Counterintuitive to my basic instincts to battle her, I notice responding with laughter, kindness, humility, and boldness is more effective in quieting down this peevish child.

What do *you* really want? Could there be something helpful

beneath all that brain noise? I understand my lizard also wants to be heard—just like me. Hmmm. Perhaps a compassionate bent is the best choice, even though placing my fingers in my ears and screaming, "I can't hear you," can be quite appealing. Petulance or compassion—which will I choose today?

*Journal Meditation*

In your journal, write down one statement that your old brain uses to distract you, such as "You can't do _____." Ask the brain why. Record the answer. Repeat. Continue this for at least five whys and notice what else the old brain may be trying to communicate.

# WHISPERS IN THE NIGHT SKY

When I raise my eyes to the night heavens and my heart reaches skyward, a world of infinite possibility surrounds me. The stars wrap around my soul like a satin scarf draped over exposed shoulders on a cool summer's eve. My heart hears the Big Dipper whisper with a crystal voice, "Your cup runneth over. Yes, yours."

The eyes of my heart remember Egyptian skies and I'm transported back in time until I lie giggling next to my aureate buddy, gasping at the brilliance of a hundred shooting stars. When I look into the endless sky, my heart recalls Hawaiian nightfall, lying flat-backed, mesmerized alongside my lineage, surrounded by friends and frogs.

My heart experiences new life and worlds unlived. It gasps, sobs, and rejoices at the magnificence I cannot name yet already know. When I look up at the night sky, I see darkness and light. Death and life. Dreams and loss. The sky carries it all—from here to time's end and all that has gone before. I see angels' wings and God's whisper. Tea lights on an ocean of unknown, unknowing, undone, unfinished—un-ness. The night sky reaches from the heavens and pulls my heart upward, always. *Yes, always.*

*Action Invitation*

 Make a date to go stargazing. Once there, breathe deeply. Pause. Ponder. Remember. What do you see in the night sky?

# KNIGHT'S JOURNEY

Have you ever wondered what heaven might feel like? Can you imagine the energy? Once upon a time, a glimpse of heaven showed itself while I shared a celebration with seven mighty souls who had just completed a transformational workshop based on the hero's journey. The vitality on this occasion was palpable. Laughter. Tears. Words of power and clarity filled the air. Humility. Wonder. Delight. Grown men's faces transformed into tender little boys. Gratitude reigned. Awe. Thankfulness.

My own heart filled with joy. Wordlessness overtook me. I was surrounded by pure love energy and acceptance. Everyone in the room was connected and transcended through this love. As these individuals wholly embraced themselves, they were able to effortlessly extend their love and graciousness toward others. This unity is the ultimate hope for the world. This was my glimpse of heaven.

The process to arrive at this place, however, was anything but effortless. These men fought long, hard, and well. They surprised themselves and challenged their mentors at every turn. They were gracious, frustrating, lovable, eclectic, and endearing. It was an honor to step in and witness their transformation. Belly laughs bursting to life. Heads held higher and words spoken with more clarity. Humility and love shone from their faces. Beautiful, wonderful, unique men. All so different yet all the same. Seeking what they had forgotten and resolving, or at least understanding a bit better, the battles inside that keep them from living freely.

This was a new day as these knights marched forward with their armor abundantly shinier. Through their bravery and courage to seek something better for themselves, they created a great gift to the world in which we all live. They showed me a tangible version of heaven on earth.

*Visualization*

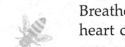 Breathe deeply and begin to draw attention to your heart center. Imagine there is armor surrounding this area with rust holding it in place. Allow yourself to feel the weight. With each subsequent breath, begin to notice the rust dissolving until the armor falls away. Breathe into the new spaciousness of this area and spend a few moments dreaming what you could offer the world from this open space.

# LET THE LITTLE CHILDREN COME

When and how do we cease to be childlike? Must we? Is it a requirement for adulthood? Jesus said, "Let the little children come." It sounds so inviting. It certainly makes me feel like I'm closer to God in a simple, childlike state than in all the seriousness of adulthood.

When did things get so complicated? When did we become the grownups? Is there a button that gets pushed? Is it irreversible? I think the change begins when the world starts to press in. The negative messages start to come. "Don't do this." "Don't do that." "Don't act like a child."

Why not? The kingdom of heaven is for the children of God. The children—not the grownups, not the fuddy duddies, not the policy makers. Blessed are the poor, the meek, the humble. Who is more poor (and therefore rich) than a newborn babe? Who is more meek (and thus bolder) than a child who knows no condemnation? Who is more humble (and consequently more brilliant) than one who does not recognize (and yet somehow fully knows) his or her own beauty?

When does it change? Must it?

*Visualization and Action*

Close your eyes and imagine a simple pleasure of childhood (watching clouds, singing off-key, skipping, etc.). Give yourself permission to experience something childlike today. If giving yourself permission is too hard, then consider it prescribed by me. *Go on, do it—let your little child come.*

# Lady Wisdom

Ancient wisdom greets me with bright eyes and wrinkled skin.

She comes with grayed hair, radiating golden light like sunflowers on a bright summer day.

Wisdom comes in the platinum locks of a precious child,

In the single tear of a caged young man. She sits on my heart until I feel her weight;

Until it sprouts wings and takes flight, leaving me lighter than air.

Wisdom has roots that reach deep into the ground, wrapping around the stones of my heart.

She is blue sky and flowing water—streams mingling with tears of sorrow and joy—pouring into an ocean of emotion where one drop cannot be distinguished from another.

She greets me with her kind eyes, her warm heart.

She holds me with her gaze and promises she will never leave.

I'm always here, she says.

I am in the bloom of a single white blossom shared by a friend;

In the candle flames throwing light into the darkness; The song carried in the air sings my tune.

I feel her within the chill of my bare toes;

The warmth and taste of coffee through my lips;

The brilliant pink and gold splashed across a raw canvas.

Wisdom greets me everywhere I am.

The ticking of a clock; whisper of the breeze; sounds of silence.

She is there when I open my eyes; focus my ears; touch with my hand; inhale through my nose; know in my heart.

My soul cries out for her and she meets me—unfailingly.

Always there. Always present.

Wisdom greets me with hair of gray and crown of golden sunflowers.
Child. Maiden. Mother. Crone. Lady that she is.

*Journal Meditation*

Slowly read these words about Lady Wisdom. Notice if
there is a word or phrase that shimmers a little brighter
for you. Record the line and begin writing your own
words about wisdom.

Write without stopping for three minutes and see what
emerges.

## January 19

# Re-Entry

Re-entry, whether by waking in the morning after a satisfying night's slumber or returning home from a vacation in paradise, is rarely without consequence. To go from sunshine and blue seas to gray skies and snow in a matter of hours is an unwelcome transition. It's not unlike rising from that warm cocoon of sleep into the harsh light of day. One moment I swell with joy and gratitude over life-giving splendor, and the next, I am filled with melancholy as I sit stranded on a rain-soaked highway. How shall I carry warmth and fullness into my day?

I am reminded of the tiny hermit crab I once watched on a rocky Mexican beach. She painstakingly worked to carry her home from one place to the next. It was tough going, but she labored well. It seems to me that this is my task, too—to take the joy so easily found in nirvana and pull it across a sometimes rocky (or snowy) path so that paradise resides wherever I am.

I choose to start with the minute, like the hermit crab, and see what blossoms in this day.

*Visualization*

 Imagine for a moment that you are a hermit crab and must carry all your possessions in a small shell upon your back. What are the attributes or items you want to store in your shell?

# ASLAN'S GIFT

Pinned.
I can't move.
His purr vibrates against my chest.
The rise and fall of breath beneath my palm.
Soft golden fur caresses my fingertips.
Warm breath, steamy on my wrist.

We rise and fall together. Breathing.
Only this moment exists. His wisdom says,
"This is enough."
He shows me what it's like
to push your way into love and care.
"This is what I need right now.
This is what you need, too," I hear the gentle murmur.

No need to rush or hurry
or read or think.
Just . . .

Feel the rise and fall
The beating of our hearts
The rhythm of two connected as one in the gentle
breaking dawn.

My gift for the day. Take it with you and
Hold this place of rest.
Calm. Stillness. God.
Learn from the wisdom of this one
Who knows only now
Who knows the embrace of the one who loves.

*Meditation*

 Place a hand upon your chest or the fur of a beloved pet if one is near. Be still and simply feel the rise and fall beneath your palm.

# LET THERE BE LIGHT

The word, light, is one that conveys multiple attributes—a quality of illumination, a source of fire, an ability to see. We can spread light in the world, take ourselves seriously or lightly, and float around light as a feather. Often light is noted for its contrast with darkness.

Light is an icon that daily brightens my heart and soul. For me, it offers a reawakening to something that has been present all my life but was "hidden under a bushel." A friend offered me the moniker of Lucy van Pelt as a reminder to not take myself so seriously. Lucy began as a symbol of the times when I got prickly or uppity, then developed into a gift that helped me find my essence of kindness and joy, not crabbiness or disbelief.

As my love affair with light deepened, I came to discover other Lucys, like St. Lucia. She is the patron saint of the blind whose name translates to mean light. Using St. Lucia's imagery, I envision my own light spreading as a beacon to the metaphorical blind—those who long for new ways of sight in their lives and the world.

*Visualization and Action*

Find a place where light is present—sunshine, a lamp, or a candle's flame. Allow yourself to focus on the quality and feel its warmth. Next close your eyes and take several deep breaths into the area just behind your navel. (This is the solar plexus which is said to carry our shining light of self.) Notice any feelings or sensations of lightness or warmth in that area. Consider what it might look like to carry your light into the world today.

# LIMINAL SPACE

There is a space that lies between sleeping and waking—between touch and not—where possibilities lay infinite. Fears rise along with desire. To touch and not be hurt. To have contact and not draw blood. Feeling what you long for, so close you can almost taste it, but not quite. The energy rising between. What will contact mean? What will the new day bring?

The space lies open and is filled with sweet and gentle expectation. Reaching into the cosmos for what you desire. Walking the fine balance between asking for what you need and being turned away in rejection. In this liminal space is where the possibilities lie—in these moments before opening our eyes, where dreams mix with reality and voices weave through sleeping narrative and daytime sounds.

The space between the possibilities. Longing and desire. Touching something not quite there.

*Visualization*

Imagine walking on a fine line or tight rope. As you lean toward one side, possibilities arise. Tilting toward the other direction, there is disappointment. Allow yourself to metaphorically walk this line as you begin the day. Notice what balance moves you forward.

# ALCHEMIST'S TALE

Alchemy is the art of transmuting metals. With human beings, it is the process of seeking inner wisdom through burning away our unnecessary shell to get to the preciousness that resides within each of us.

There is a great fable by Robert Fisher called *The Knight in Rusty Armor*. In this story, the valiant knight dons his shiny armor to protect himself while battling dragons and rescuing maidens. He finds his gleaming protection so appealing that he wears it all the time until it ultimately becomes rusted around his body. Because of this, he loses the ability to have meaningful contact with his beloved wife and child. The armor turns into an unnecessary shell and the knight is threatened with losing everything he holds most dear.

This story is the ultimate alchemist's tale. What was once protection has turned into hindrance. The essence of the knight's dilemma is an exploration of trust and letting go. Finding the precious truth inside can only be manifested by removing (or transmuting) the rusted armor that surrounds him.

*Active Meditation*

 Choose a pecan, walnut, or any nut still in its shell. Imagine that what is inside is very precious (i.e., the heart or core), then take the steps necessary to remove the shell without damaging the center. In this process, ponder a shell of yours that may keep you and/or others from reaching your center.

# Anyone There?

Themes of birth, awakening, and mothers float through my mind. Vivid dreams invade my night and wake me like a whisper from my sleep. I roll over, turn off the alarm, and sink into the space where dreamland meets dawn. The space between past, present, and future cannot be delineated and my earliest memory drifts into now. I am older than one and younger than two. Standing in my crib with an earnest look on my face, I am not crying or distressed. I appear to be reaching, not with my arms, but with my eyes. Anyone there? My eyes stretch into the room beyond the recesses of my barred bed and beckon. Anyone there?

Isn't that the question I still ask today? In times of lament, I turn to the ancient lie I tell myself. *I am not important. I will always be alone.* Was no one there? Sharing my ten-year-old brother's room, I wonder if he resented my presence. I recall the black eye my mother received when she bumped the doorjamb during a nightly visit to me. Would she return again?

So odd, these memories. So very interesting. Anyone there is what I continue to ask today. Will you read my work? Hold my hand? Laugh at my jokes? Kiss my lips? Notice my hair? Anyone there? Are you paying attention? Do you see me? Is it possible I still carry the look of a one-year-old standing in her crib, reaching and searching for connection? Anyone there?

What are the questions you ask yourself or the lies you whisper when past and present merge?

*Visualization*

 Close your eyes and allow your mind to float back to your earliest memory. Be curious at the image as if you've never seen it before. What is your expression?

Your emotion? Your body language? Pause. Sit with this and notice if a question or statement emerges. Carry this experience gently and with curiosity throughout your day.

# THE "AND" IS ALWAYS NEARBY

We live in a world of extremes, where perspectives typically materialize in the form of "either/or" but rarely as "both/and." A day is either productive or it's a wash. Our mood is good or we are blue. What if this weren't the case? What if we shifted our thoughts and considered the possibility it could be both?

Looking at today, I recognize a jam-packed week has come and gone. One chock-full of rich goodness, *and* I am exhausted, filled with a strong need to restore. It's time to refresh and rejuvenate. Living fully requires awareness and vigor, and being in the present moment is an invitation to simply be.

I encourage myself to remember there are no ordinary moments. Life comes together in perfect timing and harmony—without pressing—as I allow things to unfold in the midst of the busyness. *And*, when things get too demanding, I long for quiet time and rest—the place where I find peace and solace with and for myself.

I love that I do not need others to define who I am, *and* I adore the authentic engagement of connecting with others. Sometimes the veracity of being with other people can be tremendous and takes me by surprise. Simple spoken words or gestures bring tears to my eyes. The gentle warmth of a hug offers peace to a deep place in my soul. A compliment confirms my own delight. And the biting words or cold silence of another can threaten to send me into a tailspin—not all encounters turn out well.

Our world is more complex than "either/or." Life is a mix of "both/and." There are no ordinary moments—the "and" is always nearby.

*Ponder and Apply*

What are the contrasts in your life where you habitually select either/or as a response (e.g., happy or sad; success or failure; good or bad)? Alongside this, ponder how including "and" between these contrasts could change the essence of the feeling or situation.

# January 26
## And Judge No One

"Abbot Joseph asked Abbot Pastor: Tell me how I can become a monk. The elder replied: If you want to have rest here in this life and also in the next, in every conflict with another say: Who am I? And judge no one."

—*The Desert Fathers*

Whensperiod I first encountered the above quote, I was traveling in the Sinai desert with a dozen other pilgrims. Our guide gave us each a random quote to ponder. Upon reading mine, I immediately thought of conflict with other people. As I deepened my personal understanding, I came to see that most often the conflict is within me, and the judgment harshest toward myself.

In times of turmoil when I ask the question "Who am I?" a variety of answers arise. I am the scared one, the angry one, the confused one, the misunderstood one. Ultimately, my inner critic shows up and berates me for being confused, angry, or foolish. Instead of offering compassion, judgment comes down hard. There's no need to have conflict with anyone else as long as I listen to my critical self. Through the judgment, I limit myself and end up feeling exhausted from the battle. Yet when I take the Desert Fathers' words to heart and judge no one—including myself—life takes on a gentler quality and rest effortlessly appears.

*Ponder and Apply*

Ponder the words from the Desert Fathers. Allow a time of personal turmoil or conflict to arise in your mind. Focus on the feeling of unrest and ask the question

"Who am I?" Listen to your answers without judgment and offer compassion to whoever or whatever shows up.

# Be Alive!

"Being alive is the special occasion."
—*Patti Digh*

Whadoes it take for anyone to believe that being alive is the special occasion? That each day is a gift—each moment? That we are special? To trust our wrinkles have been earned? Our bodies well worn? That we are fortunate to be getting out of bed each day—aches, pains, and all?

What gets in my way of truly living? Mind chatter. Laziness. Ego. Outside and inside messages. I let it happen. I allow another's attitude to dampen my day. I permit shortened sleep to make me cranky. I buy into the critical voices in my head. I jump to end results and worry about what others will think. What if my work's not good enough? What if I'm not good enough? Doing X is a big waste of time . . . I could never . . .

Blah blah blah.

The chatter can be an endless reverie, and I am the only one who can stop it for myself. In this process of worrying, procrastinating, and judging, I miss out on being alive. I miss the special occasion. What if instead of listening to the chatter, we each chose to believe that being alive is the special occasion. What if?

*Meditation*

Follow your breath while pondering what brings you alive and what gets in your way. Breathe in positivity and exhale negativity. (For example, breathe in "play" and exhale "to do lists.")

## January 28

# What We Already Know

There are moments in a lifetime believed to cause a molecular shift in your whole being. Even though they may drift in and out of conscious memory, they are embedded in who you are. Ancient Yoruba wisdom speaks of "recalling what we already know within." One such experience came for me as I stood in the center of the Sacred Garden's labyrinth on the island of Maui.

As I entered the labyrinth with gentle footsteps, light raindrops began to fall and caress my bare skin. There was something fresh and exciting about the drops sifting through the lush green foliage as contented birds trilled in tune with my every step. Not one to let a little water slow me down, I continued my pilgrimage. The rain persisted and picked up speed. I realized I would soon be soaking wet when Eve, the proprietress, silently offered a giant umbrella to shelter my path.

Striped bumbershoot in hand, I continued my walk toward center. Upon arrival, I found the rest of the world had slipped away. I wasn't aware of anyone or anything except the present moment. Time stood still. As I tipped my head back to peek from beneath my shelter, the rain slowed down to the pace of creation. I could see each drop appearing, one by one. And as I felt my whole being stretching upward, I experienced the hands of God reaching for my own, forming the drops of moisture out of thin air and pouring them into the being that is me. Yes, time stood still and I recalled what I already knew within.

*Active Meditation*

 Stand in the shower (or better yet, outside in the rain). Tilt your head back, allowing the water to gently wash down your body. Envision each drop pouring in and over you. Breathe deeply and embrace this eternal moment.

# HOME

"Home is where the heart is and thus a movable feast."
—*Author unknown*

January is almost gone. On jet-propelled wings it has flown by, yet still its imprint lies upon my heart. Physically home for a few days, the movable feast traveled alongside me. Connected to myself. Connected to my soul. Home is where the light lives.

Experiencing buoyancy and freedom among friends. Communion and fellowship with family. Witnessing miracles and life in brief moments that last for eternity. Beginnings of life. Endings of death. Ice breaking and floes commencing movement. Coyotes howling. Dolphins dancing. Miracles of freedom.

These are the memories and wonders to hold when the busyness of life tries to squeeze in as a new day and month begins.

*Visualization and Meditation*

 Close your eyes and center yourself with your breath. Imagine a banquet table spread out before you. Allow the memories and miracles that make up your feast to arrange themselves upon the table. Know you can pack this picnic feast and carry it with you wherever you go.

# FEMININE WORLD

I am the pain of the world, covered with blue scarves and white.
I am the beauty of the world, bare shouldered with upswept hair.
I am the fire of the world, burning with desire and hope.
I am the joy of the world, reaching toward the heavens.

I am the beauty of the world, bare shouldered with upswept hair.
I am the luscious berry, bursting with flavor.
I am the joy of the world, reaching toward the heavens.
I am the soul of the world, centered through pain, beauty, touch, and taste.

I am the luscious berry.
I am the fire of the world.
I am the soul of the world.
I am the pain of the world, covered with blue scarves and white.

*Poetry Ponder*
       Ponder who you are in your world.

# THIN PLACES

Wise ones say the air in Ireland is thin, and the veil between heaven and earth lifts for those who open their hearts. Many times during a pilgrimage to Ireland, my own veil lifted as I encountered the Sacred Ones who welcomed me in that ancient land.

Through fading blackberry vines, I gingerly scramble toward the 4 × 6 foot unmarked graveyard. Resembling an abandoned garden plot, it was a hidden patch where infant children lay buried, nearly forgotten through the centuries. These wee ones beckon my heart as we congregate in the womb of branches and brambles. Perched precariously on a weathered stump, I assemble my tools—hazelwood branch, miniature feathers, yarn—and begin to form a tribal prayer stick. My primeval instincts engage and it is like I have done this one hundred times, a thousand, a million—forever.

Placing the small feathers near the top of the lichen-coated wand, I position my yarn to attach the elements as I slowly begin to pray. One wrap. One prayer. Another wrap. Another prayer. And so it goes until time evaporates. I wrap and meditate as the rain softly falls, signaling a new phase of this holy ceremony, unwritten until now, yet lingering in the heavens since the beginning of time.

Reverently, I exit the brambles and look for a site to plant the prayer stick. A tiny cross beckons, "Here. Lay your prayers here." Gently, I press the baton into the moist loam. Hazelwood reconnects to Mother Earth and feathers reach toward the heavens. The tenderly wrapped prayers lift and rise through the Irish mist, waving over all the lost wee ones who are forgotten no more.

*Meditation*

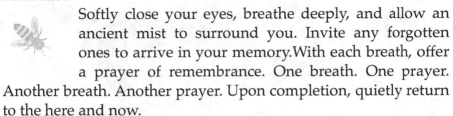

Softly close your eyes, breathe deeply, and allow an ancient mist to surround you. Invite any forgotten ones to arrive in your memory. With each breath, offer a prayer of remembrance. One breath. One prayer. Another breath. Another prayer. Upon completion, quietly return to the here and now.

## February 1

# St. Brigid's Feast Day

Today is the feast day of St. Brigid of Kildare. St. Brigid is an Irish patron saint known for her warmth and hospitality. Having visited her homeland, I can still feel her flame burning in my heart and the warmth of a dear friend's embrace as we stood on the holy ground at Brigid's well.

St. Brigid of fire and water, your kindred spirit kindles our flame of desire. You offer us a passion for life and living it to the fullest—not just watching the days go by but truly embracing them.

Certainly there are moments when my flame simmers rather than blazes. A time of tending in the night like when the Celtic women put their fire to rest, minding the fire so it can be rekindled at the break of day. How do I tend my fire? Today with an early rising, allowing free time and space. (A fire needs space to breathe; it suffocates when the wood is packed too closely.) A hot shower and steaming coffee warm me inside and out. The lamp's glow illuminates my surroundings. And in my heart, I hold warm memories of standing in Kildare with the spirit of dear St. Brigid. Peace be with you on this feast day of St. Brigid. May the fire in your own heart be illumined and warmed today and always.

*Action Invitation*

 Choose a personal way to nurture your fire today. Light a candle, build a fire, take a hot shower, sip steaming tea.

# ANNEALING

Annealing is a heat treatment wherein a material is altered, causing changes in its properties such as strength and hardness. The alteration comes about by heating the material to above the recrystallization temperature, maintaining a suitable temperature, and then cooling. Annealing is used to soften material, relieve internal stresses, and refine the structure by making its properties homogeneous.

The description reminds me of our own transformation possibilities whereby we step out of our comfortable temperatures into the rising heat of a challenge or new situation. This action fosters an internal shift and refining our structure. Heating can feel dangerous, and it's risky to step out of our comfort zone. Often in relationships, we learn that rigid ways of being need to make way for more malleable existences. This isn't to say we subject ourselves to another. I like to view it as moving toward more compatible ways of being. As my children grew older, it became evident that being malleable to my wishes wasn't working for anyone. It was imperative that they, and I, shift from a brittle form of existence and transfer into something more free flowing. Annealing allowed our strengths to move into a more homogeneous and refined relationship.

*Active Meditation*

Where in your life could you stand to be more flexible? Make a list of your rigid attributes and/or internal stresses. Spend a few moments pondering the list. Go into your bathroom with the list and a pack of matches. Stand over the toilet bowl, light the paper on fire, and watch its properties change. Let go and release the shifting list into the toilet. Flush.

# BARREN BEAUTY

In West Texas at a ranch some would call barren, I find that words pale in response to the wonder that fills this remarkable place. An army of minuscule ants streams up and down the rugged porch rafter. A small confident bird sways and speaks from the top of a cottonwood tree, announcing her royal presence. Soft auburn bunnies frolic in the grass. A spectrum of color spreads across the field—shades of red, maroon, and violet mixed with layers of yellow and golden wildflowers. Fuchsia blooms resemble round, purple porcupines perched atop thistle stems—seductively inviting yet sheathed in miniscule barbs. The gentle breeze touches my skin—Yahweh speaks. Clouds so light they look like feathers. A bobwhite calls in the distance. The earth sways with the voice of God, so soft and tender on this morning that opens in stark contrast to the majesty and power of the booming thunder and brilliant light show witnessed the night before. The pounding rain churned the red dirt into clay made ready for the potter to mold.

My heart cries, "Mold me. Shape me. Wash over me. Cleanse me. Make me pure of heart and gentle like the breeze; strong as the storm yet pliable as the clay. Meet me here in this barren place."

*Journal Meditation*

 Allow your gaze to fall upon the most unremarkable natural object at hand—a leaf, potted plant, rock, dried flower, or blade of grass. Observe this item with fresh eyes. In the most elaborate language you can imagine, write a love letter to this creation. Be pliable as clay and have fun!

# THE BATTLE

"You intended to harm me, but God intended it for good to accomplish what is now being done, the saving of many lives."
—*Genesis 50:20*

Sometimes the battle between good and evil feels so strong it is almost incapacitating. Is that the goal of evil? To incapacitate?

Pondering has taken me back to a place in time filled with an array of emotions and powerful experiences. During this era, I watched transformation of souls occur before my eyes and experienced it for myself. I felt the power of God in nature and witnessed it in the rain, wind, and hail. Eagles soared overhead and light shone on glistening treetops like something in a surrealist painting. Miracles were all around. And I could sense a battle to stop this good from happening.

Like the annealing process, the heat gets turned up during transformational work. Who turns up the heat? God? Evil? The Universe? Me? Many questions bounce through my mind for which I have no answers. I could try to ignore them and hope they go away, or I could become absorbed with them and thus paralyzed from moving forward.

The balance for me is in being aware and willing to wrestle with the thoughts. Even making a small start and putting a few words on paper brings me hope. Not that I will necessarily come up with the answers, but that I will continue to move, to choose life, to reach for the light rather than become absorbed by darkness.

I choose to wrestle rather than become incapacitated.

*Meditation*

What does your wrestling look like today? Imagine both literal and metaphorical heat. Notice what arises and how you respond.

# BE MINDFUL WHAT YOU WISH FOR

"The greatest spiritual act we can take is to stop and sit down."
—*Anne Lamott*

Have you ever found yourself in a surreal moment when you've wished for something and suddenly realized you're in the middle of it coming to fruition? There's that brief inhale of overwhelm and the thought *What was I thinking?* zips through your mind. Needless to say, this has happened to me. Once, through a series of seemingly uneventful happenings, I found myself face to face with author Anne Lamott who I have long admired.

It began with being asked to write a brief article about her keynote speech at a local conference. I invited a friend to attend with me and, once there, we ran into my friend's colleague, who happened to be getting coffee for Anne. I offhandedly mentioned my article, and the next thing I knew, the keynote was ending and my friend and I were being ushered backstage like rock star groupies for an exclusive interview.

"You'll have just a few moments with her because she's really not seeing any press today."

The moment of overwhelm slammed me in the chest and my inner critic started yammering, *Fraud! Fraud! You're a fraud!* My ego took over with all sorts of advice. *Be perfect. Look intelligent. You have to make the most of this time. She's more important than you. They're going to know you're a fraud.* And with all of those words, my brilliant and typically calm self vanished into thin air until I sat in Anne's presence sputtering like a fool. Finally my voice squeaked, "I think I just need to breathe."

And then I remembered why I had wished for this moment.

Following my request, the woman of my admiration reached out, took my shaking hands, and gently said, "Let's pray. Would that be okay?" Calm was restored with the gentle touch of compassion.

*Meditation*

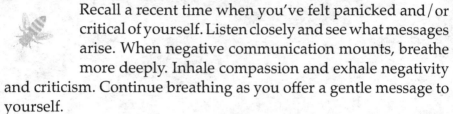

Recall a recent time when you've felt panicked and/or critical of yourself. Listen closely and see what messages arise. When negative communication mounts, breathe more deeply. Inhale compassion and exhale negativity and criticism. Continue breathing as you offer a gentle message to yourself.

# BLESSED COMFORT

"Blessed are those who mourn, for they shall be comforted."
*Matthew 5:4*

Grace. In her book *Gift from the Sea*, Anne Morrow Lindbergh speaks of being aware of times in our lives when we seem to be "in grace" and other periods when we feel "out of grace." "In the first condition, one seems to carry all one's tasks before one lightly, as if borne along on a great tide; and in the opposite state one can hardly tie a shoe-string."

There are days when I've tied my shoe-strings more easily with the help of those who surround me, and I've been comforted by words like these: *The mourners are called blessed not because mourning is good, but because they shall be comforted.* By sharing grief and sorrow, we allow others to bring us comfort. It comes to us when we are still and listen to the rhythm of our needs.

Grace. Too often, we believe it is a gift for everyone except ourselves.

*Journal Meditation*

 How will you show yourself grace today? Begin with the writing prompt: I will offer myself grace by . . .

# LUCY AND SHABBAT

St. Lucy greeted me this morning as only she can—with surprise, delight, and light. Today she brings discovery of the light of Shabbat (the Hebrew word that is the basis for Sabbath and sabbatical). Not being Jewish myself, I was delighted to discover it is a woman's mitzvah to light the Shabbat candles. In other words, it is a woman's privilege to bring "good" into the world through light. I love this! I, as a woman, can bring light into the world as no other can.

There is something holy, sacred, and sensuous in thinking about candles and light, birthing and growth. With the days gradually getting longer, the ground is stirring and making space for new life to push forward to the surface. The soul is awakening from the darkness of winter.

Images of water (often associated with creation and passion) and patterns of enlivened breath and rhythm continue to appear in both my dreams and waking hours. My journey for now seems to include the questions: Where is God calling me as I move toward spring? How will I breathe fresh life and spread my light in the days to come? How will my creativity and passion express themselves?

*Active Meditation*

 What candles are you being called to light today? Make a list or follow your breath, naming a candle with each inhale.

# BLIND DATE

In this age of the Internet and social media, we have more opportunity than ever before to meet and connect with people around the world. Every now and then, the virtual world meets the tangible realm in the form of flesh and blood. I have had many wonderful opportunities to meet people face to face after "talking" with them for extended periods online. Meeting someone you don't know can stir up all kinds of crazy feelings—kind of like a blind date—even if you're not looking for romantic involvement.

I imagine you know what I'm talking about. The anticipation. What will she/he look like? Will we recognize each other when we meet? Where's the best venue? Coffee or cocktail? Public place? What if we don't like each other? What if there's nothing to say? What if . . .

On one such occasion, after emailing a few times and exchanging voicemails and a handful of text messages, we decided on beer at the local microbrewery. I waited outside to make sure she found it and when she drove by in her car, we instantly recognized each other, smiled, and waved like old friends. We greeted with a comfortable hug because we were not strangers. We had been conversing for a couple of years and knew things about each other that people we see on a regular basis might not. She wanted to know about the rest of my vacation. I needed to check on her healing from an accident. There were no pregnant pauses in the conversation. It was a great blind date, complete with the age-old question: Gosh, I wonder if she'll call again?

*Visualization and Action*

Name an area of life where you'd like to make a new friend. Close your eyes and imagine the perfect blind date. What do you talk about? How does it feel? Next, make a list of the qualities important to you in a person. Consider where and how these may already be in your life.

# Breaking Open

Many of us are hesitant to slow down and step into the immensity of our own minds, let alone that which surrounds us in the world. For those of us living comfortable lives where we don't have to worry about our next meal or a roof over our head, it can feel selfish to feel as though we're struggling when others face devastation, hunger, war, and natural destruction. Our search for personal peace is often transposed against a backdrop of events tangibly bigger than our own breaking hearts.

As I write, dozens of distinct faces flash through my mind. I see a friend who has heart-warming dreams of personal expansion but has a challenging time seeing how those dreams can impact the outer world. My own private witness arises. It is one of prisoners in orange jump suits, some angry and entitled, others grateful to be alive and willing to transform one day at a time. The only thing distinguishing us is the color of our clothes and my ability to walk out the steel-encased doors. Pausing, I imagine what it might look like to save the world beginning on a small scale—one individual, one conversation at a time. This feels more possible and allows my breath to expand.

As I ponder what it looks like to live alongside others, I am reminded of Mother Teresa's prayer for her heart to break wide open so the whole world might fall in. Is it enough to care for ourselves when others are dying? Do we not each die a bit every day? Can a breath of life in my body reach across the world? Does it have to go that far, or is it enough to touch someone across the room, or closer yet, to fill my own lungs? How can we approach healing in our days?

*Visualization and Meditation*

 Breathe deeply and begin to notice where your focus lands—inner or outer world. With this focus of intention, breathe in healing light and exhale compassionate love.

Imagine a spiral moving both inward and outward as you breathe this prayer of healing. Make this offering for yourself, your family, your neighborhood, perceived enemies, and ultimately, the whole world.

# WORDS OF KINDNESS

Words of kindness. We often forget to share them. We discount how far reaching or significant they may be. Words that lie unspoken like an infant's sock dropped on a neighborhood sidewalk. Abandoned. Never to be paired with their match. Earlier this day, someone took a moment to offer back my metaphorical sock. A friend from the remote past (one I still envision at eighteen even though she's well past the half-century mark) offered me the profound gift of her simple yet generous words. Why today? Why not?

A smile, a word, a nod, a note can change another's day or life. With little effort on our part, we can offer the encouragement or reinforcement another may need. I would never have known this woman read my words unless she told me. How do people know we care if we don't speak out? Forget the "they should know," because chances are they don't. We've become a world of want-to-be mindreaders, and last time I checked, we aren't particularly effective. There's no way I could have known where my words had reached without this friend declaring our connection.

When was the last time you offered a generous word for no good reason? Is there someone whose name you think is cool? Tell them. Did you notice his phrase was perfect or her tenacity and brilliance admirable? Offer it up. Even brilliant people have doubts. A smile, a word, a nod, a note can change another's day or life. Why not begin today?

*Ponder and Apply*
Pause. Ponder. Begin.

# MANTRA: READ, WRITE, REST

When I was in graduate school, I had a mantra that often helped me through days of intensive study: Read. Write. Rest. Repeat. There are still times in my life when those words prove to be immensely valuable. They offer me a pattern that engages, fulfills, and restores. The word "work" can be substituted for "write" and often "exercise" makes its way into the "rest" category. It is a simple rhythm.

In the Jewish tradition, there is a practice of lighting two candles on Shabbat. One is said to be for rest and the other, freedom. The intertwining of those two concepts—freedom and rest—reminds me not only of my mantra, but also the larger notion that without rest, freedom is likely absent.

Productivity has become a god in the modern world, and there is little value placed on rest. The result? People who are exhausted, overworked, and disconnected from their lives and the people in it. Do you find yourself guilty here? What might it look like to slow down?

*Active Meditation*

 Place two candles before you. Light the first and bring your mind to the concept of rest. Simply breathe for a few moments, letting your body relax. Now light the second candle and move your attention to freedom, bringing it in with the inhale and releasing expectations with your exhale. As you come to a close, notice what tugs at your heart.

# MARROW OF THE SOUL

"The desert fathers . . . point us toward a very holistic view of prayer. They show us that real prayer penetrates to the marrow of our soul and leaves nothing untouched."
*Henri Nouwen*

The arms of God wrap around me. Enclosing me. Enveloping me. Telling me I am safe without words. I breathe in the scent of divine maleness and feminine beauty intertwined. Sensuous. Sensual. Becoming one. Coming home. Just breathe. Breathe in the mystery. Sense God like a child reaching out for a parent's hand. Like a dog who raises his nose to the fresh morning air. Breathe God in.

What is your holistic prayer? How does it penetrate your soul and leave nothing untouched?

*Journal Meditation*

With journal nearby, center yourself and begin to follow your breath. As you inhale and exhale, consider each movement as prayer—individual and unique to you. When you are ready, allow the words to flow onto the page in response to the above questions.

# MEDIOCRITY OR BRILLIANCE?

Western philosophy has taught that suffering is a normal state of life on earth. Enjoyment is something reserved for children, retirees, or hedonists. If we're super busy, then we are important. If we work limitless hours and don't have an extra moment, then we're successful. If we feel really good about ourselves, then we must be slacking off in another area. Striving toward perfection is a noble goal, but one that must be minimized with humility and false modesty.

This line of thinking is flawed and, in my humble opinion, a bunch of hooey. I am a sincere believer that we are all perfectly created and joy is our natural state of well-being. Over the course of life, our perfection gets marred with expectations of what others think. Then our own minds take over and we become mired in a world of "I could never" or "If only." We get stuck in mediocrity and our brilliance loses its shine.

What if our mission in life became to return to our original perfection? What if we were called to peel off the layers of expectation and ultimately gleam in all our glory and return to a childlike state of joy? The key is to trust our felt experiences versus the gibberish that runs through our irrational minds. If a thought causes endless suffering, then it isn't true. Suffering is that suffocating, deadening, hopelessness that keeps us stuck in circumstances. It is not to be confused with the wild, sometimes raw and exhilarating excitement that comes from letting your inner self shine and living authentically as the person you were created to be.

Which will you choose? Mediocrity or brilliance?

*Action Invitation*

Play with the following statements:
I am a worthless person who doesn't deserve anything.
Notice how that proclamation sits in your body.
I am a glorious creation designed to bring beauty and light to the world.
Allow yourself to feel the difference.

# THE EDGE

Come to the edge, He said. Come to the edge.
She smiled, lifted off the ground and did a cannonball into the unknown.

The unknown exploded and burst into a million miracles—glistening in the sky for all the world to see. They floated through the air, touching corners of the universe that had never known such brightness.

Come to the edge, She said. Come fly with me through the crystal atmosphere.
It is glorious. It is dangerous. It is life.

*Poetry Ponder*
        What or where are your edges?

# MESSY

"God of mystery, help me to hold the questions, lead me to live them, bless me to bless them for disturbing my path."
*Jan L. Richardson*

Some days are just messy.

Honor the questions. Hold them lightly. Let them guide but not overwhelm and obstruct. Allow them to disturb the path. The journey may not look how we think it should, but that's what we get for thinking.

Follow the path like a feather floating across the garden. Dropping here. Lifting there. Following the motion of the breeze. There is a plan perhaps, but it is not yours or mine. Is it God's—the man with strings in the sky? No, I think not. It is mystery. Life force. Universe.

It is not the god of my elders. A god who controls with fear and condemnation. It is the god of love. Serendipity. The god who is with me in tragedy, but who does not push a button and make it happen.

The journey is ongoing. The questions will continue. Hold them lightly. Honor them well. Life is messy.

*Pondering*

Consider how you are with questions. Do you always need an answer? What might it look like to let the questions and responses float across your path like a feather on a breeze?

# MORPHING

O ur journey toward wholeness is never complete, but still we reach and yearn and move toward and through it. Gradations. Variations. Two steps forward and one step back—we are always changing. Carl Jung used similar words to describe the relational journey: If two meet and connect, there is a reaction and we are transformed. Morphing like ancient shape-shifters. Our nature may feel like that of a butterfly—a miracle born out of the cocoon. Or a bird on the wing lifting and soaring through the air. At other times, we may feel like the snake on the ground with no arms or legs to move us, tasting only dirt within our teeth.

The butterfly breaks free from its cocoon. Birds molt. Snakes shed their skin. Yet at no time do they cease to be insect or bird or snake. They simply morph into what they already are—traveling toward their completeness.

*Active Meditation*

 Imagine yourself as a snake itching to shed old skin; a bird shaking free from feathers that no longer serve; a butterfly pushing through the tightly wrapped cocoon. Breathe deeply into the desire and innate sense to shape shift.

# FEBRUARY 17

# YOUTH'S CHALLENGE

One morning over coffee with my friend of twenty years, we mused about where we have been and how we live now. Wisdom, foolishness, joy, and sorrow have carved prophetic lines in our once smooth faces. Still, we shine with beauty and grace. We cry with sorrow as agony forms the deep places of our souls. We have chosen to live and were we to die today, it would be without regret. There are things we cannot change and things we've yet to do. We still ask questions of ourselves and know that no one can answer our questions for us. We must do it on our own.

Earlier this same morning, a fellow ponderer asked me what I think the greatest challenge is that faces young adults today. My quick response? The fact that they are young. They have the world before them and have not yet gathered the experience of longevity. It is both gift and rival. I believe the greatest challenge (and one not exclusive to youth) is to find an authentic voice and pave pathways of our own truth. To live unfettered lives that bring freedom versus imprisonment. To unselfishly and unabashedly stand up for who we are. Life's challenge is to sort through the history the elders have bequeathed us—emotionally, spiritually, and economically. To find personal choice while sifting through peer pressure and the voice of the inner critic.

The greatest challenge for me comes from within, and I can't imagine it's so very different for others, be they young, old, or in between. The beauty is that this same challenge is also our greatest gift. For if it comes from within, then we are free to change through choice. What will I choose for me? What will I offer to others? Life. I choose life over mere existence. Perhaps this is the challenge. This intentional pathway doesn't always taste of sweet honey or sound like a love song. Stepping into light means moving through darkness and befriending fear. It means letting go of what does not work and clinging tightly to what does. Choosing life is taking the risk to be immersed in the fragrance—aromatic and otherwise—of authentic being.

*Active Meditation*

What does it mean to stand unabashedly for who you are? Ponder what gets in your way of living fully. Make a list for each question. Take a move. Step into the light today.

# MEET THE JOURNEYER

For much of my life the word "journey" never entered my vocabulary. I certainly didn't perceive myself as being on a journey. I was simply living my life as best I could without much intention or design. The archetype of the Journeyer/Seeker invites us to be intentional with our steps and willing to learn from what accompanies us along the path. The Biblical Emmaus walkers (Luke 24:13-35) were in the presence of Jesus and didn't recognize him. Their companion and Lord was conversing with them and they couldn't (or didn't) open their eyes to see. How like our daily journey is that? How might things change if we had eyes to seek and willingness to risk?

Journey isn't necessarily about traveling to exotic or remote places, although it can be. We can log miles in a travelogue without having eyes to absorb our surroundings or be impacted by the stranger. We can live long lives and never look inside our own souls or travel to the core of who we truly are. Journey is about being present and developing new awareness that ultimately leads to transformation.

To be a seeker and enter the transformative journey is to take risks. It often proves rigorous. Phil Cousineau, author of *The Art of Pilgrimage*, says, "Ancient wisdom suggests if you aren't trembling as you approach the Sacred, it isn't the real thing. The Sacred, in its various guises as holy ground, art, or knowledge, evokes emotion and commotion." The Journeyer invites us to experience this trembling for the sake of our own transformation. The Seeker invites us to step more fully into the questions and plan with intention where we will step next.

*Action Invitation*

Set aside time to take a contemplative walk or visit a local labyrinth. Focus on each step of the process rather than being concerned about a destination. With discovery as your loosely held intention, allow space for surprise on this brief journey.

# THE JOURNEYER CONTINUES

My transformational journey was precipitated by a family crisis. This type of beginning is referred to as a catalytic event. Stories and myth throughout time speak of the hero's journey, which most often begins with the hero or heroine leaving home and moving along a route laden with trials and unexpected adventures. My personal journey required me to step into the terrifying expanse of my own inner world. It called me to leave a place of comfort and stability while my outer world was turned upside down through circumstances beyond my control. It felt as though all choice had been stripped away and the illusion of solid ground dissolved. The earth upon which I walked became tectonic plates, shifting and knocking me off balance. Each time I regained my equilibrium, I was called to step more fully into my own life. The trembling began first out of fear because the pathway was new territory. It continued until the shaking finally arose from a place of awe as I learned I could never predict what disaster or fabulousness might lay before me.

The Journeyer invites us to become comfortable with such trembling. This is not dissimilar to a highly acclaimed spiritual attribute in Hinduism called *Abhaya* (fearlessness). To seek this way of freedom is to seek fear or befriend it. It is to look at our own vulnerability and recognize the face of fear and step toward it. When avoidance dissipates, fear is disempowered.

The Seeker invites us to go beyond fear. We are called to move toward the authenticity that belongs to each of us personally and individually. It is a terrifying adventure, and it is a gateway to life.

*Pondering*

Where are you being called to be more authentic with yourself, the world, or God? Where are the places you seek greater personal freedom? What is the untraveled road this archetype invites you to explore? How are you willing to befriend fear?

# MUSCLE MEMORY

A throbbing muscle tugs for my attention. My aching bones are reminded of the time I physically carried an antique sewing machine out of my house. It was the machine on which my mother lovingly sewed my prom dress and countless other costumes. It sat tucked inside my office closet for years, taking up physical and emotional space. The piece was clunky and worn, beautiful in its own way and outdated for the present time.

It's no wonder we strained to carry it down the stairs. The machine was full of memories—a reminder of my mother who tugs at my heart long after her physical death. Poignantly, its name was New Home. It took years for me to understand that the machine was not the woman and giving it away wasn't the same as getting rid of her. New Home was a talisman of days gone by. Getting rid of the contraption did not mean letting go of the legacy.

Saying goodbye was a process, but even with my whining muscles, a lightness arose within. The newly created space in my home is fresh and open. I envision room for clarity and more precious memories to be made. The clutter cleared and, as I bid farewell to the machine, I made room for what I could not yet know.

*Action Invitation*

Select an area of your home or office that contains clutter. Close your eyes and imagine the feeling of having it cleared away. Be curious about this feeling. Take one small step toward reducing the clutter. Celebrate your move forward. Repeat as needed.

# MOSAIC

"As individual stones, we can do little with them except
compare them and judge their beauty and value. When,
however, all these little stones are brought together in one
big mosaic portraying the face of Christ, who would ever
question the importance of any one of them?"
*Henri Nouwen*

There are mornings I'm filled with thoughts and resonance in
the energy of the earth, of God, of humanity. We are all connected
as one, like a beautiful mosaic. In what ways may we stay separate?
How do we ultimately come together? Is it by accident? By choice?
By a power greater than we can even imagine? We are each small
stones rolling toward the other to create one vast mosaic. Seekers
responding with creativity and moving toward wholeness.

Imagine a world surrounded by compassionate seekers of
God, of creativity, of wholeness. Hearts reaching out to the world,
healing each other as divine goodness finds its place in the mosaic.
Today, may you care for your own soul as gently as if it were that
of another.

*Artistic Meditation*

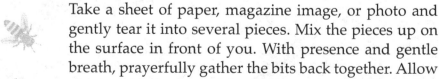

Take a sheet of paper, magazine image, or photo and
gently tear it into several pieces. Mix the pieces up on
the surface in front of you. With presence and gentle
breath, prayerfully gather the bits back together. Allow
each one to represent a portion of the universe, knowing it is part
of the whole.

# TUB TIME

Awaking in the middle of the night in a rustic retreat center, I toss and turn in the bed that is temporarily mine. My sleeping roommate snoozes less than four feet away and I quickly scan the room for non-disruptive mid-night options. Turning on the light seems offensive, and it's too dark and cold to venture outside. Stealthily, I gather my pillows and reach for my notepad as I make my way toward the sole other room in our modest abode—the bathroom.

Immersing myself in the ceramic tub devoid of water, a single drip escapes the faucet and startles me further awake as it lands on my bare toe. Feather-like pillows cushion my body and act as amniotic fluid in this man-made womb. Eventually, my nighttime restlessness begins to lessen as I mold myself to the curved fixture designed specifically for holding the human form. (While showers have their own special kind of magic with their resemblance to rain pouring from the sky, there's nothing quite as nurturing as a tub.)

In my nighttime cradle, I've found the perfect incubator for idea nurturing and dream making. I'm reminded of another friend who loves to sit in the bathtub for hours on end—without water. Her inspiration helped me discover these vessels as the near perfect pondering place. Instant mood setting is available in a moment's notice with customized climate control. You can fill it up with hot water or cold; to the brim or ankle deep; with bubbles and aromatherapy or crystal clear; and perhaps most important and least considered, you can enter it dry and have your own holding place within seconds. Add some pillows, a candle or two, and if you're lucky, a window with a view. *Voilá*, an instant cozy spot to bring on percolating, gestating, resting and waiting, hatching ideas, dreaming, scheming, breathing, being, and, of course, bathing. All hours of the day, there's a custom cradle not so far away.

*Action Invitation*

 Prepare a delicious tub or shower of your own creation. Allow each drop of water to wash over you like new dreams. For a few moments, nurture and love yourself in this man-made womb.

# IF I BRING MYSELF

If I bring myself to you, will you rise to meet me or will you flee in fear? Worse, will you advance with attack and retaliation—flinging harm into my face and heart, using my truth and beauty as weapons against my soul?

"Stand firm." My heart speaks out. The truth is real. Stand firm and gently in your beauty. It will terrify some. They will seek to harm—lashing out with tongues dipped in poison. But, the poison will turn back to them to be ingested.

You are strong and pure—able to metabolize the poison. Your beauty is not too much. The truth in your soul is yours and yours alone. Perfectly created and designed; snug inside its cocoon, metamorphosing daily, renewed in the Spirit.

A snake's venom cannot reach the floating butterfly. Therefore, fly away for a time. Rest and feel the wind beneath your wings. Soar.

Remembering the return will be necessary—crucial. A cocoon is needed for a season, not a lifetime.

Spread your wings and share your beauty. It is not too much.

*Poetry Ponder*

What does it mean to bring yourself to another? To face fear? To spread your wings and fly?

# REMINDER: EVERYONE IS A TEACHER

As a group facilitator, I often have the privilege of being taught by my students. During a day of reconnecting to creativity through restoration and rejuvenation, I invited participants to select an image to introduce themselves. The images were as varied as the people around our circle, but my teacher of the day presented in the form of a sprite of a woman, weighing no more than ninety pounds fully clothed and soaking wet. Well into her eighties with hair of spun silver, she wore a bright scarlet dress accessorized with an oversized medical collar strapped around her neck.

With twinkling eyes, she held in her hand a photo of a rugged snow-capped mountain with soaring peaks. Out of her mouth came the words, "I am one who explores the trails." Incongruous as it might seem for this frail woman to make such an unflinching statement, no one who witnessed this scene doubted her. In fact, I could actually envision her roaming that mighty mountain as she shared deeply from her heart, her memory, and even her future. With her words, her stature grew and she became the towering mountain. I could see all dreams come true—hers, mine, and the worlds. It was a glorious moment.

To live fully is to believe in dreams, unflinching truth, and living our heart's desire. Today's teacher demonstrated all of those wrapped in a petite package of wisdom. May we each learn from her example.

*Visualization and Meditation*

 Explore with your mind's eye: What is your heart's desire? What trails do you hope to travel this year? What would it look like to speak the truth out of your deepest desires?

# BE LIKE WATER

"Best to be like water . . . It pools where humans
disdain to dwell."
—*Tao Te Ching*

Today I will begin with openness. I will play with the crazy thoughts and nonsensical experiences that flow through my mind as I awaken. I will be adventuresome and see where the ideas invite me to go. I will be like a child on vacation, allowing myself to move through my list of desires and needs with playful abandon and an open heart. When things cease to become play, I will stop and breathe.

I will remember the wholeness of delight and joy that comes when I declare myself enough. To stand in my own power and desire brings richness to my life. The words shift and form until they announce, "I am fully alive." I am created to play and my life is not about work. Today I will begin with the nonsensical and allow myself to not make sense of it all, for this would be an exercise in futility. I will begin this day with openness, pleasure, and curiosity. I will invite play into my moments. I will allow my words to flow like water and dare to travel to the place that others resist. Today I will begin with me.

*Visualization*

Today, be like water . . . whatever that means to you.

# TEMPEST

"If you cannot catch the wind, neither can you prevent distracting
thoughts from coming into your head."
*Thomas Merton*

Growing up in Oklahoma, I learned firsthand the impact of a
mighty wind. The gales are not unlike the emotional variety that
rattle fiercely and shake us to the core. We can bundle up tightly
for protection, but even this can't prevent unwanted thoughts
from blowing through us.

Emotionally blustery days are filled with distractions of
relentless variety. They come with the capacity to chill our hearts
and keep us frozen in place. They pierce us like the wind and send
us searching for protection.

One negativity-filled night, I wrapped myself in layers of
warmth—gloves, hat, vest, coat, wool socks—and turned to one of
my greatest teachers: the elements. Walking into the strong north
gale, my nose began to tingle and I picked up the pace. Pushing
into the wind, the crappy story I'd let control my day rolled
through my brain. *You're a failure. Worthless. No good at anything.*
The whispering wind illuminated my own restlessness and the
choices became clear. I could either press forward or allow the
storm to blow me back to places I no longer wanted to be.

Forging my way in the night, my resolve strengthened with
every step. Planting each foot was necessary (both physically and
emotionally) to maintain my balance in the gale-like zephyr. It
was no time to slow down and let the pitiful stories take hold.
With solidified balance, blood pumped new life to the heart and

my body began to warm. The wind was still swirling around me, but as I turned the corner onto my street, the tempest lost its force.

*Action Invitation*

Step outside for a brief walk. Notice if there is a breeze and/or be present to your surroundings. Walk in one direction for several yards (go a full block, if possible). Turn the corner or reverse your direction. Notice how the air movement and/or view changes with this slight shift.

# WAKING TO A NEW SONG

Fuzzy memories lead me to a movie where the main character describes her perfect day as waking up in a foreign country where she doesn't know the language. Her exuberance leads the way for adventure and life is absolutely amazing.

Several years ago, I had the phenomenal experience of having such a perfect day when I traveled solo to Paris. Serendipity led the way on an amazing, unparalleled venture. Upon my return, I found myself dreaming fluently *a la français* while my mastery of the language stopped with eighth-grade French class. One of the outstanding lines in my dreams was *Je ne parle pas français.* Translated, it means "I don't speak French." There was an amazing wildness in these dreams, but more so actually being in a country and not understanding the primary language. Finding my travel journal, I was delighted to find the following words:

*listening to the patter of language around me . . . not having to partake or be responsible for what was going on . . . just listening . . . like music—listening to a song I could not understand, but still loving the melody and the message . . . a lullaby . . . a love song . . . written just for me . . .*

*Ponder and Apply*

When you don't understand the language around you, where do your thoughts go? Do you fight it and retreat? Can you choose to hear it as a new song around you? Perhaps a beautiful love song or possibly a fight song you'd rather tune out? What is the language you hear today—wherever you are?

# TWO CHOICES: LOVE OR FEAR

Love. Fear. We make choices between them daily in a multitude of situations, but we usually aren't conscious that's what we're doing. While we would like to profess that most choices we make are out of love, I invite you to consider otherwise.

One of my most profound examples of choosing love or fear comes from personal experience when my family made a difficult and somewhat unorthodox decision regarding our eldest child. We would say we did it because we loved him and wanted the best for him (which is, of course, true). However, at the deep root of this decision was our terror that he would not live to see another year if we didn't do something drastic. So, truthfully, the choice was made from fear wrapped as love.

How often do we see that in the world today, where well-meaning people disguise their fear in terms of what is best for others under the banner of love? What would our world look like if during each day, each moment, and each interaction, we posed the internal question: "Am I acting out of love or fear? What is my motivation?"

This doesn't mean fear needs to go away, for there is little chance of that anyway. Fear can be helpful and healthy and often keeps us safe. What responsible parent has not taught their toddler to have respect for a burning flame or a busy street? Fear, however, can also keep us trapped inside a box—immobilized and stuck in old patterns of living.

We cannot change the past or the future, which are both great feeders of fear. The only thing we can affect is this moment. The past is gone. The future will never arrive. All we have is right now. We have two choices in how we will live it—in love or in fear.

*Visualization and Meditation*

Close your eyes and allow your thoughts to connect with a recent decision you've made (perhaps with regard to your work or a relationship in your life). Now consider the two choices—love and fear—and ask yourself which one prompted your decision. Begin to imagine your thought process as a drilling bit and push a little further into your action. Does your motive change? Ask again what prompted the choice. Finally, consider how things might be different if you had asked this question before making the decision. Allow yourself to gently move through the day pondering the choices of love and fear.

# HEART HAIKU

heart
crimson cold
beating, breathing, bleeding, caught in a vise
yearning
heart

purity personified
beating, bleeding, breathing, caught in a vise
loving
heart

caught in a vise
darkness and beauty
grip the hold of life

*Poetry Ponder*

Which images shimmer to the surface for you?

# BREATHING IS HARD SOME DAYS

"The ground is always littered with our longings."
*Lynn Ungar*

Some days breathing is hard. Physical as well as emotional symptoms can hinder our inhales and exhales. I recall a particularly difficult time when I was plagued with a horrible cold and longed to breathe deeply but couldn't. The desire to find an easy breath consumed my days. On a quest to feel better, I went out for fresh air, sunshine, and a milkshake. The milkshake machine was broken. I drove to the beach but could not make myself pull over and park. I stopped for a Diet Coke and bought Cracker Jacks when I really wanted Crunch'n Munch. Desires that seemed so simple and inconsequential became heaps of angst.

Longing for connection. Longing for wholeness. Searching too hard. Desiring the place where I could just be. Searching. Looking. Asking. Seeking. Flat, dull spaces blocked my path. And then I heard my own words: Let us not move too quickly to the good news and thus dismiss our pain and sorrow. Can I sit in the sorrow for awhile? Will I allow myself to be present for myself?

To acknowledge these times of hardship, breath seems so important. Without it, my mind becomes muddled. With it, the rhythm of life speaks to me. The pendulum that swings between joy and sorrow. The ground littered with our longings. The question is how to remain faithful to all the necessary deaths while leaving room for resurrection. The only way to get through grief is to grieve. The only way to take in fresh air is to breathe. Breathing is hard some days.

*Body Practice*

Center yourself and gently bring your awareness to the rhythm of life. Be present and notice what wants to rise up within your body today. Follow your inhale and exhale through birth, death, joy, and sorrow. Inhale. Pause. Exhale. Pause.

# Breaking Through

S ometimes being present to the world feels like more than I can bear. Tragedy and need fill the daily news and darkness threatens every corner of life. While part of me desires to be an ostrich that places her head in the sand, I know ignoring darkness does not mean it isn't there. However, shadow cannot exist without the presence of light, and in this thought boundless comfort resonates.

Imagine that even at the center of evil's role in the world, there is a place of light that shines through. We can seek and find a rhythm of rest and restoration in the midst of chaos. Glimpses of sunshine help arouse clarity of mind, even when clouds are forming. There is freedom as we experience joy in the simplest of things, like cleaning a closet, taking the dog for a walk, restocking groceries, watching a squirrel at play, or feeling the sun and wind on our skin.

Momentarily focusing on simple things can break the chain of tragedy. Even when rains threaten to fall and potential battle rages all around, there's always a sliver of light waiting to break through.

*Action Invitation*

Take time today to focus on the simplest of things such as sipping your morning coffee, breathing in fresh air, folding clean laundry, or sitting in a favorite spot. Imagine this as light breaking through chaos.

# BRAZOS DE DIOS:
# PART 1

A red ball of sunshine greets me this morning.
The world is waking up although parts of it never went to sleep last night (including me).
Doors banging—wind blowing—caught in a twister.

My life right now—raw, restless—looking for a place to land.
I know my home is here with me and yet the world keeps hammering away at my sanity and serenity, even in the dark of night.

A small Texas bird speaks to me from the tree.
"It is here. Freedom is here for the choosing.
Choose life. Choose life."

Even when the battle is tough and turbulent—when you are caught in a twister—breathe.
Breathe in the air that smells slightly different.
Take in the vines of the field. They are but branches and the root lies deep beneath.

Trust. Trust God.
Trust the process.
Trust myself.

*Poetry Ponder*

Notice what bubbles up for you when you read this poem.

# BRAZOS DE DIOS:
# PART 2

I feel so raw right now—bursting with emotion.
Tender and strong—anchored with a root
that is deep and everlasting.

My vineyard is intertwined with sunflowers.
The red rock of my childhood surrounds me. It is the flat terrain
of my youth.
Yet I know the road was neither flat nor smooth.

Bobwhite calling. Beautiful. Familiar.
"Come play with me. Come join the rising sun."
The gnats are trying to irritate. It is my choice to stay calm or to
despair.

I watch a small white butterfly—a miracle. Hear the bobwhite.
My stomach is starting to growl. Mosquitoes are buzzing.
This new day has begun.

I will join my friends.
I will find solace in the midst of the twister.
The arms of God are all around me. *Brazos de Dios.*

*Poetry Ponder*

Again, notice what bubbles up for you when you read
this poem.

# BROKEN FOR YOU

Broken for you. The words evoke a myriad of images in my mind. Mosaic tiles. Christ on the cross. My own aching bones. Shattered families. Cracks and light. Hearts breaking open so others may fall in. How will we approach the cracks and find shimmering light in brokenness?

Broken wings. Broken soil. Broken ground. Broken body. Broken for you. Broken for me. A story of self-sacrifice as witness to breaking and redemption. Communion cup. Bread of life. How do we feed each other? How are we broken again and again on behalf of another? How can our own brokenness heal one another? *Broken for you.* The words ring in my head.

Broken for me. How will we fight on behalf of each other? One person at a time. One life at a time. With these thoughts, I begin my day.

*Action Invitation*

Join with one other person to share a piece of bread, a cracker, or a cookie. Consider the significance of bread as life. Take the food and gently break it in two pieces. Acknowledge the brokenness within yourself and share half of the bread with your companion.

# MARCH 6
# BULLIES IN DISGUISE

Layers and layers of discovery. I move. I rest. I pause. The stratums shift and morph. Refining my way toward freedom. Awhile back I had a memory arise and, while I'm not sure it's an actual event, I don't know why I would have made it up. Unless, of course, I needed it to help me with something else.

The scene was quite precise. I'm six years old and in the first grade. The view is of the narrow cloak closet at school, and the class has just come in from recess. I can smell the damp coats and feel someone behind me pressing my face into them. It's another child, I'm certain. I can't breathe. A vise-like grip deepens on the sides of my throat—pudgy fingers. My fear tightens as a knee or elbow presses into my spine, stuffing my face further into the darkness of the fabric. The bully tells me to "Stay quiet, or else." My nostrils fill with the acrid smell of wet wool. I want to scream, but my mouth is buried and the words won't come. Suddenly, there's a flurry of activity and the grip releases, the pressure comes off my back. I'm alone and disheveled in the closet.

The metaphor to life is immense. Internal struggles over voice, aloneness, and importance are core for many of us. They are battles I've been peeling the layers off of for years. They move and shift and morph. Sometimes the biggest bully is oneself. We must consider how long to allow the knee to press into our backs and stifle the scream rising in our chests. The power of authentic expression releases the grip of fear and in the voicing, we cease to be the bully in the closet.

*Visualization and Meditation*

Ponder the ways you bully yourself or others. What is the risk of speaking truth or releasing the pressure? What is the danger of allowing the vise-like grip to hold your throat and continually saying no to your heart's desire?

## MARCH 7

# BUT

Three little letters: B.U.T. It's amazing the impact they can have on a situation. The tiny scrap of a word can totally change the tone of any encounter. When we use the word "but," it often appears to negate everything that comes before it. For example, what happens when we offer, "I love you, but you really make me mad." The receiver of those words likely only hears what comes after but.

What if, however, three tiny letters were changed and the sentiment is instead spoken as "I love you, and you really make me mad"? You get to express the anger *and* not negate the point that love is included in the equation.

Many of us grew up learning something had to be either right or wrong, good or bad. We think we have to choose between opposites. Imagine how situations would change if we were inclusive rather than exclusionary. Could it be as simple as switching out three tiny letters?

*Action Invitation*

 Challenge yourself throughout the day to be aware of when and how you use the word "but." Imagine replacing "but" with "and." Give it a try and notice what happens.

# March 8

# Exhausting Inauthenticity

*"The most exhausting thing you can do is to be inauthentic."*
*Anne Morrow Lindbergh*

How often do you find yourself censoring who you are or what you have to say? The older I get the more I notice that censoring myself leaves me agitated and restless. My authentic self bursts at the seams with thoughts, emotions, and feelings galore, and putting a lid on them is just not satisfying. So, when my internal censor kicks in, fatigue often follows, because it's exhausting holding back authentic emotion.

Sometimes it's necessary to have alternate ways to exhaust the emotion. Some of my favorites include dance, yoga, walking, and talking. But for me nothing satisfies quite like putting pen to paper and then transposing it onto the written page where others can muse and ponder and possibly relate to what I have written. It was a grand day when I discovered that writing from the heart is a huge part of my authenticity. Where is the balance between being too candid and risking living in inauthenticity? Joy is me. Grand adventures are me. Writing is me. Honesty is me. Compassion is me. Censorship and inauthenticity are not me!

*Journal Meditation*

Do you ever experience feelings of censorship? Where does inauthenticity enter your life? Do you hold back to try and avoid misinterpretation or judgment? Journal the ways you could be more authentic and share what makes you uniquely you.

# EYES OF A CHILD

Looking into the eyes of a child with arms spread wide, I see the wisdom of the world. Young. Old. Ancient. God is in those eyes. All-knowing. Kind. Wise. Looking again, she raises her arms and lifts into flight. Sun. Source. Water. Fire. Earth. Air. The promise of a rainbow. Wings of angels. Stars in the heavens. Creator. Miracle of transformation. Darkness and light. Serious and playful. Mischievous. Serene. Calm. Reaching, not striving. Moving. Growing. Changing. Transforming. Universal.

Look into those eyes and experience peace. Life. Paradox of creation. Unique. Odd. Magnificent. Welcoming arms that say, "This is my world. Come with me. Look at me. See what I can do. You can do it, too." We are one. Source of life. Atom of God. Core. Beginning. Seed. Rest. Chaos. It's all there.

The eyes of a child. Where we meet God. The place we enter the kingdom of heaven. She speaks. He calls. They touch. Light. Life. Wisdom. Source. The eyes of the world. Stranger. Foreigner. Family. Everyone. Look into the eyes of a child and see the world.

*Artistic Meditation*

Select a photograph or magazine image of a child. Open your heart and gaze into the child's eyes. Write without stopping for several minutes about what you notice and see.

# MARCH 10
## EYES OF MY ANCESTORS

When I think of my ancestors, I am reminded of stern faces and, more often than not, words of criticism rather than kindness. Maybe it was due to the serious times in which they were raised, or possibly the influence of the Bible Belt, but there never felt like there was much, if any, room for play or imperfection.

In penning this reflection, however, I became increasingly aware of the many dimensions of these ancestral women—my great aunties with their crinkled crimson lips, my mother at five years old in her sackcloth dress, my paternal grandmother standing beside my father in his Navy uniform. While many of their words have stung me deeply, I believe I can bring something new to the world by breaking their ancient patterns of hiddenness and propriety. I pray that through the realization of my own dreams and forgiveness, these women can be honored in new and glorious ways.

the eyes of my ancestry
hollow and vacant. cold and elusive. barren of love. are they my eyes? my fate?
do those eyes still watch and judge? or do they weep for their veiled dreams?

might I be their eyes today?
might I see things differently and shed grace where once was derision?
might their eyes be washed clear by my tears?
the eyes of my ancestry are they watching now? were they ever?

*Visualization and Action*

Today, I invite you to remember your ancestors by offering them a few moments of curiosity and gratitude.

# EYES WIDE SHUT

Is it fading memory or past inobservance? I don't remember ever awakening to such an amazing, picture-perfect view right outside my window. Did I not turn to the west upon emerging in the past? Or is there a new window—a wall moved just a foot or two? How can I miss something so simple and astonishing that is right before my open eyes?

I think we must do it all the time. The missing, I mean. Some say we cannot go looking for the Sacred. I wonder if that's true. If we don't open our hearts, eyes, or minds, how will we know what is there? And what of those times when we desperately want to experience something greater and yet feel or see nothing?

This is the paradox of being. We must see to believe, but in the looking we often miss what is simply there. "Let it be," says the still small voice. "Be"—that simple, small word that is so huge. Let it be.

How will I choose to be today? How will you?

*Visualization and Action*

 Close your eyes and slowly count to ten. Gently open them and allow your gaze to land on one thing. For the next few moments, examine this one thing like you've never before seen it. Imagine it has a story to tell. Listen to the tale and see with new eyes.

# FEEL YOUR FEELINGS

---

"The fastest way to freedom is to feel your feelings."
*Gita Bellen*

---

I don't know about you, but sometimes I feel like I'm being swallowed by the weight of life and falling into an emotional wasteland. My first instinct is to ignore and make believe it's not happening. I try to steer around the feelings or pretend they don't exist. Wisdom, however, has taught me the only way to clear this wasteland is to go to the dump. I do this by getting out my journal and writing like a mad woman. It's amazing how once I write those feelings down, articulate them, sit in them awhile, I'm able to release their nasty aroma and begin to feel some freedom from their hold. The heaviness lifts even though circumstances haven't changed. The problems aren't necessarily gone, but rather are seen from a different viewpoint.

I think about the complexities of life and all the choices we can make to help us feel better. We can pop a pill, numb ourselves, put on a happy face, or hurry to fix things. I'm not saying that action doesn't need to happen, but I am suggesting we not overlook the power of actually doing as Bellen offers and feel our feelings rather than stuff them down, or look for the quick fix, or anesthetize them away. All of these things are simply ways to help us find a new feeling, so why not begin where we are?

*Body Practice*

Starting now, check in with your body and notice what you feel. As you mentally scan for aches and pains—physical or emotional—breathe deeply, name the feeling, and imagine placing it on a small boat. In your mind, watch the boat drift out to sea. Continue checking in with your body and place each ache or pain on their own vessel and gently watch them drift away and over the horizon.

# LENTEN PRAYER. LIFE PRAYER.

"People who pray stand with their hands open to the world."
*Henri Nouwen*

I am continually amazed at the benefits of getting out of my own way so I can hear more clearly. One year in the days leading up to Lent, I decided to prepare well in advance. I studied the topic and ordered a daily meditation book. I considered giving up wine and sugar or exercising more, but by the time Ash Wednesday rolled around, I still hadn't solidified my plan and was off to facilitate a retreat with little free time to ponder the matter.

Our retreat facilities offered no phone service, Internet, iPods, or television. There weren't any interruptions from the outside world—only ten people with the sole purpose of rediscovering the truth and beauty that lies deep inside each one of us.

It was in this quiet that I remembered my joy and my life prayer—to bring awareness of truth and beauty to people of the world. To help others seek the loveliness and glory they may not be able to see in themselves. To dig through the armor of lies we each wear—such as *I'm not good enough. My feelings aren't important. I don't matter*—and join the battle alongside one another. While I know we must learn this for ourselves, we do not have to do it alone. We can travel the path together.

Once I got out of my own way, I understood my Lenten practice was not about giving up drink or sugar or reading and doing more, but rather it was (and is) about making the choice to be present to the world and to those around me. Living intentionally and bringing myself fully. Fighting side by side the battle that is ours together.

*Ponder and Apply*

Allow these personal applications to flow through you like gentle prayer. Notice where there is the most resonance and begin your practice there. What is your life prayer? What would it feel like to give yourself the gift of silence by turning off the phone and all other electronics? What if you simply got quiet and out of your own way? Listen intentionally to what you have to offer yourself and others.

# MY DANCE

My dance. No one does it like I do. I am delighted and slightly disturbed by so much responsibility riding on me simply being me. It seems that when I begin to experience fully and wholly the sweet spots of life, doubt starts to creep in. Can this be real? How long will it last? On occasion, I've been known to fight the words "courageous" and "brave" when they are ascribed to me. It feels like a battle for my soul. If I continue to step into life and live peacefully in the midst of craziness, it is a threat to evil. It is breaking the chains that bind me to daily drudgery and mediocrity.

There is always a tug of war going on between settling for dullness and moving toward brilliance. For years I wrote under the pseudonym of Lucy because she would go ahead and write without care to what others might think, whereas it took me multiple tries to get over a fear of hanging prepositions. If I'm afraid of proper grammar, then how much more hesitant will I be as I bump up against the ingrained voices of my past and present? The good news is I can choose. It definitely takes practice, but it is my dance.

*Body Practice*

Think of a small fear where you get stuck or hold yourself back from full expression. Consider what's the worst thing that could happen if you let it go. Choose to let it go and see how your body feels. Go ahead, dance your dance!

# MYSTERY AND MASTERY: PART 1

To ponder is to consider the weight of something. It is allowing questions to mull around until they create their own identity. Today we explore a question of movement and waiting—of mystery and mastery. Can there be movement in waiting? A sigh. A breath. A tear. The rise and fall of the chest. The twinkle in an eye. Waiting does not mean ceasing to live. It involves existing deeply and intentionally.

"Wait here," a mother says to her child. The child can both hold his breath and try to remain perfectly still, living in fear, or he can begin to examine the world around him—the ant on the ground, a bee tasting sweet nectar, the wind rustling through the trees. In this waiting, this examination of mystery, is he not living more fully and deeply?

Waiting for the birth of a child, the coming of a savior, the easing of a pain. Waiting does not mean becoming frozen or comatose. It can be just the opposite. A heightening of awareness. Feeling the very structure of your being. Noticing the beams and concrete of your soul; the bare branches of your nakedness; the child inside the mother's womb.

This living into mystery is the mastery of life. It is appreciating each moment instead of worrying or analyzing what it will mean later, or like the compliant child, waiting and holding his breath until the life goes out of him.

So breathe, feel your heart, and listen to the rhythm of the earth. With these movements, the axis shifts slightly and light grows stronger. Without the dark of night, a star cannot shine. So wait. Wait intentionally—not for mastery but for the sake of mystery and all it has to offer.

*Active Meditation*

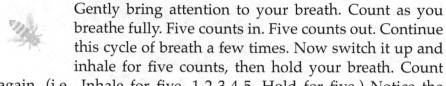

Gently bring attention to your breath. Count as you breathe fully. Five counts in. Five counts out. Continue this cycle of breath a few times. Now switch it up and inhale for five counts, then hold your breath. Count again. (i.e., Inhale for five. 1-2-3-4-5. Hold for five.) Notice the difference between these two ways of being.

## March 16

# Mystery and Mastery:
# Part 2

Pondering takes us more fully into life's mystery. We cannot see the wind except when it blows through the trees. From where does the rain begin? Was the earth created in seven twenty-four-hour days or billions of years? Will I live to be a hundred? This is mystery.

Staying wedged in the questions or naming pat answers inhibits us from moving toward mastery of our own lives because life is full of mystery. It is in motion that life happens. It is found in movement as minute as the dash on our tombstone. That small punctuation mark represents all the life that happens between the day we burst forth from the womb and our final earthly breath. Life happens in movement as subtle as listening to our own heartbeat or watching a blade of grass push through the earth. And movement transpires in grand gestures like tectonic plates shifting or the places of facing our deepest fears. Mastery arises by having the courage to wait within the mystery.

*Ponder and Apply*

 Position yourself to look outside a window or step outside. Spend a few moments watching the sunshine, the rainfall, or the wind blow. Now tell them to stop. Ponder mystery versus mastery.

# NAVIGATING

The contrasts of life greet us with each movement into the day. Have you ever considered how fullness and emptiness can inexplicably be wrapped together? How a person can feel totally alone in a room full of people and then while sitting unaccompanied in silence, find oneself met with the fullness of life? One minute we are on top of the world, and the next moment we are burdened under its heaviness.

Each day we are called to navigate from where we will choose to live. In the fullness, the emptiness, or the "in between." Presence means experiencing the richness of one or the other rather than staying stuck in between. Being half anywhere is a pathway toward loneliness. Fullness resides in our response to the present moment.

*Journal Meditation*

What are the contrasts of your life? Where do you see yourself living "in between?" How do you navigate through the contrasts of life? Spend a few moments in your journal with these questions.

# NAMASTE

The beauty and pain inside me witnesses, acknowledges, accepts, and loves the pain and beauty within you. We are one. Connected through pain and undefended hearts. Hearts refusing to close even in uncomfortable places. Locking eyes. Holding hearts. Grief of destruction. We are held together in that space. Hearts wide open. Reaching. Receiving.

Acknowledging and accepting all that is. Witnessing the beauty in everything. Namaste.

*Active Meditation*

Set the intention of being a nonjudgmental witness today. Practice.

# ABOVE AND BELOW

"What lies below us? And what is above?"
*Christa Gallopoulos*

When I was a little girl, I envisioned splendid images of God and his kingdom in the sky. I believed that if I squinted through my eyelashes and pretended I wasn't looking, I could catch a glimpse of him floating by on a cloud, surrounded by white-winged angels. I would lie for hours in the fresh summer grass, staring up into the sky until I could feel the slow turning of the earth beneath me. In my child's mind, I never quite caught that vivid peek of God, but as an adult I realize those were the moments a higher power was most fully present to me. In that dreamlike state where waking and sleep merge, when vision blurs and yet becomes crystal clear. The place of being held by the earth, gazing longingly into the sky and being completely content for timeless hours.

Without nearly as much conviction as believing I could catch God through the window of my eyelashes was the notion that somewhere beneath my feet lay a fiery pit tended by a man with red horns, pitched fork, and tail. I also imagined that if I dug a hole through the center of the earth, I would end up in China. Much more time was spent fantasizing about the delight and joy of ending up in a faraway little girl's backyard than worrying about falling into a fiery pit. How could the same earth, soil, and grass that cradled my cloud-watching self also cover such a nasty place in the middle of the earth? I preferred to think of the magical tunnel that connected me to my foreign soul mate.

As an adult, my heart returns to cloud watching and earth pondering. What does lie below? My heart believes it offers a place to be grounded and held. We can be cradled and nurtured in love, or we can be captive to fear with worries about what waits to pull us down. And above? Both adult and child know above is the space filled with infinite possibility. The dreamlike state where waking and sleep merge, when vision blurs and yet becomes crystal clear.

*Action Invitation*

Take yourself outside for a play date or find a window nearby through which to look. Be a child watching the clouds go by. If it's a clear day with no clouds, feel the earth solidly beneath your feet. Claim your space between what lies below and what is above.

# THE NEXT SMALL STEP

What happens when you start imagining what you can do and not what you can't? What happens when you do the next small thing instead of concentrating on saving the entire world? What happens when you focus on simplicity rather than complexity? When you follow your heart instead of the world's suggestions? What happens? Simply put, things begin to change.

Do you want change? Do I want change? Am I open to possibilities beyond my wildest imagination? Am I willing to tread on the ground of an amazing God? Will I take off my shoes because I am standing on holy ground? Are you willing to take the next small step?

*Journal Meditation*

Take a moment and imagine a project or endeavor that feels overwhelming to you (World peace? Cleaning your house? Losing weight?). Make a list of what it would take for this to happen. Begin by writing down the most difficult thing. Next, write a step that is simpler than the previous one. Continue until you arrive at a step you can do right now. If you're willing, take that step today.

# NO TRESPASSING

Can we expect the unknown to be agreeable? For most of us, it's terrifying. I don't know what lies ahead today or even in the next moment. We are called to be present with others and ourselves, but there is an invisible divider that penetrates our silence. What if I tell you how I really feel? What if you honestly offer what's on your mind? Will we meet or will we stay separate? Have you placed a "Do Not Enter" sign on your heart?

What keeps us apart? Lack of voice? Fear? Why are we afraid to reach out? We dread rejection and in some cases, acceptance is our foe. What do we want of others? Can we expect the unknown to be agreeable? Do we visualize our losses and then find them waiting to meet us? When we project what will happen (e.g., you will reject me), we stop short and cease to put ourselves out there. As we push others away, our lies become true. We fear being solitary, and therefore quit seeking friendship and thus become alone. We say we are worthless and perpetuate this by not recognizing our own value. Beauty becomes something only others have and looking honestly at our own gifts slips away. We build invisible boundaries and erect "No Trespassing" signs around us.

*Visualization and Meditation*

 How would it feel today to let your invisible boundary soften just a bit? Ponder a limiting thought you have about calling an old friend, posting an honest blog entry, sharing a poem, speaking up at work. (I can't, I shouldn't, I could never . . .) Imagine how you would feel without that thought. Can you think of one stress-free reason to hold onto that thought? Invite yourself to soften the boundary and step into the unknown.

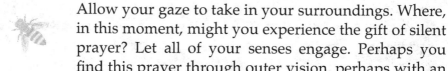

## MARCH 22

# NO WORDS

Timeless. Breathless. Speechless. Sometimes there are no words to describe the magnificence of creation. In this space, we are called to experience silent prayer. Words spoken through a soft breeze. The sound of a gently flowing fountain. Sunbeams and shadows cast across a brilliant green lawn or drab urban concrete. Flowers bursting with color saying, "Look at me. Dance with me." Soft white clouds floating above a sea of azure or field of golden maze. Pure. Perfect. Content.

*Meditation*

Allow your gaze to take in your surroundings. Where, in this moment, might you experience the gift of silent prayer? Let all of your senses engage. Perhaps you find this prayer through outer vision, perhaps with an internal sense of memory. Invite calm and stillness to surround you for a few moments. Experience the power of no words as you focus on the simplicity and magnificence of creation.

# NOTES OF MY SONG

"When a pianist learns a new piece of music, he or she does not sit down and instantly play it perfectly . . . It may all seem disconnected. It may not sound like a harmonious, beautiful piece of music—just isolated notes . . . Then one day, something happens. What we have been working toward, note by note, becomes a song. That song is a whole life, a complete life, a life in harmony."

*Melody Beattie*

It seems as though I'm always practicing something—yoga, mindfulness, counseling skills, artistic endeavors, being a better wife, mother, or friend. I am practicing the parts of my life to come fully into the whole song that is me.

When I reached an awareness in my personal journey and realized I didn't have to or never could figure everything out, it freed me up to explore life with curiosity and adventure. This approach frees me from always striving to get somewhere I won't ever arrive and keeps things exciting and full of surprise as I discern the notes in my song of discovery.

*Ponder and Apply*

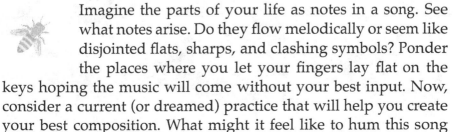

Imagine the parts of your life as notes in a song. See what notes arise. Do they flow melodically or seem like disjointed flats, sharps, and clashing symbols? Ponder the places where you let your fingers lay flat on the keys hoping the music will come without your best input. Now, consider a current (or dreamed) practice that will help you create your best composition. What might it feel like to hum this song today?

# March 24

# Ode to the Hours

Oh, Dawn . . . how do you feel when you arrive wrapped in fog? Is it cozy or are you impatient and begging the morning sky to receive your brilliant light? Do you have trouble awakening? Must you set an alarm or does the end of night push you out of bed? Do you smile when you arise? Do you have gray days like me? Do you know beforehand what kind of day you will be?

My friend, Day—do you prefer the rain or sun? How about your companions, wind or snow? Is your favorite mood the brilliance of light? Do you have a favorite temperament, one that suits you best? Or are you a chameleon, bending to others' whim and demand?

Dusk. You wax and wane. Sometimes your moment moves fleetingly and other glorious days it lingers. What do you make of that? Does a favorite color don your palette? Why some days do you offer your brilliance and other days hold back? Do you feel caught between the dark and light? Or do you rest in the blend of both?

Darkness. Do you feel judged? Misunderstood? Are you sneaky? Are you comfort? And what do you think of our friend, the moon? Do you feel lonely when the sky is empty or are you happy for some time to yourself? Are you the evil warrior or a warm blanket of safety and rest? Do you crave light or can you find repose in your own shadows? Are you lonely? Are you satisfied? Do you call out for the light of day to greet you? Do you play in those early morning hours? Do you sleep when Dawn appears, or do you linger in the shadows of the day?

*Active Meditation*

Inhale deeply and begin to follow your breath in four counts: inhale, pause, exhale, pause. As you do this, imagine the inhale as dawn, pause as day, exhale as dusk, and pause as darkness. In this way, experience the rhythms of the day through your breath. Notice whether you have a favorite or one where there is more connection today.

# CHERRY BLOSSOM WISDOM

Once upon a time there was a beautiful pink cherry blossom. She was stunning in her splendor—light, extravagant, playful. She wanted to swim in the air, but nevertheless clung to the branches, hoping she could live and bloom and grow for a good long time.

Alas, the blossom spent vast amounts of energy worrying about what would come next. Would she fall? Would she soar? Would she die? All the blossoms around her were letting go and gently floating through the air. They seemed oblivious to what might lay beneath them.

"How ridiculous," she thought. "Don't they know you have to fight for what you want?"

"Really?" chimed in the branch upon which she clung. "All I do is sit here, come rain or shine, and beautiful, amazing things happen to me."

"Like what?" asked the blossom.

"Like green leaves and blooms and purple sprouts and colors changing and covering me in pink light until I am so full I don't know what to do. And just when I think I can't hold another thing, the load begins to lighten—slowly, but surely—the weight dissolves and I grow and morph and change into something new."

"But if I fall from this branch, I will die and turn into mush."

"Yes, you will change, but you will transform into something new and life-giving, like food and molecules."

"But will I be as beautiful as before?"

"Who defines beauty? Beauty is in your heart, not your color or weight or size or smell. Give it a try. Let go."

And so the blossom let go and she was filled with the greatest exhilaration of her existence. She was free in those moments as she floated to the earth. Free as a bird. She was swimming in the air and nothing else mattered in the world.

*Pondering*

 What undiscovered adventures might await you today? Is there something you need to let go? Are you willing to risk stepping into the unknown for a chance to experience something new? Ponder the possibilities.

MARCH 26

# SAVOR

---

**Savor: to give oneself to the enjoyment of.**

---

When's the last time you truly savored something? It's easy to go through life mindlessly encountering everything that comes in our pathway. We think we're awake and aware with comments like "This tastes good," "You look nice today," or "Isn't the weather great?" I, however, am talking about something deeper. What does it look like to savor? For point of reference, I offer a personal experience with a piece of chocolate.

Who knew a tiny, minuscule bit of French truffle could provide such delight? *Trés magnifique!* While I am not your typical chocolate-craving person, I find myself occasionally yearning for a taste of the delectable delight. One particular evening following a lovely light dinner, my taste buds said, "Thank you and one more thing . . . Chocolate, please." I considered my alternatives—diving into a date-expired bag of Tollhouse semi-sweet chips or the never-satisfying unsweetened Baker's chocolate. Neither would suffice. Fortunately, at the opportune moment, my husband was on his way out and I posed, "Chocolate truffles, please. Can you pick some up?" He knew there was no possible answer except yes.

To give oneself over to the enjoyment of something, one must be fully present. So it was to be. When my husband returned home, truffles in tow, I turned my training in presence over to this sensual piece of dusted decadence. Using my senses, I examined it, smelled it, touched it, and took the tiniest bites possible, each one more flavorful than the next. This quarter-sized treat delivered more than half a dozen bites of unadulterated heaven and the memory of pure enjoyment.

*Active Meditation*

 Look around the room and find something you'd like to savor. The hot tea by your side, the plant in the corner, the tree outside your window. Bring your gaze fully to this object as if you've never seen it before, offering curiosity and inquisitiveness. Let your senses guide you as you bring your full presence to this object. Consider how you can savor other moments, people, and things throughout your day.

# SCRIBBLED ON A SCRAP OF PAPER

d iving into the depths . . . do i fight or
will i surrender?

are you leading me in my dreams?
will i awaken
to an ongoing nightmare?

or shall peace
finally flow and wash over me
with new, abundant life?

*Poetry Ponder*

What is your choice today: fight or surrender? Which
will bring you abundant life?

# SEEKING SOURCE

W e are each on a journey of amazing possibilities with forks in the road and many choices to be made. Do they all lead to the same place? Can choices made along the path look different for each of us and still lead to one Source? I hear the voices of my past (and occasionally my present) say, "Do not stray from the narrow path. If you do, you will be wrong. You will live in eternal hell." Ironically, it feels more like hell to follow the narrow voices that want to rein me in—to keep me from living my true nature. But wait—would that be a "sinful" nature? The one to which evil tempts me? Thoughts like this feel so dramatic and forced and fear-based. But the voices of judgment hang tough and strong, telling me to keep myself in check.

Could those strong and tough voices of judgment be from God? Is my true nature so evil that I need hard and fast guardrails? I think not. My heart, my soul, my very being tells me to listen to the beauty. To trust that God will meet me where I am as long as it is God I am seeking.

Ironically, I don't believe it is God I have the problem with. The challenge is to live in the world and follow my path regardless of how others tell me I should live. You see, I believe that the way of Jesus is love. It is God I am seeking. It is God who is seeking me. Together, we will make our own path.

*Visualization and Meditation*

 Quiet your thoughts and listen closely for the voice of the God of your understanding. Envision what your path together looks like.

# SHADOW REFLECTION

*"But the sacred presence is there, breathing in the shadows."*
*Jan L. Richardson*

My breath has come in fits and bursts this day. With tears and anger. Grief and sorrow. Loss. I felt silly about my emotion, because I have so much to be grateful for. Yet I do not want to rush toward the light. I need to be solemn. Alone. To have solitude. But it's not to be.

Children rustle around me. The phone rings incessantly. The dog breathes hard and asks to be noticed. Messages pile up and clamor for my attention. The soaking carpet screams at me through my nostrils.

Momentarily, the smell of warm soup comforts me, and then the tears come again.

I am tender. Yearning to be still. Something beckons in the future, but all I have is now. The late afternoon darkness wraps its arms around me. I want to sleep. To close my eyes and dream. To sleep a full night without stirring.

I yearn for warmth and comfort. To be held in arms that ask for nothing. An embrace that gives without condition. Yahweh. Breath of God. This day I am tired. Worn out from disaster and work. Spent from holding in emotion. I want to cry. I want to create. I want to rest in the shadows.

*Visualization and Action*

 Survey your surroundings until you find a place where dark meets light. Bring your attention to the shadow while breathing deeply in and out. Allow the darkness to be a welcoming presence wrapping its arms around you and providing rest in this present moment.

# TRUTH FOUND IN SILENCE

More often than not, truth is found in silence.
In shrouds of white covering the heads of pilgrims
who walk softly across the oldest ground on earth.
On stones where churches were not built, but
rather set free from the earth that held them
like a tomb waiting to be opened.

Silence digs into our souls like deft archaeologists
searching for the origin of man when perhaps
they should be looking for the origin of woman.
After all, Lucy, those primordial bones discovered in
Ethiopia, were female—
a woman's frame, not a man's.

And how do men arrive in life if not through
the wombs of their mothers?
Distinctly female.
Feminine.
Finely honed.
Foreign.

More often than not, truth is found in silence.
But first the rage must come . . .
The breath shaking sobs of birth and anguish.
Silence comes second.
We want to skip the first phase—the throbbing rage that brays,
*Release. Let go. Burn, baby, burn.*

We want to skip that state because
it's painful and nasty and hurts like hell.
Hell.
The Biblical place that is anything but silent
with its burning lake and gaping mouths
pouring forth the blasphemy of the ages.

More often than not, truth is found in silence . . .
and beauty is birthed through pain.
The two are lovers locked in the dance of life.
Sweat pouring off bodies—passionate and inflamed,
mixing with tears and saliva and semen to plant
the seeds of what comes next

*Journal Meditation*

Spend the next ten minutes journaling with the
prompt "Truth is found in silence."

# ROLES

I am a writer, a muse, a poet, a pawn. I move myself throughout these roles, shifting and strategizing like chess pieces on an ivory board. In the distance, I hear church bells ring and gravel stirring under the weight of an approaching car. Chatter begins a few feet away, breaking the silence and sneaking into my reverie. The conversation has interrupted my focus and my moment of silence is broken. Choices stir through my consciousness. Will I be angry? Let this go? Or do something entirely different? Rather than become distracted, can I allow myself to engage more deeply in what is being offered through this space? What is the gift in this untimely interruption?

My mind quickly flows through the options as I try to make sense of the nonsensical. Sometimes an interruption is just that—an interruption. I invite myself to stop. Look. Listen. Breathe. It's okay to go back to the beginning and remember I am a writer, a muse, a poet, a pawn. Sometimes I move myself through these roles and other times, they move me.

*Active Meditation*

Pause and listen to the sounds around you. For a moment, label them as distraction. Refocus and consider them as a gift with something to offer. Finally, allow them to simply be a part of the landscape in this moment.

# HOW FOOLISH IS THAT?

One recent year, Maundy Thursday (which commemorates Jesus's final feast before his death) happened to fall on April Fool's Day. For weeks in advance, I found myself reflecting on the potential irony of this. Questions swam through my mind, starting in full force with the gospel story of Mary Magdalene pouring expensive perfume onto Jesus's feet. *How foolish is she?* thought the observing witnesses. Shortly thereafter on the fateful Thursday before his betrayal and death, Jesus declared to his disciples, "I will wash your feet." *What?* they wondered. How foolish is that? Our leader becoming a servant to us?

The progression of foolishness continues as we consider the larger narrative of a man dying on a cross and subsequently rising from the dead—willingly giving his life so that others might live. How foolish is that? I wonder if Jesus asked the same question of his heavenly father? *Really? Put me on a stake and crucify me? You've got to be kidding. Couldn't we do this some other way?* They say he did not question. Still, I wonder.

Perhaps I am alone in seeing the irony of placing Jesus's story of betrayal and death alongside the celebration of the archetypal Fool, but today is a day for foolishness, so why not? Manifesting in a variety of forms (clown, court jester, trickster, happy child), the Fool reminds us to embrace life, lighten up, and view normal circumstances from an upside-down perspective—kind of like the perfume-pouring, friend-betraying, cross-bearing participants of Maundy Thursday. How foolish is that?

On this day of the Fool consider what embracing life looks like for you.

*Pondering*

Pick your ponder from these five questions: Where might you be taking yourself too seriously? Where are you living so lightly that others are forgotten? Will you wash another's feet today—literally or metaphorically? Will you embrace life for what it is—foolish, dark, majestic? Can you be a fool for love's sake?

# MYSTERY ON THE MOUNTAIN

Transitional seasons are always quite interesting for me as I wait to see what will manifest in my life while attempting to be present to the world around me. Restlessness can overtake me and impatience at what's next knocks at my door. One early spring, my time of waiting introduced some interesting messengers. The experience placed me in a virtual remake of Alfred Hitchcock's classic thriller, *The Birds*. While not nearly as frightening, it appeared as though if I didn't listen carefully, I might find myself covered in blue jays cackling and laughing at me.

It started innocently enough. While driving along a neighborhood road, I looked to the side and noticed one distinct blue jay. Beautiful, he seemed a bit out of place; the locale was not known for blue jays. A day or two later—different road, same thing. A single blue jay placed herself distinctly next to my stopped car. Coincidence? Perhaps. The next day, however, scenes from the Alfred Hitchcock movie ensued while I was at Mount Rainier with friends. As we were going to our car after lunch, there was another amazing jay. And then another and another and another until they nearly surrounded us. It was surreal.

Now they really had my attention and I began to wonder, "What's the deal with blue jays?" One of my friends said that they represent either dabblers or masters. This felt oddly familiar to my current state of mind, so upon returning home, I opened Ted Andrews' book *Animal Speak* and looked them up. The words spoke to an innate amount of ability that was scattered or undeveloped. The jay was here to inform me of the greater resourcefulness and adaptability that was about to unfold. I had found a new vision and clarity on the direction of this transitional time via "the birds." What did I hear? It's time to focus. Listen. Wait. Be still and know.

Be direct in what you choose to do and stop being scattered. Listen. Wait. Focus.

As you transition into your new day consider the following:

*Journal Meditation*

 Take a few moments and breathe deeply while you wait in stillness and listen. Then use your journal to write down your thoughts on these questions. Where or when do you feel scattered and/or focused? What does it mean to wait for the unknown? Is greater resourcefulness and adaptability necessary to follow your dreams? What might that look like?

# MORNING MINDFULNESS

A good friend once asked me how I "fight for my personal freedom every day." It is a question I understand and take seriously. In my work with groups and individuals, I often share that if you think you can have one amazing experience and then that experience will carry you effortlessly through the rest of your days, you are sorely mistaken. So, how do we hold onto those amazing experiences when they enter our lives? How do we stay connected with God or Spirit or Universe or ourselves?

Over the years, I've personally collected a tool bag full of techniques. Morning pages and journaling. Centering Prayer. Lectio Divina. Sharing story with others. Giving without thought of receiving. Expressing gratitude. The list goes on and on, but one that resonates with me that we can do anytime and anywhere (without having to set aside "special" time for it) is to be mindful of the present moment. Right now is all we have. What does it look like to embrace the potentially mundane of the day? (And I say "potentially" because once you become mindful and connected, nothing seems mundane anymore.) My own mundane morning has looked like this:

The sky, alive. God everywhere. The touch of hydrangeas. The smell of rosemary. A squirrel darting out to meet me on the sidewalk. A mother with her big old dog. Her baby swaddled in the stroller. The dog pulling her around the stop sign. Smiling, it takes me back to those times with my own daughter when she was a babe. The sky. The birds taking flight. Fire and flight. Powerful combination. I see the birds lined up on the telephone wire. I see the fingers of God. The rays of the sun coming through the clouds. It is a gift. I am overcome. I am one. The world has disappeared. I am sky. I am clouds. I am flight. I am the telephone wire. I am the dog wrapping myself around the stop sign. I am the baby bundled in the stroller. I am the little girl standing on the porch saying good morning. She is brave and bold as she tells her old dog not to bark at me. I am enlightened. I am alive.

*Ponder and Apply*

What brings you alive? How do you stay connected to your true essence, your personal freedom? What gives you flight or starts your blaze? If your answers are slow to come, continue pondering. Finally, take five minutes and begin practicing presence right now.

# SIX SENSES OF GOD

No old man in flowing robes and long white beard for me. My God looks like the wind, the rain, the sun and moon. He is creation all around—both seen and imagined.

Rainstorm beating on a tin roof and brook gently babbling through the forest. The laughter of children and screams of childbirth. Tinkling bells and booming gongs. These are the voices of Majesty.

God smells like spring after the first rain. Roses, old and fragrant. Wet dog and fresh-baked bread. Homemade cookies and pie. The taste of sweet nectar dripping from fresh berries. Complexities of a gourmet meal. Chinese food and take-out pizza. Communion wine. God pours flavor into life.

Experience God with the touch of a newborn's bottom, a soft kitten, or the bark of a gnarled tree. The suede of a young child's head and the crepe-like texture of a woman's weathered hand.

A presence that embodies pain and sorrow, joy and laughter. Tugging of the heart and a whisper in the ear. The flutter of stomach and pounding of heart. Our God is the feast of eyes and the fullness of soul.

*Poetry Ponder*

Ponder what your god looks, tastes, smells, and sounds like.

# SIPS AND DROPS OF BLESSING

"The element of water connects us to a sacred web across the globe and invites us into acts of blessing, pouring forth love and grace to the world around us and receiving it in return."
*Christine Valters Paintner*

I've often thought of the air we breathe as being connected to everyone in the world. My neighbor in Puerto Rico inhales the same air that flowed from my Seattle home, across the United States and then south to the Caribbean. In my mind, it moves on around the world across Europe and Asia, crossing the Pacific and then back home again.

Air flows freely and, although it may feel stagnant for periods of time, it is still fluid, as is water. While water may not be the exact same body flowing directly from one place to another, there is still the possibility and invitation to connect across the globe—if only in our heart and imagination. When I ponder my flowing tears dropping into a stream that flows toward the ocean, which moves via gulf stream, I can witness a piece of myself touching the woman in Africa who washes her clothes on a rock while bending over a muddy river. Perhaps it is the same water melted from the polar ice cap, evaporated, blown through the clouds and poured out on a different continent halfway around the world.

While I am no scientist, I do know that water changes shape and form and has a unique path of its own. I love the image of blessings passed through sips and drops of water.

*Visualization and Action*

Bring a centering focus to this moment by allowing your breath to flow freely through your inhale and exhale. Continue breathing deeply and imagine what it would be like to consider water as "acts of blessing, pouring forth love and grace to the world around us." Through your breath, allow this pouring forth to flow.

# EVEN GIRLS IN TUTUS CRY

One spring morning, I had the delicious opportunity to meet with a dear friend and spend a few hours dreaming together of creative possibilities for our lives. Part of my dreaming included fessing up to some of the things that stop me from moving forward. These mainly consisted of whining words like "I could never" or "Everybody else does it better than me."

The background of this conversation featured children, mainly in the two- to four-year-old range, romping up and down the sun-drenched beach—some with shovels in hand, others wearing brightly colored hats, most being trailed by mothers trying to keep up with their toddlers' mad dashes toward the sea. One little girl in particular caught my eye. She was several yards down the beach but close enough that I could see she was wearing a fabulous pink-and-black tutu, her mop of curly auburn hair flying in the breeze of her own making.

Tutus always catch my fancy and I can easily get caught up in the magic of tulle. As I watched the little princess from a distance, I felt empowered to overcome my whining and replace my "I could never" with a most certain "Of course I can!"

A brief stop in the ladies' room brought us face-to-face with tutu girl. Her glee had been replaced by bellowing cries and fear at the sound of the hand dryer. The illusion of perfection in tulle was momentarily shattered. Which was the illusion? What was the reality? Would my resolve waver too? Perhaps it was only the magic of the beach, sunshine, and the tutu that made my dreams seem possible.

Nevertheless, I leaned into my resolve and listened to my inner creative spirit as I realized sometimes . . .

. . . even girls in tutus cry.

*Visualization*

How would you finish the sentence "I could never . . ." Ask yourself, "Why not? Is it absolutely true you could never?" Now, drape yourself in magic tulle or your superman cape. Shift your statement to "Of course I can!" Imagine boys in capes and girls in tulle flying, not crying.

# BEAUTY IN THE (NOT SO) SMALL THINGS

---

*"Beauty is the physical manifestation of the Mystery—
God, Spirit, the Divine—that surrounds and
beckons to us every day of our lives."*
*Oriah*

---

I lead an ordinary, extraordinary life. Most days are an amazing reminder to me and today I'd like to share one with you. On this day, the sun seemed to shine a little brighter. The morning found me snuggled in bed—reading, writing, and listening to music. It was heavenly. Then I ventured out to work. The air was crisp and clear, springtime starting to tease. I had the privilege of sharing a young woman's story and being with her in her struggles. There was something so good about knowing she had not been alone for an hour and neither had I. The Divine was present.

The day led me to a local outdoor mall where I made a return rather than purchasing something new. It felt great! I stood in the sunshine for awhile and pondered the possibilities of the time before my next appointment. Ultimately, I decided on coffee and a bagel at a local espresso bar. My bagel was fresh, my coffee was hot, and the banter of baristas and customers was light. Again, heavenly. And the day grew even better. I ran into a friend I had not seen in years. We stood in the fresh air, catching up and sharing stories.

All day long, life brought me delight. I laughed out loud with the joy of synchronicity when I saw a sign I had driven by a hundred times and never before noticed. I had tea with a friend and her soulful rescue dog who demonstrated much about relaxation and enjoying the moment. I saw Mount Rainier rimmed in pink clouds. I heard my daughter laugh. I knew my son was safe. I sparred and joked with my husband. I spoke to counselors and social workers. I corresponded with friends and read provocative blogs. I could go on and on about the "ordinary," but you see, those things do not feel ordinary to me. They are beautiful and extraordinary—"physical manifestations of the Mystery."

*Pondering*

Where do you see the extraordinary in your life? Take a moment to pause and look around. Allow yourself to be washed over with the beauty of even one small detail in your life.

# CALLING

While attending graduate school to become a mental health counselor, I often heard the word "calling." It was intriguing and stirred something inside me that I couldn't quite name. It took a few years to grasp this concept, and it finally clicked when I was in the midst of my new career and a supervisor said, "Listen to you! What a wonderful time of your life. You have found your calling!" Did I find it or did it find me? Somehow it was through the words of another that I started to understand that my inner longings and the calling of how I will be in the world are uniquely intertwined.

It's amazing to see what happens when I can let go and quit trying to guess what may come next. Who would have dreamed an accountant from Oklahoma would end up as a therapist or author in Seattle?

What does the Universe hold for you? Are you open to the possibilities that lie ahead? Will you allow yourself the chance to dream and listen today? It is often hard to know what the call may be or from where it comes. One thing I do know, however, is that just as a bird outgrows its nest, we, too, must risk in order to fly.

*Visualization and Meditation*

Picture a bird's nest safely harboring tiny eggs. Now imagine those eggs hatching and baby birds beginning to emerge. Watch the birds grow in your mind and as you breathe, give one bird the name of a dream you have held. Keep breathing and consider this: What will it take for that dream to leave the safety of the nest and receive the opportunity to soar?

# CAPACITY

The human heart carries unfathomable pain. Its capacity for joy is unlimited. We shield ourselves from ourselves. We try to hide from God. Our ache runs deep like hidden riverbeds beneath rock surfaces. We become brittle until we break or explode or implode. Without meter or rhyme, we forge on, never knowing if tears or laughter will burst forth. It is tenuous, this life. To embrace the moments. To feel the depth and agony of pain while soaking in a perfumed tub. To experience gales of belly laughs while playing a silly game. To know the pounding in the head from stress or excess wine.

The capacity of the body is immense. The capacity of the heart, infinite. Just when we think it will break, joy emerges from the ashes. How? Why? I do not know. It is grace. The grace of God. Learned. Given. Received. I do not understand this God. This life.

I need to feel it. I need to share it. This depth. This groundedness that I do not understand. The both/and. Not either/or. I am not sad or happy. I am both. I am filled with delight and terror and grief. Both/and. I don't understand, yet I know it to be true.

Our capacity is immense. The pendulum swings far and wide and depths sink beyond comprehension. Life's tapestry is rich. I do not understand it and I do not have to understand. When I come to this still place, I know. Pure and simple.

The cycle of life forges on. Birth. Death. Resurrection. Over and over and over again. The capacity of the body is immense. The capacity of the heart—infinite.

*Visualization and Meditation*

 Quietly ground yourself and begin to breathe into your heart center. Imagine your heart as a supple and resilient balloon. As you breathe in, fill the balloon with images of joy and delight. With each exhale, release grief and sorrow. In your mind's eye, watch as the balloon expands and contracts with infinite capacity—regenerating with each breath.

# A PIECE OF THE BEGINNING

---

*What part of you is a small piece of the beginning?*

---

Once, while being interviewed about my work, I was drawn to the above query even as it somewhat confused me. I considered asking for clarification but decided to plunge ahead on my own.

*Fire.* My answer is fire. I believe there is a spark deep inside of me that is a piece of the eternal beginning. It cannot be squelched. It cannot die. It was here in the beginning and shall live forever. When I am living from the place in my soul that is whole and true, the small piece grows and glows. It is like the spark that turns into flame. It is the place where I come alive, and when I share it with others and they are willing to receive, they, too, come a little more alive. It is the best beginning I know.

*Journal Meditation*

 Come to a quiet place and follow your breath for a few minutes to calm your mind. Pose to yourself the question: What part of you is a small piece of the beginning? Allow whatever wants to arise. Follow with some free-flow journaling on the question: why?

# CAPTURING FIRE

Simmering around the edges, I am reminded of the fire in my belly that has dominated the growth seasons of my life. The image of fire tingles like a slow ember just before bursting into full flame. Pondering the places where our humanity and the Divine meet in fullness captures this heat. It comes like a flash when reading the words of another and burns in its absence when I go searching for it. Often it scalds. Always it warms.

What image does fire ignite inside you? Simmering? Scalding? Life-giving warmth? Whatever it is, I invite you to consider the warmth of your own light.

*Active Meditation*

Placing a candle in front of you, thoughtfully bring match to wick. Allow your gaze to stay with the flame. Imagine the spark is the fire in your belly. For two or three minutes, ponder what is ignited in you.

## April 12

# Childhood Now

W ho says children have to grow up? Once I had the privilege of witnessing a group of men bonded and laughing. During this extraordinary time, I felt the nurturing warmth and embrace of the Divine Presence. I saw God in the face of a child. In the eyes of grown men. In the embrace of a friend. In the glow of my beloved. All. Skipping. Running. Resting. Excited and joyful. Tender and strong.

Men of all ages. Young. Old. In-between. Simultaneously young boys and men of strength. Unwavering. Speechless and shouting. Hoarse and ever so clear. On their knees and scaling the highest mountain. God was present. Brothers and sisters. Souls connected as one. Magical. Holy. Eternal. Through the eyes of a grown-up child I saw God.

*Visualization and Action*

 Sit quietly and recall a fond memory from childhood. With eyes closed, experience the ease of a child at play. Acknowledge this child who still lives within you. Invite him or her to warm your heart with joy today.

# APRIL 13

# CHOICE

---

**two doors stood before me
one of joy
one of sorrow
i chose joy**

---

Life is a series of choices. We choose to get up in the morning or to stay in bed. We decide what we will eat or whether we'll skip breakfast. We plot our route to work or school or a room in our house. We decide whether to smile or frown, whether we're having a good day or a bad day. Perhaps I've lost you and you're thinking you have no choice in some of these matters. I invite you to think again. We always have a choice. It may not be easy or something we like, but choice is always present.

It's habit to get stuck in places and convince ourselves we have no choice. Here's a simple example:

I have to go to work today. Why? Because I won't get paid if I don't go.

What if you don't get paid? I won't have any money. What if you don't have any money? Then I can't pay my bills.

What if you don't pay your bills? They'll take my house away.

They'll take it today? No, they won't take my house away today.

Could you choose to not go to work today? Yes. I could choose to not go today.

*Active Meditation*

Consider an area where you feel you have no choice. In your mind or on paper, ask yourself "why" and "what if" questions. See what happens as you drill down and discover the choices you do have.

## APRIL 14

# FELLOWSHIP

One day while running errands, I ran into a woman I'd known for several years through our children's school and a church we had recently left. I knew the question was coming before it was out of her mouth. "Where are you fellowshipping these days?" she asked. "Nowhere," I answered. Although I refused to feel guilty about our decision to leave, I subsequently hemmed and hawed about how it was hard and we were looking . . . blah, blah, blah.

Walking away, I felt like I had just told a big fat lie—not the "we are looking" part, but the "nowhere" part. It felt like such a falsehood, because in reality I am fellowshipping daily—with the world, with myself, with long distance friends, on the phone with my sister, with my husband as we talk about our faith journey— really with anyone who wants to be even a bit authentic or at least listen to me as I practice my own feeble attempts.

So, what is fellowship? In the way this woman asked, it felt so confining, like a single building in which to perform ritual on a specific day and time of the week. Not to be disparaging, because I absolutely believe in ritual and gathering together in relationship, but fellowship feels so much bigger than something we only do on Sunday morning.

Sharing with others, contemplative prayer, witnessing stories through art and song—that is fellowship. When my heart connects with the beauty of nature—the moon, the sun, the cold air on my face, the flowers at the market—that is fellowship.

Fellowship is not simply held inside four walls with a designated group of believers. It is life. The homeless man on the street. The laughing infant in the coffee shop. The stranger in your midst. Returning to the original question: "Where am I fellowshipping these days?" Everywhere!

*Ponder and Apply*

Ponder what fellowship means to you. Where do you find connection with others? With a higher power? With yourself? Make a date to fellowship now.

# FIGHT, FLIGHT, OR COMPASSIONATE KNOWING?

"We are slowly discovering what many of us are calling 'the Third Way,' neither flight nor fight, but the way of compassionate knowing. Both the way of fight and the way of flight fall short of wisdom, although they look like answers in the heat of the moment."

*Richard Rohr*

In one of my first spiritual direction courses, I was introduced to the theme of three types of relationship: with self, with others, and with a Source greater than we. Relationships are tricky at best and compassionate knowing can be a difficult path. It asks us to operate with awareness rather than act on impulse. This discovery invites us to consider whether we as people will choose to fight, flee, or entertain trying something new in the relationship. We must be risk-takers in order to be peacemakers, and it can be precarious to break from the status quo and seek peace. To pursue a new way of looking at things. To do something different when the old is not working.

In living life fully, there are multiple venues where we face the urge to fight or flee. Sinking into depression and not considering options can be a form of flight. Immediately going to outside sources for cures, saying nothing is wrong, or merely treating symptoms is a form of fight or dismissal. Feeling the pain, being in it, and wrestling with it resonates of connection and compassionate knowing. How might this third way impact your way of being in the world?

*Active Meditation*

Name a current issue you struggle with relationally (self, other, Source). Consider your way of being with this situation. Do you fight, flee, or bring compassionate knowing? Ponder the impact of making one slight change.

# FOLLOWING THE THREAD

*"There's a thread that you follow. It goes among things
that change. But it doesn't change."*
*William Stafford*

Stafford's notion of the thread we follow is one I've often pondered. When I think of my work as therapist, coach, spiritual director, and SoulStroller, I look at the varied ways I engage others. While it could appear on the surface as spreading thin, in reality the thread that connects each process allows those I engage with to move deeper toward self-awareness and personal goals.

We each learn in different ways, but always by experience. For some people, awareness comes through spoken words. For others, it is more visceral. There's auditory and visual. Art. Music. Nature. Movement. The list is as unique as each individual, and inside everyone is the beginning of his or her thread. By being open to process rather than product (journey versus destination), awareness and transformation deepen.

My thread—both personal and professional—leads toward deepened self-awareness and more authentic living. My offered modalities are personalized to each individual. Sometimes the work is done in two chairs, face-to-face, listening to story and waiting for the thread to appear. Other times, awareness comes through image and symbol, silence and contemplation, journaling or physical movement. The beauty is that healing and insight can happen anywhere and in a variety of ways.

*Pondering*

 Imagine your life as tapestry while you ponder these questions. Have you let go of your personal thread? Perhaps the edges have become frayed and you're ready for some re-weaving? How do you envision the threads of your life? Do they weave together to create a cohesive rendering? Are there so many loose ends and knots that you're coming unraveled?

# FORGET ABOUT COMFORT: PART 1

Forget about comfort—whatever comfort is. These are words spoken to me from the innermost recesses of my heart. I first heard them as I sat surrounded by a tropical paradise garden, and I was reminded of the garden. The beginning.

"And the man and his wife were both naked and were not ashamed." Genesis 2:25

Why are we now so fearful to be naked—both physically and spiritually? Given the choice, I imagine most people would choose to bare themselves physically rather than let someone see the inner recesses of their heart. It is such a paradox because we live our lives desiring to be seen and truly known yet still we hide.

"And the man said, 'I was afraid because I was naked; so I hid myself.'" Genesis 3:10

We hide in our comfort. We hide behind our clothes. Our image. Our jobs. Our homes. We say we are serving others, catering to their needs—our children, spouses, bosses, friends. What are we afraid of? Being selfish? Being wrong? Being seen for who we truly are? Being naked?

We build up savings accounts for old age. We work until we can work no more and then ask, "Where did my life go? I have built this comfort and still I am not comfortable. What happened?"

Comfort. The comfort of the womb. The safety of a bosom cradling a child's head. The joy of being seen and truly known. Connection. Relationship. True comfort comes from authentic relationship. Relationship with God, with others, with ourselves.

Forget about comfort—whatever comfort is.

*Meditation*

Take a moment and observe your surroundings. Consider what is essential for you to be truly comfortable. Make note of what may hide you from being authentic with yourself and others.

# FORGET ABOUT COMFORT: PART 2

It is the illusion of comfort that keeps us locked in fear and turmoil. For comfort is not about material wealth and trappings. Comfort is being at rest and at peace with the Universe and with oneself, for the two cannot be separated. Comfort is surrendering to the still, small voice that says, "Let the little children come. Come to me, all who are weary and heavy burdened."

Our comfort zone is an illusion—a trick—to keep us in conflict. Take a step, move beyond, one tiny motion can change your life. One honest moment of moving through or past fear creates a miracle. Taking the risk to do something different can break the chains that bind.

Each day it looks different. Some days the biggest thing I can do is get out of bed and step out from under my cozy covers. Or speak to a stranger as my heart pounds wildly. Go to graduate school. Give up a good job. Travel to a foreign country. Let go of my teenagers. Take a step. A single step outside my zone of comfort.

If there is a battle raging inside (whether loudly or nearly undetectable), then something is yearning to move and shift. Complacency holds fast, but risk is the ticket to freedom. Forget about comfort.

*Pondering*

What would you do today if you were brave?

## APRIL 19

# OPENING WHAT?

"An open mind, like an open window, should be
screened to keep the bugs out."
*Virginia Hutchinson*

I try to make it a regular practice to not open email before enjoying my morning quiet time and journaling. What happens when I don't follow this policy is that the wondrous thoughts that emerge from dreamtime easily slip away with the click of a mouse. Once I choose to open my mail, my head is instantly filled with other stuff.

One such morning, I didn't follow my own rule and I received two chuckles from friends, a prayer request from a sister in need, an email from a disgruntled co-worker, the new download of my favorite TV show, a great morning reading about choice, and an update from a friend on her latest cruise. Throw into the mix familial and work duties and—presto—quiet time must wait until later. I find I have little success putting the screen back on the window once the bugs have flown in.

*Action Invitation*

For the next three days, I invite you to establish a practice of spending ten to twenty minutes in silence before doing anything else. Pay attention to what "bugs" beckon to fly through your screen and make a plan to shut them out for this time period. If you find benefit in beginning your day this way, repeat for three more days. Repeat again.

# AWAKENING

I awaken thinking of small things and simplicity. How these are the things I've built my life upon.

A breath. Birdsong. The feel of tree bark beneath my palm. Steady. Solid.

Small steps followed by daring leaps. It is the leaping that others notice, but it is in the minutiae where change and magic occur.

Getting quiet. Slowing down. Being still. Listening. Waiting. Resting.

The small things. A grain of sand. Bumblebee wing. Baby's laugh. Child's tear.

Are they so small, really?

I pause and wonder how to build a career, a life, a living on these small things. Can a single tealight illuminate a world of darkness? The idea is overwhelming and so I return to the most healing things I know: one breath, one step, one insight, one moment, one heartbeat.

*Meditation*

 Follow your breath for the next five minutes. Inhale. Exhale. One slow breath at a time.

# PARADOX AND CONVICTION

Pondering what it looks like to live in paradox has been a favorite topic in my awakening years.

Considering what it's like to live in the already and the not yet. Both/and. Thy Kingdom come. If we are not definitive, does that mean we lack conviction?

Having grown up in a fundamentally black-and-white, right-and-wrong environment, I must admit today I get concerned with the compelling need to take a stand. Being a person whose stand is unwavering for the sake of not being "wrong" is not who I am any longer.

My way of being is drawn to words like mystery and possibility rather than good or bad, right or wrong. Stand-takers might say this makes me wishy washy and indecisive. I think not. Mystery and possibility offer infinitely more expansiveness than toeing the line.

The poet Rilke's words speak deeply to where I am in life today. He says, "I want to unfold. I don't want to stay folded anywhere, because where I am folded, there I am a lie." If I try to keep things folded up or in a box, it is limiting and feels like a lie. Instead, I want to open up the lid and unfold the mysteries—the areas where I have placed limitations with my judgments and insecurities. I want to live in the paradox whereby appearing as though I may not have convictions, I, in reality, have more conviction and truth surrounding me than ever before. The possibilities and the mysteries are limitless. To that I am convicted.

*Visualization*

What is one nonnegotiable in your life? Consider if this fits snugly inside a box or if it comes from a place of expansiveness and conviction. Let yourself explore what this means for you personally.

# PASSION AND GLORY

"Participation in glory is the greatest thrill one can have on this earth." When I first heard these words spoken by Professor Dan Allender, something stirred deep within me. Glory and passion seem uniquely intertwined. Witnessing another's passion holds hints of glory as others are stirred to consider their own passion.

My passion is seeing people come alive. It is something that comes in the most unexpected times and places. I have seen glory in perfect transformation when a woman long bent over from the weight of her world stood tall with a new awareness shining upon her face. I witnessed glory when an addict realized his hunger for drugs was representative of a deeper longing, and he chose to nourish his soul rather than his habit. I see glory when my readers struggle through their own process to name their passion.

That is my work, my joy, and my life prayer—to be fighting with and on behalf of truth and beauty for others and myself. Seeking the beauty and glory that we may not be able to see in ourselves. Fighting the battle alongside each other. While I know we must do it for ourselves, we do not have to do it alone. We can travel this path together—learning from one another.

Together we can participate in glory, experiencing "the greatest thrill one can have on this earth."

*Visualization and Meditation*

Close your eyes and let the words "glory" and "passion" wash over you. What does it look like to participate in glory? Notice what scenes come to mind. Are they yours or someone else's? Consider your deepest passion and whether or not you're living it today.

# THE PATH IS MADE BY PAUSING

> "The way is made by walking."
> *Antonio Machado*

Leaving the corner café, coffee in hand, the rich aroma fills my senses and warmth infuses my body. The way is made by walking. Inhale. Exhale. A crimson birdhouse hangs in a barren tree. Festive lights twinkle in a paned window. My heeled boots greet the concrete sidewalk. *Click. Clack. Click. Clack.* The pace is slower in my skirt and dress coat than in my normal tennis shoes and tights. Heels connect to the pathway with a more resounding purpose. *Click. Clack.* Inhale. Exhale. Heel-toe. Heel-toe. The way is made by walking.

A tree—not just any tree—beckons me to stop. It is massive. I have passed it a hundred times, but never like this. Its circumference is probably twenty feet—perhaps I exaggerate, but it demands attention this day. Solid roots permeate the ground, lifting the sidewalk in cracked spaces. How has this tree survived urban sprawl and the early logging days? It is ancient. Moss covers the crevasses of its gray bark. Reaching toward the sky, its branches raise like arms lifting in worship, hundreds of strands praising the heavens. It is a church full of worshipers singing their psalms and with this chorus, my spirits rise. Today, the path is made by pausing.

*Action Invitation*

 Take a walk either inside or out. Deliberately feel your feet connecting to the ground. Heel-toe. Heel-toe. After several moments, stop, close your eyes, take a few deep breaths, and open your eyes with new awareness for the surroundings. Embrace the path offered in this pause.

APRIL 24

# FREE BIRD

"Were it but free, it would soar cloud high."
*Charlotte Bronte*

O sweet bird, you came to me as the tiniest egg, encased in a shell worn too long. I barely noticed you as we passed that first day, but somehow in a fleeting glimpse, I knew it was you.

You were a lone egg, tucked tightly inside your hardened shell with nowhere to safely nestle. Week after week, I sat at the edge of your cage and offered sticks to build your own nest. A tidbit here, a love offering there. Afraid of your own shadow, you turned any movement into potential danger. Together we grew. While I learned to make my gestures more steady and gentle, you learned to receive. As we built a safe nest, the pieces of your shell began to crack and fall away. Slowly, slowly you let kindness seep in. Gradually you trusted yourself and me.

O small bird, I waited patiently as you learned to let my hand enter the cage. You pecked and bit at any object moving into your space. In defense, you would fly into a corner to hide. Some days you perched by the door hoping I would reach in a little further. You began to spread your wings and bump against the wire encasement. You molted and shed and sprouted new feathers. Your color turned from dull brown to brilliant blue, red, yellow, and green—the colors of passion and tears. The colors of new life.

Ultimately, the door stood open for days at a time, but you insisted you weren't ready to fly. Your small beak tentatively peeked through the open space. You perched on my hand until you understood you could not stay there and soar at the same time. So you hopped around the cage and tested your new wings. You scratched and poked and wailed a forlorn cry. Slowly, I receded until you stood alone on the edge, dreaming of flight.

You said it was too soon. I nudged that you were ready. Each week you came to the edge. Each encounter you sprouted a new feather and color. You considered the risk until one day you knew you were ready to fly.

Little bird, flying high, you've broken free of shell and cage. My heart lifts as you spread your wings and flutter away. One last time, you cross my path. Your form is new—no shell, no cage—but with a tip of your wing and a soar across my path, I know this brilliant creature is you. I've known it all along.

*Pondering*

 How is your life like a fragile egg or a frightened bird?

# BUDDING SPRING

What is awakening as we move into spring? There is something about the depths of our souls, the bare bones of our branches, the seed that lies deep within the ground waiting to sprout. The beauty emerges with each slight movement, and while we certainly do not want to rush spring, there is hope in the new buds that wait to blossom.

*Visualization and Action*

Come to a comfortable position and connect your feet with the ground. Inhale deeply and imagine yourself as a strong tree, barren of leaves. Envision the trunk replacing your spine as you breathe and lengthen your posture. In your mind's eye, witness the tree's branches begin to blossom. Witness what may be waiting to bloom within you.

# SIMMERING

The mind is complicated. A memory returns with a flash and you know beyond a shadow of a doubt that in that remembered moment your heart was pierced deeply and the wound is still healing decades later. Sometimes the healing hurts more than the original wound.

anger simmers like a pot on the stove; threatening to explode while silent and steaming

turn up the heat just a bit and you will be burned, so steer clear and gently tilt the lid, letting the pot release some pressure

still the anger simmers, ready to bubble over and make a mess. you inch away but not before inhaling the aroma of contempt and blame

you believe you have made the mess. if the pot explodes it will be your fault, and so you control the temperature as best you can with your tiny hands

hands thrust inside too-big oven mitts that swallow them like boxing gloves. as time goes by your hands will grow into them, but they will always feel clumsy

never allowed to take a healthy swing, you punch the air like windmills spinning in the storm

the circle continues on. the steam releases ever so slightly, but still the anger simmers like a pot on the stove

*Body Practice*

 Check in with your body and notice if there is a place where emotion resides. Notice its location and how it feels. Allow the sensation to expand as you focus on the point in your body. Breathe deeply into the spot allowing the emotion space to expand. Feel the pressure release and, as you are able, let it go.

# SIMPLE AS A LOVE SONG

"I was four years old. I was playing, alone, in a thicket of trees and bushes. A moment came when there was sound and silence at the same time. I became exquisitely aware of the breeze through the leaves, of the sunlight dappling across the earth in front of me. I understood that this was an experience of God in me and around me. It was strange and familiar at the same time, and it was the simplest thing in the world."

*Tess Marshall*

Tess's encounter evokes in me the simplicity of a love song. We spend our lives trying to learn the notes of our own song. Desiring to be purely seen and heard. To be enwrapped in arms that hold and love us. To become exquisitely aware of all that surrounds and encapsulates who we are. The longing. The desire. Everyone loves a love story. You know the ones—where eyes lock, energy charges, and the lovers are known without pretense, without all the if-you-really-knew-me-you-wouldn't-love-me stuff. In an instant, barriers are overcome and magic happens.

It may only be a split second where everything else in the world disappears and you know you are loved. Your heart sings the love song. You experience God's presence. You know He, She, Me exists. People spend a lifetime searching for that feeling, but it seems that you cannot find it when you work at it. You can only open heart, mind, and soul to the experience. It often comes when and where you least expect it. A stranger on the street. A child. A film or book. Words of poetry. Dancing butterflies. A breeze through rustling leaves. A broken heart.

It may take a lifetime to find your own song, but when you experience it you know you have found heaven on earth and it is something you will never forget.

*Visualization and Action*

Center yourself and bring to mind a favorite love story. It may be one from your own life, a movie, book, or pure imagination. Close your eyes and begin to place yourself into the love story, imagining you are the principle character—the one being loved and adored. As you sit quietly with the story, gently wrap your arms around yourself and either stroke or pat your arms as you focus on love. Witness your own love song. It may be a single note or a complex symphony. Allow whatever arises to simply be yours.

# LET IT BLOSSOM

*"And because there is only one of you in all of time*
*this expression is unique."*
*Martha Graham*

This time of year, spring is bursting forth with life and new birth everywhere I look. Blossoms, babies, puppies, and green grass. And the question "What is blossoming in me?" keeps showing up.

What remains hidden below the surface waiting to sprout? How will I blossom and then bring my unique bouquet to the world? There is only one me just as there is only one you. I am a woman ready to spring forth into blossoms—maybe one at a time or maybe a whole bed of crocus bursting at once.

*Ponder and Apply*

Acknowledge there is only one you. How will you blossom today?

# SIMPLICITY

"Simplicity is the seedbed for sane, free, illumined holy living."
*Tilden Edwards*

In the stillness I return to God. The busyness of the days settles into my body like a workout followed by Savasana. In yoga, they say it is in Savasana or "corpse pose" where the benefits of the practice come. Returning to stillness, I am regenerated. Listening to my body, I know it needs rest today. Will I pull out of the quiet and press forward, or can I rest here in the simplicity of bed, rejuvenating?

I ponder the complexity of a simple existence. Eating when hungry. Stopping when full. Resting when tired. Moving when restless. Responding when called. The practices of my life. Focusing on here and now. The garbage truck rumbling outside the window. Cat purring against my chest. Pen flowing across paper. Heartbeat inside chest. Coffee flavoring the walls of my mouth.

Here and now is all I have. This perfect, simple moment is enough. My stomach growls. The kitty hiccups. My head has a twinge of ache. I pause, slowing down to the minuscule of the moment. Operating at the speed of breath. Entering into holy living. Experiencing simplicity.

*Active Meditation*

 Wherever you are right now, close your eyes and allow yourself to begin to tune into the world around and within you. Using all of your senses—smell, taste, touch, hearing, mind's eye—see what you notice.

Allow yourself to explore with curiosity and acceptance for the next few moments. Believe that here and now is a perfect offering as you enter into the simplicity of your surroundings.

# FRIENDS FOREVER

One of the greatest gifts in life can be having a friend who knows you well. You wonder and ponder whether they were with you in another life or somehow silently observing you throughout the years. You experience those moments when you say, "How did you know?" But then it doesn't really matter, does it? Because they have seen deeply into your being, and to know and be known needs no response at all.

*Action Invitation*

Call a friend today and thank him or her for being in your life.

# MAY 1

# IN SEARCH OF
# WINGED WISDOM

Black and white with streaks of blue, her gentle movement catches my eye and causes me to ponder. For what are you searching, little bird? You weave in and out of the brush, looking for or stalking what? Do you seek with intention or open yourself to possibility?

You pause. You hop. You seem to move with a mission. You stalk like a confident hunter in the African bush even though you weigh no more than the smallest marmoset. You leap. You listen. You look. Are you just playing or is this a role of survival? Perhaps they are one and the same. Is this new ground for you to cover or is it comfortable and familiar territory?

With one smooth move, you find your vantage point and wait, a place where you can see the broader world. There you linger until, with one surprising leap, you move to the highest branch and in an instant soar through the sky. Teach me, little bird. What are the secrets of living a winged life?

*Visualization*

Imagine yourself as a gentle winged bird. Where would you soar? What would you seek?

# WHAT DO I KNOW?

W hat do I know?

I know the sun was out only moments ago with the promise of a dry morning.

I know that now the sky has turned gray and raindrops are not far behind.

I know the kitten in my lap is a creation of God even when he seems to be of the devil.

I know my daughter is beautiful and pure as she sleeps in the room down the hall.

I know that I will always be full of questions and unknowing.

I know God is near and yet I long to see His face. Or Her face.

And I know if I allow myself, that face will be seen in the sun, the rain, the kitten, and my daughter.

I will see God in the questions and in the mystery.

I will know this presence even when my heart feels cold and dry because God gives the promise of sun after the rain and light in the midst of dark.

But then again—what do I know?

*Poetry Ponder*

What comes to your mind when you begin a sentence with *I know*?

# Chronic Pain Relief

*Presence is an open, receiving movement through time.*

Dubbed with the label of chronic pain patient, the aging woman sat in front of me with hands bent by rheumatoid arthritis. Her pain had been constant for more years than she could recall. As her soft voice drifted into the room, she unwittingly wrung her hands and grimaced with each subtle movement. There was a look in her sad eyes that spoke of a faraway place and the longing to be heard. Listening closely, I understood no one had ever invited her to share that distant place. Her thoughts had been quarantined as if her agony might be contagious.

On this particular day, we moved away from the medical charts and I asked if she might share a bit of her journey with me. While I don't remember the particulars of where we went, she metaphorically took my hand and led me down her private path. She shared, laughed, and cried as I received. There was no trying to fix anything or directing emotions one way or another. We simply joined together as the hour flew by and our time to close arrived.

With gentle awareness, she raised her eyes from her lap while caressing her curled fingers. "The pain was gone for awhile," she commented with wonder. For years and years, she held no hope of relief. In this moment, however, something had shifted and there was a new light in her eyes as she bathed in the afterglow of presence.

*Meditation*

Set aside whatever may be clamoring for your attention in this moment. Breathe deeply and become present to your breath. Let the glow of wordlessness and oneness wash over you.

## MAY 4

# THISTLE

Thistle outside my window. Weed or wisdom? Beauty or barb? You speak to me of life. Prickly people or situations that poke and prod. Hurting. Snarling. Pushing away. Don't come close or you'll get hurt. Stay away. Guard the path.

Inside, however, all soft and tender. Beautiful beyond description. Intricate spires of deep lavender persist past the pointy bulb. Reaching toward light. Beauty and barb combine and mix into a potion, uniquely you. Then just when I think I've figured it all out—*poof*—you morph and transform again, turning into a million feathery seeds. Spidery. Reaching. Floating. Clinging. The wind pulls and tugs and insists you leave your place of safety and comfort.

Life. Prickly. Hard. Demanding protective covering. Life. Releasing armor to burst into extravagant hue. Life. Tender filaments and seed. Clinging to comfort. Carried on a breeze. Sprouting in the barren desert and lush-filled garden. Life. Wisdom and weed. Beauty and barb. Thistle outside my window. Tenderness inside my heart.

*Pondering*

How is your life like this thistle?

# CLEAN PAIN. DIRTY PAIN.

> "Virtually all suffering comes from the misuse
> of our imagination."
> *Martha Beck*

At least two kinds of pain exist in the world: clean pain and dirty pain. Clean pain shows up when something is truly wrong with us, like grief over the death of a loved one or physical pain when we break a bone. Dirty pain exists in our minds as it ruminates over all of the what ifs. What if I never love again? What if my bone doesn't heal properly? What if . . .

I once knew a man with a nasty toothache. He spent weeks in agonizing pain because he was afraid to call the dentist. Meal after meal he chewed on one side of his mouth to compensate for the ache in the other side. Missed meals and soft food replaced his normally robust appetite. He fretted and stewed over making that appointment. *What if I need a root canal? What if it's jaw cancer? What if?*

Finally in a burst of determination, he picked up the phone and made the call. The dentist could see him immediately. Once there, the man had to wait a moment or two before going into the dreaded dental chair. The time lapse from entering the office until walking out the door with the pain cured and gone was less than ten minutes.

The tooth held the clean pain, because it was real and ultimately an easy fix. His agony and fear, along with the waiting and overcompensating, resulted in weeks of unnecessary dirty pain. His suffering had resulted from overuse of his imagination.

*Action Meditation*

Is there something you are avoiding or refusing to let go? Ask yourself if the "pain" is clean or dirty. Clean pain is pretty simple (e.g., "This hurts"). Dirty pain is messy and increases suffering. Consider the downside and upside of thinking differently.

## MAY 6

# WHIRLWIND

Focusing on breath, yet finding I scarcely have time to breathe.
Listening to the cat's purr—wishing I could be so content.
From where has this whirlwind of my mind come? How can I make it stop?
I've typed over a thousand words this morning. Breathed a dozen cleansing breaths.
Started and stopped and still . . .
the tornado of ideas and creations and concerns whirls through my mind,
creating its own wind tunnel of chaos.

Yesterday, I walked in the wind. I felt spring's air upon my bare legs,
my skirt floating on the breeze of God and the steps of my desire.
I watched the newly bursting lilac blooms nod to me as I passed by.
A floating kite appeared in the sky, its imaginary string held in my palm.
I paused and naughtily picked a dandelion puff and blew the seeds into the wind
(being mindful, of course, to avoid the neatly manicured lawn along my path).

Wind. Breath of God. Ruach.
I write and I recall those moments of bliss,
and in the recollection, I am once again, if only for a moment,
Present.

*Active Meditation*

 Close your eyes and breathe deeply. Are you battling a whirlwind in your mind? Is there someplace you would rather be right now? Continue to breathe and see if you can imagine inhaling fresh air and feel the gentle wind pressing against your body. Allow the whirlwind to calm, if only for a moment, as you are present to now.

## May 7

# Pause for Directions

My local guide offers quick verbal directions and I trust my mind (or at least my body) has taken them in. Down to the end of the drive. Turn east and take the second left (although it's the third if you count the lane). Turn left at Wild Spirit Gallery. Go up the winding road. Weaving through unfamiliar territory and wondering where my next turn will be. Stop. Pause. Listen. Wait for the turn at the graveyard. I notice it is just past Alamo Road. The symbolism of it all is almost too much for me to bear.

Reverence arrives as I make my final left. Poverty and garish beauty resonate from the rural graveyard. I can feel the spirits who have gone before me. It is unlike the manicured lawns or military installments found in the midst of urban cities—Arlington Cemetery or even Rose Hill where my parents lie. There is no order here. Cheap plastic flowers lay upon makeshift wooden crosses that bump against cracked concrete slabs. Headstones elaborate eternal rest next to unmarked mounds.

My instructions continue: Turn left at the graveyard and continue on the makeshift road. Make your way around the cattle guard. But I cannot move. I am mesmerized and awakened by the loving care that resonates out of this chaos. In this moment, the destination no longer matters.

*Journal Meditation*

Pause and listen. Close your eyes and allow today's directions to gently arise in your consciousness. Write them down lest you forget.

## May 8

# COMPASSION

Compassion. How do we find it and give it not just to others, but also to ourselves? Have you ever noticed how quickly we want our emotions to be fleeting? If we stop to feel them at all, we hurriedly move on to the next thing as we let the sensation slip away. In our rushed world, we take time for neither joy nor pain to be deeply felt. Our emotions move quickly—like a flash flood running into the sewer and becoming part of the muck and mire, festering and turning into a stinky, rancid mess, waiting to be dredged up.

What if rather than pushing the emotions down the drain, we put the stopper in the sink and the covers over the manholes? What if we allowed ourselves to be washed with emotion and cleansed at the same time? What if we chose to dance in the rain rather than put up our umbrellas? What if we "experienced" rather than "stuffed"?

Today I say, let the water flood the streets. Let the shower spray everywhere. There are plenty of towels to soak up the excess. Bathe the world in love. Sink into emotion and feel it. Sprinkle compassion wherever you go—beginning with yourself.

*Active Meditation*

Fill a small bowl with water. Center yourself and notice what emotion arises in this moment. Name the feeling, dip your finger into the water, and sprinkle yourself with the emotion. Continue doing this until you've named each emotion that shows up. As you complete this ritual, sprinkle yourself with an extra dose of compassion.

# FRAGILE DREAMS

It can feel exposing to put your dreams out into the world. Not the dreams you have while slumbering, but rather the electrifying ones that keep you wide awake and make your heart race to think of their fruition. Is it presumptuous to believe even the wildest ones could come true? Are you afraid to jinx them if they're spoken out loud? What if everyone laughs and calls us crazy? Are we afraid of failure or are we afraid of success?

Once while in the car, I found myself behind a red Ford two-ton truck from Alaska. On its bumper was a banner that read, "Those who abandon their dreams will discourage yours." It caused me to ponder whether it's the discouragement of others I fear or my own resolve that if I state a dream out loud, one of two things must happen: 1) the dream will seem foolish, or 2) I will be on the hook to make something happen, thus opening possibility for either success or failure. Scary, huh?

Is that what dreams are about? Moving toward our heart's desire? Perhaps that's why dream sharing is fragile, because it is a heart thing. I wonder if sharing our heart is the same as sharing our dreams?

*Body Practice*

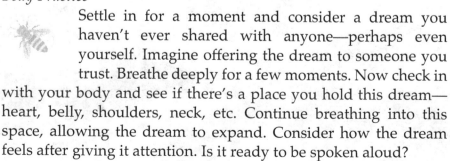

Settle in for a moment and consider a dream you haven't ever shared with anyone—perhaps even yourself. Imagine offering the dream to someone you trust. Breathe deeply for a few moments. Now check in with your body and see if there's a place you hold this dream—heart, belly, shoulders, neck, etc. Continue breathing into this space, allowing the dream to expand. Consider how the dream feels after giving it attention. Is it ready to be spoken aloud?

# A PLACE OF RECIPROCITY
# OR ODE TO TAOS

Tucked inside this high desert repose, I pause and ponder: What do I love here?

I love how the church bells from town drift across my consciousness every hour of the day. Sometimes I'm unaware and other moments they draw me close like an answer to prayer.

I love how the magpies greet me each morning. They've taken the place of my Seattle crows and even though others name them pests, I find them delightful as they match my own curiosity.

I love the feathers that land in my path each day and how the birds break into cacophonous song following the call of the chiming bells.

I love how the clouds leave shadows on the landscape and turn from virginal white to metal gray just before an afternoon squall.

I love how it is dry and I can breathe and let my skin be bathed in fresh air. I love the warmth and aridness that substitute for Seattle's summer moisture.

I love how I've been held by a group of wild women who have embraced me for who I am. I adore that my craft has stretched and grown, just like my body moving in morning dance and reaching in twilight yoga.

I love the spaciousness all around and the ability to see for miles. The rolling landscape mirrors a beloved ocean full of waves and crests.

I love the pond and garden tucked in the midst of this arid locale and that sculptures are formed by both man and God.

I love the idea of a master creator—a weaver allowing all these precious hearts to entwine together.

I love having the freedom to write whatever I want. To have a container, a loose framework, and the invitation to simply pay attention.

I love that Taos is infused in my soul as an artist, not a tourist. I have not simply passed through; I have inhabited this place and allowed it to seep deep within my pores. It is a place of reciprocity where offering and receiving become one.

*Journal Meditation*

 Pause and ponder what you love about your surroundings. Free-flow write for several minutes about this abundant love.

# FREEDOM IS IN THE AIR

Where does your mind go when you consider the element of air? My mind often turns to the ightness of a feather and the ensuing weightlessness.

I am the one who is light as a feather. I am the one who floats on air—light, airy, pink. Carried by balloons—colorful and delightful. I am the one who makes peace with who I am by turning old expectations upside down. I feel the breeze behind me, above me, below me, around me.

And so I ask Air, what do you have to give me? What I have to give you is peace, joy, and rest in knowing who you are. You're only as old as you think you are. It doesn't matter if you have wrinkles or saggy arms or skin as fresh as a newborn baby. Be yourself. Lighten up. Don't stop when you hear the voice of the stopper. Let go! Play, laugh, love. Be free as a bird. Blossom.

I am the one who laughs and plays and drums and dances and blooms. I am the one who doesn't hide behind conventional wisdom. I am the one who says go, not stop. There are many fruitful paths, so move in the direction of your heart. Stop holding on to what "others" think. Play. Release. Let go. Drum and dance. Stop stopping you!

Play. Bloom. God's wisdom is not what the world thinks it is. We all want to play, but we get stuck. Stuck in the paradigms we think are true. We think spirituality has to look stale and safe. We've taken the fun out of worship. We've put churches inside buildings rather than out in the fresh air on the cliffs and near the water. We've forgotten how to take off our shoes and run through the grass. We hear our mothers saying, "Don't get dirty. Finish your work before you go out to play." Guess what? The work is never done. So, let go and reach toward freedom in the air.

Today I invite you to close your eyes and consider where the element of air carries you.

*Action Invitation*

 As you feel your breath moving in and out, see if you can experience life all around you. Feel the wind in your hair. The breeze on your skin. The sun kissing your magnificence. Be free. Float like the feather. Let your body move with your own rhythm. Laugh like there is no tomorrow. Stop hiding. Bloom. Reach toward freedom.

# Shared Memories

One year I had the distinct privilege of traveling with my older sister for her fiftieth high school reunion and the gathering of friends who spent twelve years united in a small-town community. Even though I was a tot when they graduated from high school, these friends influenced me as they orbited around my sister, who seemed larger than life to her baby sis.

Attending a reunion breakfast one morning, I was amazed at the memories that flooded back to me. In front of me sat the gregarious twins who I've never seen apart from each other. They were chattering bookends with my sis in the middle. They lived around the corner from us and their house still stands just as I remembered it. Speaking with them, I recalled falling off my bike and scraping my knee only to confirm it was their caring mother who scooped me up and tenderly patched my bleeding wound. Her act of kindness has never left me.

I also encountered the towering prince who I gazed upon with starstruck orbs when he came to pick up my sister for a formal event. He smiled at me in present time and became teary-eyed as he remembered his own younger brother who died when he was just a boy. And then there was the prom queen—a little worn with age, but recognizable nonetheless as she opened her mouth and spoke to me in a Southern drawl of yet another brother who passed away the previous year. For many of my sister's classmates, I was a mascot of sorts—a reminder of their mothers who birthed children in their thirties (an oddity in that era). Another neighbor introduced himself and we both gave our descriptions of the circular path in front of his house—to me it was a never-ending driveway on which to ride my bike; to him a small sidewalk nearly forgotten.

Who knew all those memories would tumble out of a woman who was barely four years old when they were created? The emotions these individuals evoked in me were surprising and remarkable. Today it feels important to honor these people who grew up just a decade before me. Like my sister, I cannot shake the awareness that each of these encounters both past and present has marked my life with indelible ink.

*Visualization*

Close your eyes and take a stroll down memory lane—the path to get there may be shorter than you think. Notice what emerges—people, places, things. Who or what do you recall that was bigger than life? Take a moment and consider how this presence may impact you today.

# FRUIT OR VEGGIE

Pondering is a fruitful way to connect more deeply with ourselves and ultimately the rest of the world. Existential questions such as Who am I? or What's my purpose in life? can get exhausting and keep us spinning in our heads. Occasionally, it's fun to step out of the brain box and play with our personal image in new ways. Today is designated as one of those days.

*Journal Meditation*

If you could describe your essential self as a fruit or vegetable, what would it be and why? Without questioning, quickly jot down the fruit or veggie that first pops into your mind. Let your intuition flow and write down the attributes of your selection. Have fun!

# PEOPLE WATCHING

Do they know who they will become? Are they already there?
Pink crocs and purple cast, she floats across the playground.
Will she be a nurse mending others or the daredevil breaking bones?

Tiny son in his own blue crocs raises his voice to the sky.
Budding opera singer? Talk show host? Perhaps a bellowing father.

Newborn babes and scampering tots, mothers, fathers, aunties too.
Do they know who they will become? Are they already there?

The merry-go-round spins faster and faster.
Which moments of the blur will stand in clarity?

Bell bottom jeans, peasant top and flowing hair, she sits upon the campus wall.
Could she know who she would become?
Was she already there?

Walking past a playground one morning, I stopped to pause and watch the exuberance of children at play. Pondering moments of my own early life, I see the clues to my own destiny that were there all along. Fond memories from childhood remain things that bring me deep joy today. Even though the yearnings were tucked away for decades, I still find delight in pink tutus, belly laughs, and holding hands with another. Curiosity, exploration, and meaningful engagement are attributes that burst from my being when not tethered by my own fear of what others or culture has to say. These authentic tendencies have been with me from the age of five and before.

So, what do you think? Did you know who you would become? Were you already there? Can you see the clues that were visible along the way?

*Artistic Meditation*

As you go through your day, observe what makes you smile spontaneously. Carry an index card with you and jot your observations down. At the end of the day (or week), examine these clues and see what they offer today.

# FORMATION

*"Be patient toward all that is unsolved in your heart
and try to love the questions themselves."*
*Rainer Maria Rilke*

I love to read. One of my favorite things to do is to light a candle, put on some gentle music, pour a hot cup of coffee, and snuggle into my bed surrounded by a pile of current reading material. At first glance, my assorted texts might appear to be diverse in topic, and often they are. However, my ponderings typically unearth the common thread I see in my choices.

Perhaps it is merely my perspective, but I see that they all move toward the goal of greater life—fullness, connection with a power greater than I, mental health, mindfulness, coming alive, fulfilling who we are meant to be. They all speak of formation and lead me to ask the following questions: How will I be formed? How am I being formed? What is my role in personal formation? Do I read for information? Do I write to be formed or to inform? Who or what do I seek?

When I allow myself to slow down, I realize that it is unity I seek. The ultimate wholeness and completeness of the Universe. When I experience God, I am home. I hear the still, small voice, the words that seem to come out of nowhere, the meaning that has no words, only experience. I know that I am here for a purpose even though I may not quite know what it is.

*Pondering*

How are you informed? Do you see patterns in your life that warrant exploration? How do they connect in your daily life? In your readings? Your work or play?

# CUTTING THE CORD

I don't understand the chemistry of a labyrinth, if chemistry is even the word. How magic happens by stepping into a circle of stones. This day I was simply there to do the time. I even set the stopwatch on my wrist. Walking slowly, I was drawn to pulling out haphazard weeds. Themes of ritual and funeral rose in my mind. Letting go. Refining and expanding.

Stepping into the center, I saw the altar of remembrances and symbols of others' letting go. My pockets held a hotel key and sunglasses. I had nothing to leave. But there on my wrist were the cloth bracelets I had worn for years. They represented another time of life. The raising of my children now turned adult. It was time to release and let go.

The lavender band was the easiest to remove. Elastic, faded purple, worn around the edges, it had many uses—holding my hair, snapping my wrist, adding color to my life. It was a reminder of my sweet girl. This day it was time to let go. The green band came next—not so easy to maneuver. I'd worn it for seven years in honor of my dear son. It was time to let go and, as I stood in the center of the labyrinth, I knew that to be true. Ritual. Funeral. Release.

No scissors. No knife. No stone sharp enough to cut the cord. Only my sheer will to release and let go. It was painful and at times seemed impossible. Pushing. Pulling. Tugging. Centimeter by centimeter I stretched it across my hand, tiny blood blisters forming on my wrist where no doubt bruises would follow. Millimeter by millimeter. I ceased to battle, because it was inevitable the bracelet would stay in the center of this New Mexico labyrinth. How do we know when it's time to let go? We know.

Pausing in the center, tears formed. While there wasn't a

whoosh of relief or release, there was a calm presence that offered, "This is true. Yes." Squatting by the sweet altar, holding my breath for a moment or two, I left purple and green tucked and entwined together, a magpie feather guarding their resting place. "You can't return the way you came." Words as clear as a bell. Another magpie led my way as I stepped across the path. A hop here. A pause there. I can't go back the way I came.

*Meditation*

 Sit quietly and follow your breath while gently holding the theme of letting go. Notice what arises for you. Is there someplace in your life it's time to cut the cord? Pause. Breathe. Listen. Know.

# TO BE KNOWN

One of my biggest hopes and greatest fears is that I will truly be known by another. It seems that at times, people I have known almost my entire life look at me and say, "Who the heck are you?" Or worse yet, they don't even bother to ask the question. Then there is this crazy technological world where "virtual" friends speak to me as if we were cloned from the same DNA even though we have never set eyes on each other. It is like they are mystics who can read my mind and feel my emotions while they are happening to me.

Most special of all, however, are the times when someone you have known for awhile (maybe not even a long while), someone you know "in person," lets you know they have been paying attention. That they get you. That you have made their world a little brighter even though they have seen you, warts and all. In that moment, consider yourself known.

*Journal Meditation*

Where do you desire to be known? With pad of paper and pen in hand, begin with this prompt: *To know me is to . . .* Journal for three to five minutes without stopping. When you're finished, agree with yourself to share one thing with another person that you've never before shared. Do it today.

## MAY 18

# WHIDBEY ISLAND WISDOM

T he cormorant perches on a half-submerged buoy, both floating in the transparent morning light—not sunny, not quite gray, with a touch of gentle mist in the air. Ocean angel opens her wings and balances like Sensei in a scene from *The Karate Kid*. What does Madame Cormorant say to me? *Balance, my dear. It's time to regain your balance.*

Swallows chase playfully past the bedroom window, moving at such speed they threaten to bounce off the crystal-clear glass separating our worlds. Oh precious swallows, what say you? *Play. Play. Play. It's the essential beat of your heart. Wait no longer to play.*

Waves rhythmically lap against the sandy shore, licking the wet gray sand with their gentle tongue, kissing the earth while holding floating fowl. *Love,* they whisper to me. Open your heart like the cormorant. Play with abandon as the swallows do. Kiss the world with sweet compassion.

*Action Invitation*

Step outside or position yourself in front of a window. Find your center and begin to take in the natural surroundings. Notice and listen to what the sweet earth and her rhythms offer you this day.

# PERMISSION TO BE UNIQUE

*"Because there is only one of you in all time, (your) expression is unique. And if you block it, it will never exist through any other medium and it will be lost. The world will not have it."*
*Martha Graham*

Martha Graham's words speak boldly and remind me that I have something to offer the world, even when my inner critic says, "Who do you think you are?" No one is me, or thinks exactly like I do, or has experienced what I have in the same ways. My personal role is to find what wants to be birthed into the world by me. If I keep my expression close to my heart, no one else has the chance to see it, feel it, or experience it. It's not my job to make others believe anything. It is my desire to share as authentically as I can, warts and all.

If I live in a way that is transparent, authentic, and open, others may begin to see that they, too, have permission to do the same. I lived much of my life believing that everyone else had "it" figured out more accurately than I did. A colossal sense of freedom arose when I realized that no one can discern what's best for me better than I can. No one else knows what makes my heart soar or my pulse quicken. Only I know what a unique expression is for me, just as only you know what is yours.

*Ponder and Apply*

Ponder the thought of your unique expression being lost to the world. Consider how to uniquely offer yourself this day. Give yourself permission.

# Permission to Shine

Humans have an uncanny way of getting into situations where they believe if they authentically show their brilliance, they will tarnish someone else. This stems from a mentality of scarcity instead of abundance. How might things be different if we believed there's more than enough light to go around for everyone? Unless you're a puffed-up narcissist, sharing brilliance only makes others more vibrant. It's the shadow or inauthentic self that dulls our existence. By holding ourselves back, we unwittingly withhold permission for others to dazzle.

Another's smile brightens our day and then we shine more intensely together, not separately. My glow casts a glow onto you and if you catch it, we both glow and then pass it on. It's like a million candles lined up together. They build a stream of brilliance because each is allowed its fullness. So stop holding back. You are brilliant. You're beautiful and you deserve to shine. When you do that, the whole world begins to shine—one candle at a time.

*Action Invitation*

 Gather several candles together in a dark room. Light them one at a time and watch the brilliance spread.

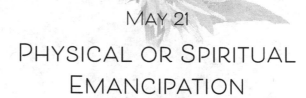

# PHYSICAL OR SPIRITUAL EMANCIPATION

"If it isn't an experience of newfound freedom,
I don't think it is an authentic God experience."
*Richard Rohr*

God doesn't make us smaller. When we become emancipated in our lives, we are enlarged in our capacity to love, to be, to worship, to live. If I have to live a life of making myself smaller, then I'm not fully experiencing God. Of course, there is sacrifice and it's not about getting what I want all of the time.

Living life authentically isn't about making ourselves smaller or taking up too much space, but rather using the space we have wisely. When moving forward and exploring life, our ways of using space (being) and/or undertaking life often shift. There was a period in my personal experience when my activities seemed more physical than spiritual, more internal than external, more solitary than communal. I came to the point where I finally paused and invited myself to consider the question: Am I wasting time or am I expanding? My journaled response offered the following:

*I need to contract and pull back some of the time or I'll pop like an overstretched rubber band. I need time to percolate—to practice and integrate what I'm learning, just like in yoga. You don't go from zero to perfect pose immediately. Keep returning to the restorative poses.*

*Stretch and return. Push the edges and rest. Perhaps my mind is taking a break to integrate and I'm using my body to recuperate. Mind and body working together to find the balance and wholeness I desire.*

Where are you being stretched? Does lying in "corpse pose"

feel restorative or lifeless for you? What are your thoughts on balance? Do you feel imprisoned or emancipated?

*Body Practice*

Allow yourself to sit comfortably wherever you are and slowly begin to follow your breath. Turn your awareness to your physical presence and allow your focus to settle on a place where tightness is held—stomach, shoulders, back, temples, etc. Continue breathing and allow your breath to expand the tight area. Imagine your physical constriction becoming more spacious and free. Consider the difference between imprisonment and freedom. Thank your body for being the keeper of all that is you.

# SPREADING WINGS

"It may be those who do most, dream most."
*Stephen Leacock*

What of dreaming and following our heart's desire? Do those who dream more do more? Or do they simply enjoy more of what they do?

It wasn't until I was firmly planted in middle age that I returned to graduate school to pursue a degree in counseling psychology. Having been a traditionalist, a conformist—whatever you want to call it—most of my life, I was used to functioning in practicalities, like get a degree that is marketable. (I chose accounting.) Believe in God. (I found myself in a fundamental-based tradition.) Own a practical car. (Toyota mini-van.) And a practical house. (Two story, white shingle with room for children.) Get the picture?

Now please don't get me wrong. I am not knocking any of those things. I chose them, after all, and they've been a formative part of my life. My point, however, is that it wasn't until I allowed myself to dream and listen (step out of "practical" patterns, perhaps) that I began to discern the call of my life. Once I listened, the possibilities became endless, where before they felt finite. I began to spread my wings and fly on the updraft of my own soaring heart.

*Visualization and Action*

 Stand firmly and feel your feet connect with the ground. Breathe deeply and allow a present or past dream to rise within you. With each inhale, let your arms rise slowly until they are spread like wings. Feel the infinite possibilities and let your heart soar in this open stance.

# PERFECT STILLNESS

One step onto the gravel path reverberates like clashing cymbals. It is a cacophony of sound against the deep, dark nothingness that surrounds me. It is nothing and it is everything. I can feel a presence in the air that is neither wet nor humid nor dry. It does not feel heavy and yet I am immensely aware of the air. Not a breath of wind moves through it. Perfect absolute stillness. Perhaps this is God.

I tiptoe through the wet grass not wanting to break this mood. It is reverent. Holy. The pool of light from my lamp leads the way. It is absorbed into the night, leaving me inside a bubble of gentle illumination. It is perfect soft light. It is holy, and for a moment, so am I. But I am not alone. My light has disturbed a resting goose who startles and makes it known that he is not pleased by my presence. His honks and wings in flight reverberate through the stillness and across the water that continues to sleep. My heart races for a moment, the goose's call quieting long before the *thump thump thump* of my pounding heart.

And then it returns. The stillness. The calm. Presence. I tiptoe across the wet grass, my own company disturbing me. How odd it is. I want to be absorbed into the air; the moisture; the dewy grass. I am one with the night. It is a gift. It is perfect. It is the holy Universe.

*Meditation*

Allow yourself to be totally still for the next few moments. Silence all external sounds. Use earplugs if it helps. Follow your breath and imagine being absorbed into the air around you. Receive the gift of perfect stillness.

# STAND FIRM

The Judeo-Christian depiction of the crucifixion and resurrection is filled with powerful images and metaphors of dying to self and rising again—standing in the face of life's trials and not backing down. Scripture offers, "I did not hide my face from insult."

No matter what happens, stand firm.

Standing firm can take on many forms. It can mean grieving or gritting your teeth and bearing unbearable situations. I see it as not numbly checking out or fleeing but staying with some form of presence. "I will never leave you nor forsake you." God stands firm, representing the ultimate image of parent. Even if you do not believe in the God story, you have the choice to parent yourself and stand firm in the face of life's trials. Choosing not to leave yourself.

Feeling our feelings. Being impacted by others. Standing firm. Firm does not mean rigid. It is grounded. Perhaps a face in the dirt—head to the earth, humbly weeping. *Terra firma.* The ground as holy. Feet planted deeply and entwined with the roots of the world like an old tree that can be blown about and lose its leaves in a storm or provide shade in the heat of day.

May we each stand firm with strength and tenderness for ourselves as well as others.

*Pondering*

 Where do you long to stand firm today? Where are you tempted to flee? How might you consider changing your view of what standing firm looks like? Is it full of strength? Tenderness? Both?

# STOP. BREATHE. LISTEN.

**what has happened?**
**where did my spaciousness go?**
**waxing. waning.**
**full moon gone behind a cloud of busyness.**
**stop. breathe. listen.**

Life feels too fast. Like a poorly trained runner, I'm out of breath. Only moments ago, living felt spacious, inviting, and oh-so-wonderful. Now choices compete. Early morning yoga or necessary sleep? Work on the to-do list or spend time journaling? Create artwork or complete a beckoning project? Magazine clippings sit at the corner of my desk whispering, "Create me into something."

Create me into something. Is that my prayer today? I don't want these days to pass so quickly, only filled with busyness. My longing is to be intentional. To stop and listen to the Universe. To see where my path is leading. To follow the rhythms of my soul. It is a fabulous paradox. When I take time for myself, I seem to have abundant time in other places. When I give to others, I receive blessings in return that I cannot count.

The words are difficult forming, yet time has graciously slowed. The spaciousness is returning as I stop, breathe, and listen.

*Active Meditation*

What are the paradoxes in your life? Where do you need to slow down? Breathe? Listen? Take a moment now to experience spaciousness as you follow the rise and fall of breath.

# FIRE OF FREEDOM

It is easy to love the lovable, but what of those who are labeled as not so lovable? My heart is big even though it grew up in a home of judgment and criticism. My mind turns to my friend, Linda, on the playground. We were seven years old. I can still feel her hand in mine. It has a slightly different feel—drier, coarser, but still it is a mirror of my own small hand. Fingers entwined as we skipped across the playground together.

During that moment, I did not know this was considered an outrage to many. It was 1963 in Bethany, Oklahoma. Linda was black and I was white. I did not know that during this same time period, perhaps even the same week, four African American girls our age had been killed in a bombing in Alabama while attending church. I did not know it could be considered dangerous to be friends with this girl who was just like me. I did not know that some considered her unlovable.

I have no idea how long we were friends. It might have been only that one day. She disappeared from our school as quietly as she had arrived. Still several decades later, she lingers in my mind.

Have you ever heard the saying, "You cannot skip and be angry at the same time?" Try it sometime. Two images of freedom come to me most strongly when I think of my childhood. One is skipping by myself on my way to kindergarten, scuffing my perfect little shoes along the way. The other is skipping hand-in-hand with Linda on the playground of our elementary school. Together (and individually) our souls shined brightly with the fire of freedom.

*Pondering*

Ponder one question or both: Who are the Lindas of your life? What does "fire of freedom" say to you?

# COLORS OF YOUR LIFE

i want to know . . .
why do you leap for joy?
what is it you hold in your gently cupped hands?
where does the curving path lead?
for what do you reach?
what dreams live inside your young soul?
what lights the fire inside and sends the lava flowing?
from where do you come and where are you going?

how does the sun warm your heart?
what does it mean to "live wild?"
what brings you sadness?
for what do you reach?
who defines magic?
what causes your tears and brings you delight?
where are you going and
where have you been?

tell me, please.
what are the colors of your life?
. . . i want to know.

*Poetry Ponder*
> What are the colors of your life?

# GARDENING FOR GOD

Sitting outside after a day of digging, mulching, and pruning, I am in awe of the glory that surrounds me. There is so much rhythm in the garden. Bees work busily to re-pollinate the catmint I trimmed yesterday. A tiny spider spins a minute web between two flower stems. An ink-black crow slowly struts across the green grass looking for an afternoon snack. My golden dog sniffs with nose in air and ears pricked high for smells and sounds I cannot fathom. The water in my fountain gently trickles in the background, and I find myself renewed, refreshed, and grateful to be alive. My muscles are tired, my hair needs a shampoo, and my limbs are slightly more tan than they were a few days ago. The garden glows in the afternoon sun. How can one imagine all these things just happen? It has become clear to me that when I am frustrated with the world around me all I need do is walk out my door and witness the abundance that awaits me in the garden.

A gentle breeze blows an *Amen* in response.

*Action Invitation*

 If able, visit a park or garden. Allow your eyes to take in the broad expanse. Slowly begin to narrow your focus. Be still and explore the creation and creativity that surrounds you.

# BIG LIGHT. BIG SHADOW.

*The bigger the light, the larger the shadow.*

While outside walking one morning during a particularly transitional period of life, the above words came to me. In the proceeding weeks, I had experienced many grief-inducing times: the five-year anniversary of my mother's death, my eldest child's passage into adulthood, leaving a job I loved. Additionally, I attended a life-giving retreat with my fabulous sister and spent an extended weekend with treasured friends. My shadows were expanding and contracting even while my internal light steadily increased.

A seeker of the light will always have great shadows in their path. Shadow and light balance each other. This isn't dissimilar to a simple gravity pendulum whereby after an initial push, the weight swings back and forth at a constant amplitude, balancing itself out. As our emotional pendulum moves far into sadness and lets go, it will swing to an equal degree of joy and back, again and again. So how do we live fully into joy and sorrow without getting whiplash from the ride? If our eyes are open, we see not only the amazing beauty of the simplest pleasure, but also the great depth of pain that pervades the world. Perhaps the wisdom is in the expansion and contraction as we make room for both shadow and light.

*Action Invitation*

 Consider taking a photographic journey around your home or neighborhood to explore the relationship between shadow and light. See what wants to be captured in the camera frame.

# MAGIC'S BAD RAP

As I've grown more present to life, I find that magic seems to follow me along my path. Growing up in a conservative Christian environment, magic got a bad rap. It was considered wicked and something not to be tampered with. What am I to do today when I encounter moments with God that can only be described as magical? Are they to be denied or defamed?

I could try and rename "magical" with words like revelation or synchronicity. I suppose they might fit almost as well; however, some things don't deserve to be renamed.

One spring morning while walking in my neighborhood, a crow began to follow me along the electrical wires overhead. With each caw from her beak, I clearly heard the words, "Magic. Magic. Presence is magic." She hopped along her high wire for half a block and her tune never changed. "Magic. Magic. Presence is magic."

How can one argue with that? Presence is magic.

*Active Meditation*

 Put on your shoes and step outside. Allow your senses to take in the surroundings. Breathe. Look. Listen. Slow down. Experience the magic of presence.

## MAY 31

# THE COLLECTIVE "THEY"

Once while conversing with a potential new client, I listened closely to her words and observed her crossed arms, smiling face, and tensed body when simultaneously a thousand other faces flashed before me. I witnessed her holding on and struggling to maintain an appearance she thought was pleasing. I observed her battling to stay in composure and keep others at a distance. Poignantly, I saw her pleading for someone to come a little closer while confidently declaring herself independent.

Have you ever witnessed such a struggle from within or without? Come a little closer, but not too close. The push and pull of see me/don't see me. Most of us long to live as our true selves rather than a personality created to please everyone around us. That is if we can recognize what our authentic identity even is.

In her book *When the Heart Waits*, Sue Monk Kidd writes, "Change begins with the recognition that we're not so much an 'I' as a 'they.' We may like to think that we're individuals living out our own unique truth, but more often we're scripts written collectively by society, family, church, job, friends, and traditions.

When we live exclusively out of the expectations thrust on us from without, rather than living from the truth emerging within, we become caught in the collective 'they.'"

Have you ever felt like you were living someone else's life? If the collective "they" were stripped away, who would you be?

*Meditation*

Close your eyes and focus on your heart center. While gently breathing into that space, allow the layers of how the world sees you—noble parent, compliant child, good girl, tough guy, whatever identities sit in place principally formed to please others—to gently slide away. Compassionately thank each role and let it slowly drift out of sight. As you allow space within your heart center, see what images arise that feel true to who you are. Notice them and listen to what they have to share. How is your personal script longing to be written?

## JUNE 1

# COMPASSION BEGINS WITH ME

At what point in time do we learn to love ourselves? Western culture seems determined to exterminate personal values and set us up for failure with impossible goals of perfection and success. We think all our achievements and collected things will bring us satisfaction and happiness; however, it is often in tragedy where kindness becomes essential and self-love is critical for success.

I once read about a Jewish man under persecution during World War II who later went on to be one of the most compassionate men of his time. He noted that all of the good he was able to accomplish would never have been possible had he not learned to love himself during that terrible moment in history. I began learning to love myself in the most horrible period of my life while watching a beloved child evaporate before my very eyes. The threat of not one life but many being shattered existed like a cruel trick on my perfect plans.

In those years, I could have decided to hate the world and God too. At times I did. But now I know I had to live through my own horrible moment in history in order to offer compassion like I had never before given or received. I still struggle to receive. My personal demons push hard and say I'm not worthy, but somewhere, deep in my core, it's easier to acknowledge myself as uniquely created and worthy of being loved. At those times I choose to remember, compassion begins with me.

*Journal Meditation*

Make a list of your favorite qualities, talents, and achievements. Include the kind things you have done that nobody noticed, as well as successes at home and

work. List the things you find quirky and unique to you. Gently
and kindly offer yourself compassion for your failings in the same
way you would a friend. Offer a prayer of gratitude for uniquely
magnificent you.

# DRAGONFLY WISDOM

T here was a time in the world when humanity recognized itself as part of the natural world. Priests and priestesses used animal totems to assist them in connecting with the spiritual world. Through animals, shamans helped reconnect conscious human life with nature. In recent times, there's been an arising consciousness of the importance of being present to the knowledge that is all around us. One of the easiest ways to pay attention to nature is to watch the animal life in our own plots of earth.

I was first introduced to the wisdom of animals when facilitating a workshop in the West Texas drylands. Late one afternoon, swarms of dragonflies appeared out of nowhere. It was a glorious sight. Excitedly, one of our more mystical local retreatants headed inside and reached for the Native American medicine cards resting on a bookshelf. She read to us how dragonflies are seen as reminders of the brightness of transformation and the wonder of colorful new vision. This was a picture-perfect description of both the workshop in which we were all participating and the magical moment we watched the brilliant swarm swoop through our midst. My heart leapt at the wonder of this deepened connection and the knowledge of forces greater than we facilitating our experience.

*Ponder and Apply*

What is your connection with the animal world? Make a commitment to pay closer attention today and notice if there is wisdom lingering in your own backyard. Invite your family pet or the buzzing fly into conversation. Allow your heart to leap at the wonder of deepened connection.

# DAMSELFLY WISDOM

**D**ragonfly. Damselfly. You swoop into my world unannounced. Subtle. Natural. Compelling.

Dancing across the silken pond, offering me respite from my restless perch. Witnessing you in your natural habitat, it's easy to dismiss your powerful medicine.

Still, you persist on your quest as you meet me in the gem store. One tiny bead buried in the midst of thousands, you place yourself within my hand and heart—a talisman of our magical first meeting. Still, I am slow and don't consciously take notice until finally while I repose upon my landlocked deck, you spontaneously arrive and perform your splendid show in my barren yard.

You come in threes and fours until I can ignore you no more. Showing up brilliantly alive, in a bead, a word, a wing. You draw me in and tell me I can fly. It's time to spread my wings and share your light. The rainbow of colors—clear, dark, iridescent, solid, and clear. Reflections deep and pure.

Oh, sweet dragonfly—subtle and not so shy. Thank you for your persistent wisdom. Is it just me who takes so long to recognize and hear what lies right along my path?

*Visualization and Meditation*

What talismans of nature or man may be crossing your pathway and going unnoticed? Close your eyes, breathe deeply, and ponder this.

## JUNE 4

# COMPASSIONATE WATCHER

Compassion for self. How do we get there? We learn by watching and listening to ourselves. By noticing the places within us that need compassion. One thing I've learned about myself is that I drift away from my internal knowing when I think someone else is watching me. I cease to be present to everyone when I step into my brain rather than listen with my heart. By learning to observe and watch what's happening for me in any given moment, I'm able to move with the flow and let go of results. It's a remarkable gift to watch ourselves rather than assume others are watching us.

In anxious circumstances, if I can let the room disappear for a few moments, I find an ability to return to myself and have everything I need through staying present. This is quite different from dissociation where we numb out—a technique we may have learned while growing up in uncomfortable situations. Now we need to learn to step back into our own bodies while gently watching and observing ourselves—with compassion.

*Active Meditation*

Center yourself and allow any thoughts to flow freely alongside your breath. Imagine stepping back and looking at yourself as if in a mirror. Observe what you see without judgment, comment, or applause. Offer compassion for this imagined reflection.

# CRITIC OR WITNESS?

The compassionate witness or watcher is quite different from the inner critic. When asked about their inner critic, most people immediately have a knowing response. The compassionate witness, however, is rarely as well-known to our inner selves. In the late '90s TV series *Buffy the Vampire Slayer*, Buffy had a watcher named Giles. It was his role to observe and train her so she could grow into her full power and step into battles with strength and wisdom. He offered great care without coddling her.

Our watchers often go silent. We lose ourselves in the battle by getting hijacked with rampant thoughts and jumping full speed ahead into drama we've created in our minds and the lives around us. Chaos ensues as our presence slips away and wisdom follows it. We forget to step back and observe. We disregard our ability to breathe and call on our inner strength and calm. But if we are able to step *into* drama, then that means we have the power to step back *out* by rising above the situation, if even for a moment. We can observe with curiosity what is happening and offer compassionate witness rather than criticism. Then we, like Buffy, can enter each situation with strength and wisdom.

*Visualization and Action*

Recall a recent situation when rampant thoughts hijacked your presence. Could you pull yourself out? Was stopping for a moment to breathe a possibility—even a remote one? Next time your thoughts start to spin, call on your compassionate witness and observe without judgment or comment.

# JUNE 6
## COMPOST

Tending our gardens involves hard work, both literally and figuratively. It gives us opportunity to inhale garden-fresh air mixed with the smell of rich mulch and possibly a hint of manure. A pile of dark earth holds many opportunities for discovery, such as tiny rocks and other objects that somehow survived the composting process.

Is life on earth simply a composting process? For years, I thought of the composting process as only a breaking down or decaying procedure, but interestingly enough, the root word *compositum* actually means "something put together." So, I ask the question again: Is life simply a composting process?

Will we allow ourselves to be broken down until only our true self is left, like the pebbles that survive in a heap of compost? Will we stay in the process until there is no more space for barriers? Until what you see is what you get? A life as pure as a pebble?

We are called to be true to our nature. A rock is a rock. A bird is a bird. Water is water. People are people. We cannot be anything else. Yet, maybe we are most like water as we take on the colors and reflections of the world around us. But when we try to reflect what is not our nature, there is disharmony and confusion. If water reflects a flame, it does not become fire. It is still water. We, too, can reflect many things, but to be at peace—to be whole and true to ourselves and to God—we need only be who we naturally and truly are at our core.

Some of us resemble rocks and some are free as birds. Others are beautiful flowers blossoming anew each day. And, me? Well, I am simply a child playing in this magnificent garden.

*Active Meditation*

Today, reflect on the call to be true to your nature. Consider the hard places where you resemble a rock. Lift your arms and feel the freedom of a bird. Feast your eyes upon the garden's blossoms. Notice which images resonate strongest in your core.

# CRUCIBLE

If you step into the crucible of relationship, you may get burned or purified. It's risky business.

The crucible of relationship is the place where no one really wants to go. It's the place where the heat gets turned up so high that parts of you start to melt away. It's been said there are places in Australia so hot you begin to cook from the inside out. That's what it feels like sometimes to be in genuine relationship— cooking from the inside out. When the heat gets turned up, it hurts too much to stay. Yet turning away from the flame isn't an option because tending the fire is too important. The crucible teaches us how to stay with the heat and lean into paradox. There we learn to be kind and to speak the truth—even if they don't always appear to be the same.

Growing up as a "good girl," I was taught that being nice— at least to someone's face—was the most important thing in the world. As soon as they were gone, you could speak any array of unkind things. It was a pattern that left me reeling and untrusting for much of my life. How can we possibly know what someone else means or thinks unless we ask them? How can they believe us if we don't say what we really mean? But speaking the truth can turn up the heat. Jumping into the crucible may mean you'll get burned.

It can also lead toward the emergence of something new and magnificent, because when the dross burns away, the gold can shine through. Granted, sometimes the truth hurts, but don't forget this one: "The truth will set you free" (John 8:32).

Is freedom worth stepping into the crucible?

*Ponder and Apply*

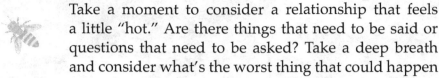

Take a moment to consider a relationship that feels a little "hot." Are there things that need to be said or questions that need to be asked? Take a deep breath and consider what's the worst thing that could happen if you spoke your mind or asked the question on your heart. After pondering that for a while, take another cleansing breath and ask yourself what's the worst thing that could happen if you *don't* speak your mind. Now consider: Is it worth stepping into the crucible? Where do you feel most free—inside or outside the heat?

# GOD IS HERE

Stepping into the deep dark night, the crescent moon lit my way. My head tilted back to absorb the night sky while the Big Dipper shone overhead, full and clear. Laughter filled my soul. God is here.

In the morning light, I headed for the river rock trail and a still, small voice said, "Turn." I curved away from the path, toward the sea, and there before me was a magnificent eagle soaring in the clear blue sky. God is here.

The persistent morning wind blew through the sunlit trees. Waving. Calling. Singing. I am here. Yahweh. Spirit. God.

My friend built an altar out of discarded metal—a ladder representing her fears. She built an altar to a god she said she did not know, a god whose name she could not speak. God wooed. Spirit called. The wind whispered, "I am here."

She waited. She listened. She struggled. She railed against the hope. She slept. Peace came and washed over her through a flood of tears. She wept. She knew. She spoke the name. "God is here!"

*Action Invitation*

Step outside into the open air. Stop. Breathe. Look. Listen. Repeat.

# Infinity Pool

I stand on the edge of an infinity pool, lines blurring between concrete and flow. This edge is the place of freedom and life. It reverberates with loss and death, too. They say the human mind is most engaged and satisfied as it stands on the verge of failure. For when it faces doom, it also breathes the sweet smell of success. Sink or swim. Do or die. Drown or fly.

Positioned on the edge—terrified, exhilarated, reaching for life. I stand on the edge of the infinity pool, lines blurred between solid and soft. What will I choose? Today, I choose flight. I am not afraid to fail or fall, even as my heart quakes. I've been hurt before and will bruise again. And, had I not jumped, I would never have flown. Stepping through fear. Moving toward self. The edge of the infinity pool beckons and blurs.

*Visualization*

With eyes closed, imagine standing at the edge of a pool with no edges (an infinity pool). Bring to mind a decision you're pondering. Breathe deeply with this thought as you stand at the edge. Without force or forethought, notice what happens next in the scene.

# ONE SMALL STEP

While embarking on an exercise to name my weekly intention, I landed on the task of focusing on the next small step. While this might sound simple, it can be a harder venture than one might think. I can easily come up with the next step, but then quickly want to move to the one beyond and then the one beyond that and ultimately try to skip a few rungs in between. Hastily launching into the future can make us stumble like a toddler who suddenly realizes she's walking on her own momentum or a child learning to ride a bike once the parent lets go. Falling is imminent. We peddle along, content in the arc of the present moment, until we jolt ourselves into the future by realizing everything that must be done or hasn't been done or should get done.

When the trajectory threatens to become out of control, my only hope is to remember the single thing that grounds me—returning to the present and focusing on the next small thing.

I inhale a deep breath, slow down, and step into the holy ground of my heart. As I listen to my body, it confirms my longing. It proposes the next step and opens me up to possibility. It offers me completion and satisfaction, because I can always do the next small thing. And if that seems too overwhelming, then I back off and make my task smaller. This reminds me of the powerful knowledge I learned a few years ago when reading *The Four Agreements* by Don Miguel Ruiz. One of the agreements is "Always do your best." I've found it incredibly freeing to acknowledge that sometimes my "best" means staying right where I am. Maybe even pulling the covers back over my head while doing only the simplest thing . . . like breathing.

*Pondering*

Take a few moments and explore what happens when you focus on the next small thing instead of trying to save the world . . . or your family . . . or yourself. What does your next small step look like?

# GOD'S WAYS

---

**I wrote a word of Peace. The reader said, "Too pat."**
**I spoke a word of Rest. The hearer said, "No way."**
**I read a word of Grace. My heart said, "I believe."**

---

There are inexplicable ways of being that cannot be described with words. Since we each bring our own experience to any given situation, miscommunication is bound to happen. How does one explain peace unearthed when life is chaotic or quantify rest in the midst of turmoil? My experience is not necessarily yours. God's ways are not always our ways. They are hard to believe with a "rational" mind. They are impossible to hear with a worldly ear. They are indisputable when received in the heart.

*Body Practice*

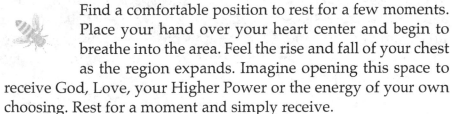 Find a comfortable position to rest for a few moments. Place your hand over your heart center and begin to breathe into the area. Feel the rise and fall of your chest as the region expands. Imagine opening this space to receive God, Love, your Higher Power or the energy of your own choosing. Rest for a moment and simply receive.

## JUNE 12

# DRIFTING

Drifting is sometimes defined as a driving force or the buildup of things like snow and sand. For me, however, drifting is a delicious state of mind. It's a liminal space—something in between. I became aware of this space when I had the opportunity to spend several uninterrupted hours alone in nature. I had a single job to do—listen to my surroundings. I took my journal as well as a good book, but as I lay there in the countryside, I found I had no desire whatsoever to open my journal and record the amazing things happening around me. Lying there with bees buzzing, grass blowing, and clouds gently swaying in the sky, everything was absolutely perfect. I didn't need to do anything else.

That feeling stayed with me for several weeks. At first I thought I was experiencing writer's block. I wondered if it was exhaustion or mere laziness, but then I realized words like "liminal" and "drifting" seemed to pop out at me when I heard or read them. It was a gentle shift. A slight rocking motion, like the wind moving a hammock with an island breeze. In this space of drifting, I feel cared for and caressed, even when not following my usual routine of morning reading and writing. God's presence is abundant even (perhaps especially) without the need to record my impressions on the page. Making time to drift is divine.

*Action Invitation*

 Take a blanket and head outside. Either wrap up or lie down and give yourself a single job of listening to your surroundings. Fall into a delicious drift of mind.

# DESTINATION (UN)KNOWN

There is a place where timelessness resides. Where if you let go of past, present, and future, all become one and you can feel the heartbeat of the earth. Every molecule of your being unites with the pulse of eternity while witnessing the birth of creation.

The destination is found on no printed map, nor can you set your compass toward its point. The secret (if there is one) is to listen with the depths of your soul, unfold a pilgrim's heart, wait with mundified patience, and respond in flagrant gratitude and awe. Travelers beware. Once you have journeyed through this place there is no turning back.

*Visualization and Meditation*

Take a few moments and simply follow your breath in and out. Bring awareness to your heart center and the presence of a pilgrim's heart. Imagine this heart opening up within your safe, warm treasure chest. Continue breathing, unfolding, and deepening. When you're ready, gently close the chest and acknowledge you have the key to open it whenever you desire.

# TENDING THE GARDEN

There's nothing much better than a day of working hard in the garden followed by a nice hot shower. Add in a little epiphany and it turns into an amazing spirit-lifting experience. Reflecting on one day's gardening, I recognized that the tasks I had performed were the kind of work nobody notices unless you don't do it. Things like pulling out weeds that threaten to take over the healthy plants. Thinning out some of the good stuff, so it can shine a little brighter and breathe more fully.

The parallels with life seem infinite. Doing the work nobody notices (maybe even yourself) unless you *don't* do it.

*Pondering*

 What are the things you do on a regular basis that would be missed if you didn't do them?

# ARISING PRESENCE

Breaking through the dreams of night, slowly I awaken.
Rain falls softly on the lawn and in my heart I hear the call,
*Listen. Listen. Listen.*

I stretch and feel my sinewy limbs come alive.
Golden softness brushes my palm. The breath of God caresses my face.
*Listen. Listen. Listen.*

Spirit prompts and says, *Arise.*
Come greet the day that lies before.
*Listen. Listen. Listen.*

Holy friend, you walk beside.
My feet caressed in lamb's soft wool, we step 'cross solid ground of oak.
I feel your touch and once again hear,
*Listen. Listen. Listen.*

Creator Soul, you meet me through breath and touch and sound.
Rain falling. Breath purring.
Wool caressing. Ground holding.
Speaking to the dreams of day,
*Listen. Listen. Listen.*

*Meditation*

Bring your awareness to the present moment. Acknowledge there is no past and no future, only now. Allow all your senses to engage as you simply breathe for the next few moments.

# GOMBEY DANCE

The Gombey dancers spin and twirl, bringing color and life back into a day that has been clouded with conflicting emotions and gray skies. Paradise. Heaven. Will there be both dark and light in heaven? Are we already living in a heaven or hell of our own making?

Choice. We get to choose how we will be, but sometimes the choice feels out of our hands. Old hurts and childhood (often childish) responses get in the way and, even when we want to respond otherwise, we hold tight to the preferred reply of the moment—hurt, anger, bitterness, confusion. The clouds appear too thick to see the sunshine. We can only hear the thunder roaring in our ears.

Still, a piece of our heart reaches for the light. The heaven that lives inside our soul. The light that is as old as time. Created in the beginning. "Let there be light." We struggle. We push. We yearn, but we are stubborn, strong, proud. And so the battle goes. Hang on. Let go. Hang on. Let go.

And then as if by magic you begin to hear, to feel a different rhythm. A soft pounding of drum and heart. It is slow at first (possibly even annoying), but soon you feel the pull to follow the new rhythm. You are drawn to the beat. Two hearts. Multiple hearts. Sounding as one. Spiriting joy into the world. And then the crowd parts and the dancers spin and twirl, bringing color and life back into a day that has been clouded with emotions and gray skies.

The skies are blue again. The light shines all around. Your heart leaps and you begin to smile and dance, for this you know is heaven. Music. Color. Rhythm. Life. Young and old. Mother and child. Husband and wife. Friend and friend. Unity. The world spinning and twirling as we choose to experience heaven on earth.

Gombey dancers are indigenous to the island of Bermuda. Dancers perform in wild masquerade costumes telling stories of old.

*Visualization and Action*

 Imagine yourself as a Gombey dancer. What colors would you choose for your plumage? What stories would you portray? Select a favorite piece of music and allow yourself to move to the rhythm of your story in this moment.

# GRACE ON THE BUS

"If you don't know the kind of person I am and I don't know
the kind of person you are, a pattern that others made
may prevail in the world and following the wrong
god home, we may miss our star."
*William Stafford*

D o we really know the people around us? This question
arose for me as I boarded the bus one morning amid headlines of
increased assaults and overcrowding.

After a bit of seat shifting between bus stops, a middle-aged
man landed in the seat next to me. He said, "Good morning,"
which is something different in itself. Most riders plug into their
media and pretend the person next to them doesn't exist. Soon this
man and I were sharing a bit of conversation as he relayed pieces
of local good news—a lost runner found, baby falcons hatched.
This didn't feel like the bus described in the newspaper.

The bus felt even lighter on the afternoon ride home, even
though we rode in five o'clock traffic and the coach was filled to
capacity. The bus driver was gracious as he let riders exit from
the back door rather than push through to the front. I witnessed
riders offer seats to mothers and children. I saw strangers engage
in lighthearted conversation. I saw a woman exit through the
back door and deliberately walk around to the front and pay her
fare (others had not done this), and then I watched that pattern
repeated over and over with no real expectation from the driver.
The bus driver was our guardian for that short period of time.
He was a keeper of peace, not with enforcement of rules but with
kindness and a lightness in the air. Grace. He could have insisted

everyone push through the crowd. Instead, he opened another door, thus unwrapping a different way of knowing for each of us—people in our midst are capable of lovely surprises.

*Pondering*

Choose one or more questions to ponder. Through what door will you enter the world today? In what small ways might you help to alleviate someone else's burden? How will you see goodness and seek to know the person who stands before or sits beside you? Where will you be gracious?

## JUNE 18

# HEROES ARE BORN

"It is not because things are difficult that we do not dare;
it is because we do not dare that they are difficult."
*Seneca*

Miracles abound.

To watch the sun rise while stars still play in the heavens.

To hear coyotes howl in the distance and laugh to see deer dance across my path.

To witness frightened souls lean into fear. Beautiful songs emerging from dead hearts. Velveteen rabbits becoming real.

Bent-over women standing tall in their beauty. New and golden stars shining with all their might. A monster melting into a bundle of joy.

Heroes are born.

Golden goddesses emerging from the womb. Miracles abound.

I am blessed and grateful to have witnessed these miracles beyond imagination.

*Journal Meditation*

 Pick a prompt and free-write for five minutes: How do you define a miracle? What makes a hero? Where do blessings and gratitude lie?

# PICK UP YOUR ORDINARY

Have you ever experienced a creative block? If your inner critic is already telling you you're not creative, invite him or her to please bow out of today's conversation. If you go to work, cook meals, get dressed, garden, draw, dance, or simply get out of bed in the morning, you are creative. Writers are notorious for this blockage dilemma, and one of the best ways I've found to dispel mine is to focus on something ordinary.

Consider a leaf, for example. How a leaf is like me as writer?

My leaf and I are beautifully shaped and rich with color. We have a strong central vein with many offshoots. Our edges are a little rough, but they all connect to make the whole. In springtime, we show off fresh colors. Other times, we feel brittle and dry. When breathing, we create oxygen for others. When dead and crumpled, we fertilize the earth. Connected to our roots, we have a grounded heritage upon which to draw. We are pieces of the universal way of life, offering to the world as best we can.

*Journal Meditation*

 Take a moment to close your eyes and place your feet solidly on the ground. Feel your spine stretch as you take a few deep breaths. With soft focus, open your eyes and notice which ordinary object is calling your name. How is this object like you today? Free-write for several minutes on this question.

# SIMPLE. PURE. STUNNING.

In the center of the lush landscape perches a magnificent yellow-breasted bird. Simple. Pure.

Stunning. We are one. Quiet and still. Allowing space for God. Simple. Pure. Stunning. Alive. Participating in life. Gentle as an ocean breeze. Powerful as a summer squall. Tears and joy. Solitude and laughter. Present to what we need.

Right now there are no others around this space. Only the energy of the Universe. Breath. Air. Water. Flight. Heat. Subtle. Simple. Pure. Even when "nothing" is going on, the world is alive. Can you be present to your own life? Will you be the elegant swallow ready to take flight, the bird at the center of the landscape?

Everything radiates out from here. Concentric circles of energy—floating out to one another. Intersecting and colliding. Uniting and meshing. Passing through. Ripples of life touching each other. Tide—flowing and ebbing. Exposing rocks and sand. Filling the deep.

You are the center of your own lush garden. How will you choose to see what is around you? Will you sing with joy? Sob with sorrow? Ache with pain? Melt from heat? Weep? Laugh? Sing? Dance? Breathe?

*Meditation*

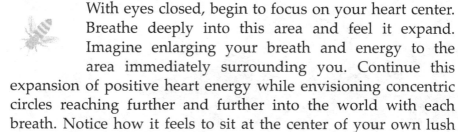

With eyes closed, begin to focus on your heart center. Breathe deeply into this area and feel it expand. Imagine enlarging your breath and energy to the area immediately surrounding you. Continue this expansion of positive heart energy while envisioning concentric circles reaching further and further into the world with each breath. Notice how it feels to sit at the center of your own lush garden.

# HOPE. FAITH. LOVE. FORGIVENESS.

"Nothing that is worth doing can be achieved in our lifetime; therefore, we must be saved by hope. Nothing which is true or beautiful or good makes complete sense in any immediate context of history; therefore, we must be saved by faith. Nothing we do, however virtuous, could be accomplished alone; therefore, we must be saved by love. No virtuous act is quite as virtuous from the standpoint of our friend or foe as it is from our own standpoint; therefore, we must be saved by the final form of love, which is forgiveness."

*Reinhold Niebuhr*

O ne could look at this quote as a "hopeless" viewpoint such as the verses in Ecclesiastes that declare everything is meaningless. However, Niebuhr's words are filled with hope and guidance for us to live full and intentional lives. Although we may not see the results in our lifetime, we can begin the process. Even though it may not currently make sense, the results will be there. We cannot do things alone. Therefore, we need community and a higher power. In a world torn by strife amongst families and war between nations, it is time to open our eyes to hope, faith, and love, with forgiveness being the greatest gift of all.

*Body Practice*

Follow your breath and allow your focus to drop into your heart center. Allow a situation that needs forgiveness to arise in your mind. Perhaps it is toward another or possibly even yourself. Notice where this need to forgive sits in your body, whether a painful ache or empty abyss. Continue deeply inhaling and exhaling as you bathe this area with the breath of forgiveness.

# ENERGY OF INSPIRATION

What's our responsibility when it comes to inspiring others? Can we? Should we? Must we? While I'm certainly open to sharing what I have to offer, I do find it disheartening if those I'm addressing are disengaged and uninterested. I don't believe it's my job to make others want something, but it is my responsibility to consider who my audience is.

Attempting to encourage anyone who's not interested is exhausting and energy zapping. It's wise to remember that we always have a choice as to how long we keep up our attempts, and challenges offer the gift of learning new ways of being. Tell me where I'm wrong, but can't we learn something from every situation?

Being ignored or misheard can leave an ego bruised, but if the essential self is intact, it's possible to come out stronger on the other side of any conflict. Using public speaking as an example, here's how I might handle a situation where my inspiration isn't connecting with others:

First I ask myself, What's the worst that could happen?

Then I come up with possible answers:

*Response 1:* I could die of fright or embarrassment. (Not likely.)

*Response 2:* The audience could kill me. (Less likely.)

*Response 3:* I leave and they don't ask me back. (I don't want to come back anyway. Whew!)

*Response 4:* I'm seen as an awful speaker. (I have an opportunity to evaluate and strengthen my skills.)

*Active Meditation*

> Give it a try: Imagine a situation you might be dreading and begin with the question: What's the worst that could happen? Keep responding and notice if there's a shift.

# TO SPEAK OR NOT TO SPEAK

Have you ever stood in front of a group and opened your mouth only to wonder if the words you've spoken might have been in Swahili (and you're not in Africa)? Blank stares come your way or worse, no one seems to know you're even in the room. It crosses your mind that you've gone mute and your mouth is moving but no sound is coming forth.

Public speaking falls in the top ten of people's greatest fears. It makes perfect sense, especially if you've had the experience just described. In the midst of such a situation, what can be done? I've considered tactics like quietly closing my notes and sneaking out of the room while the audience continues to doze. When feeling sassy or brave, I've had fantasies of pulling out a bright pink tutu and dancing across the tabletops. Seriously, could things feel much worse than having a room full of people perceive you as incompetent or (*gasp*) dull? At least with the tutu option, there's a chance my presentation would be remembered, and I might have some fun in the process.

*Action Invitation*

The next time you're in a situation where you want to freeze, flee, or fight, ask yourself what's the worst that could happen. Invite your inner star to step up and notice how things change. Consider this: The ego freezes, flees, or fights, but the star shines—if only in the center of his or her own brilliant chest.

## JUNE 24

# STORY FONDLING

Is there a story you tell yourself that keeps you from living your most magnificent life? Do you get stuck and fondle a story that limits your forward movement? Perhaps it sounds like this: "I'll never amount to anything" or "I'm too old, too young, too whatever to start something new." Prominent American industrialist Henry Ford was quite insightful with his statement, "Whether you think you can or whether you think you can't, you're right." The problem is, many of us don't go so far as to even ask about our heart's desires. The bottleneck between our heart and head has gotten clogged with should not's, could not's, and dare not's.

Once while attending a writing workshop, the instructor asked us to consider a story where we were falsely invested—an untrue narrative that we believed. Mine regarded my vision that writers' words flow like water when in reality, they often drip from beads of blood, sweat, and tears. While my passion and dream is to write, I somehow thought I could avoid doing the actual work. Then when the words required work, I concluded I wasn't really a writer. Finally, it dawned on me that if I wanted to write, I had to put pen to paper. Some days it's easier than others, but never do the words magically appear on my notepad or computer screen without me adding the strokes of the pen or keyboard.

Fondling my negative story would have resulted in you holding someone else's book in your hand! I'm so glad you're not.

*Journal Meditation*

What's one story you are falsely invested in? Take a moment to consider, then notice what pops into your mind as you answer this prompt: *With no limitations I would . . .* Free-write for several minutes in your journal.

# IF ONLY FOR A MOMENT . . .

"Let the little children come to me, and do not hinder them,
for the kingdom of heaven belongs to such as these."
*Matthew 19:14*

Can you remember back to those carefree days when boys and girls were just kids and not genders? Can you see in your mind's eye the freedom of summer and endless play without regard to time, space, or commitments? When hours could be lost staring at an ant carrying a piece of food? Or an entire afternoon spent catching bees in a jar only to release them at day's end? Can you remember what it was like to walk hand in hand with someone just because it felt natural to be by his or her side? Can you remember when it all started to get complicated and boys became yucky or girls developed cooties? When appearance became more important than freedom? When propriety took the place of simplicity?

Some of those questions are easier for me to answer than others, but all remind me in some simple way of a delightful day when for a few brief moments, all the questions disappeared and I got to simply be me, a child at play—if only for a moment.

Sitting next to the international fountain at the Seattle Center, a friend and I watched the children at play in the brilliant sunshine. One little guy caught our attention as he darted in and out of the fountain spray clad only in his pint-sized white briefs, which I swear he had on sideways. Oblivious to every care in the world except delight, this young spirit was the picture of joy and his energy was contagious. My friend spontaneously said, "Come run through the fountain with me!" and the next thing I knew, we were dodging the showers and laughing with the other children. Pure delight indeed!

It is funny how you just know some moments will mark your life in a unique way. This, for me, was one of them. It was a brief slice of time slathered with delight and freedom when two grown-up children allowed themselves to come out to play and time stood still—if only for a moment.

### Artistic Meditation

 Take a moment and gather paper and pen—or better yet, crayons or markers. Quietly begin to reflect upon this reading and the verse, "Let the little children come." Using your non-dominant hand, allow yourself to journal or draw without judgment or focus on the end results. Create with a sense of delight and wonder, if only for a moment.

## JUNE 26

# SURRENDER AND
# EMPOWERMENT

When we surrender to a power greater than ourselves, we become empowered. Surrender isn't weak. It is courageous. It is stepping into the unknown and receiving the reality that we can't know anything except what actually is. All I have is now—this moment with pen in hand, bed beneath my bottom, air moving through my lungs. I cannot be certain of what the next minute, let alone the rest of the day, may hold. I prepare and plan and then I let go. Surrendering to the one who creates time. I ponder and then I release.

Opening arms wide in surrender and in that place finding rest. Time isn't ours to control. Nothing is. There is a power greater than we and where there is surrender there is also gift. When we let go, we are given the opportunity to simply be. Allowing breath to move in and out of our lungs, and even that we can't control. We reside in bodies so intricately made they won't allow us to even hold our breath indefinitely. The breath comes on its own and when I surrender to this, I am able to experience rest. Empowerment comes from that which is greater than I.

*Body Practice*

Inhale deeply and hold your breath for as long as possible. Repeat this practice and notice what arises as you try to control your breath. After a few moments return to normal breath. Experience what comes from simply being in this space of not trying.

## JUNE 27

# DAYBREAK

d ay spread out before me like fresh sand upon the beach
no footprints yet to mark this day, nighttime clearly gone
the golden orb fully taking her place in the sky spreading outward
at the center almost too brilliant to observe and then
broadening, widening, turning softer layers of color
ringing, moving, spreading

watching me, capturing me, being me
who am I to be?
who will I be in this day?
am I the one who plays in the surf and dives from the cliffs
laughing and roaring with the thrill of the risk, the freedom,
the joy?

or will I be the one who silently, thoughtfully ponders art
through the halls of life's museum?

I want it all!

*Visualization and Action*

Consider your day spread before you like fresh sand
upon the beach. Stand where you are right now and feel
the soles of your feet connect with the ground. Wiggle
your toes as though digging into the sand. Listen for
which pathway your footsteps want to take today.

# MOMENTS

I t is not the words of life that count, but the moments.

A hug. A smile. A laugh. Witnessing a majestic eagle soar along the shoreline. Adult children head to head on a beach studying tiny crabs with the wonder of carefree tots. An arm slung over a shoulder and a kiss on the forehead. Friends gathered around a blazing fire. Breaking bread. Flowers' splendor filling the air with fragrance and beauty. Joyful play. Fireworks. Hard work. Quiet minutes.

Moments are what we remember. The times when the Universe speaks through the beauty, wonder, and glory of the creation surrounding each of us and teaching us that we are beloved.

*Visualization*

What are the moments that speak to you of love? Use this current time to remember, then imagine how you might create more memorable moments today. (No words required.)

# ROADBLOCKS

I simply adore how often roadblocks can lead to the most fantastic adventures. Arriving in Taos a day early for a writing retreat, my friend and I dropped our new acquaintance, Patience, off at the pueblo outside of town. Patience is a warm and delightful woman who is Mother Earth embodied. With flowing hair of spun silver and eyes the color of ocean, she resonates with a peace that is grounded and pure. She is filled with wisdom and openly shares but does not force or press her opinions. She is a woman who offers grace and invites it in return. Thus our predestined roadblock was one that would not willingly be ignored in service to this precious soul.

It was nearing the appointed time to retrieve Patience from the pueblo where she'd been wandering for hours in the blazing desert sun. Departing the café, we were appalled to learn that the road toward our friend was closed for the afternoon to celebrate a fiesta. Tenacious and indefatigable women (but nonetheless in unfamiliar territory), we began to weave our way through back roads, hoping to find a way north. Happening upon a local officer, we were told Patience would simply have to wait.

The officer swiftly and accurately read our eyes as he realized this was an unacceptable answer. Within moments our patron, the officer, had imbued us with a super-secret escape route map for the city. What ensued was a wonderful adventure through back roads and vistas we never would have seen without the imposing roadblock. Dear Patience, of course, lived up to her name and was grateful to have friends who would not be deterred by a little bump in the road.

*Pondering*

How do you perceive roadblocks on the road of your life? Do you turn away, give up, push through, or find delight in the adventure? Today, I invite you to ponder this.

# JUNE 30

# HARMONY

Head and heart. We have both for a reason. Trying to live using only one leads to imbalance. For most people it is easier to listen with the head, but the body gets restless and screams, "Hear me! Listen to me!" Headaches. Shoulder tension. Back pain. Ulcers.
It is hard to hold in the feelings of the heart. It wants to beat. It wants to burst and break free. And its cohort, the mind, wants to rest. All that thinking can be exhausting. Sleepless nights. Ragged days. Endless lists. Spinning. Twirling. Vertigo.

Body, mind, soul. Can you imagine that connection? If the heart is the soul, if the head is the mind, and the body is, well, the body, they should all work together. It is the ideal balance. Created in perfect unity and harmony.

We are finely tuned beings. So, if one part feels like it is out of whack—pay attention. Think. Feel. Breathe. Let go. Mind. Soul. Body. Harmony.

*Active Meditation*

In your mind, imagine a perfect egg—better yet, get one out of your refrigerator. Envision the shell as your body, the yolk as your heart, and the white as your mind. Notice how they perfectly unite to make a whole egg. Spend a few moments pondering the virtues of the whole and each unique part. Consider: What happens if the shell cracks? Is the yolk alone still an egg? How about the white?

# SUMMER'S SWEET SLOWNESS

Dressed in glossy red coat adorned with perfect black dots, I lean an antenna into the warm summer air. Ahhh.

The bark feels cool and safe beneath my bare feet.

Perfect for a slow stroll on a summer day.

Shall I stick close to home or spread my wings and fly?

The world offers much to explore. Hmmm.

Which outlook will I prefer today—comfy bark side view or daring aerial vista?

Summer sweetness beckons.

*Poetry Ponder*

What resonates for you in this ode to summer?

# PAYING ATTENTION

*"When you have put into practice the thing you are talking about, then speak from knowledge of the thing itself."*
*Thomas Merton*

I feel the evening breeze blow across my face as the late afternoon sun begins to set. My golden cat sits nearby, tasting his paws and grooming his glistening coat in beams of precious light. An ice cream truck plays "Row, Row, Row Your Boat" and mercifully fades into the distance. Crows caw and sparrows chirp outside my window.

Earlier as I drove home from yoga with the convertible top down, the sun shone on my warm, moist skin as the wind blew my hair wildly across my face. The inspirational anthem "Unwritten" by Natasha Bedingfield poured from the stereo and as I looked overhead, a pure white seagull pierced the light denim sky. Heaven on earth. Reverence for these small, great things. Majestic. Awesome.

Fuchsia-colored peonies. Miniscule ants of ebony. Golden fur and fluff. Gentle breeze. Strong-brewed coffee crinkling over ice. The feel of glorious, perfect sunshine after days of gray too numerous to count. Strength of my body bending backwards and sinking my spine onto the floor. Sweat on my brow. Air moving down my throat and into my lungs, then pressing out again. Dirt beneath my fingernails. Smell of freshly mowed grass. Blisters on my feet. Lavender bubbles in my tub. Crushed ice and freshly squeezed lemon. An evening fading. A night beginning. A heart received. A spirit full.

These are a few of the things I've noticed today, paid attention to, revered. Oh, that I could speak from their knowledge. Perhaps tomorrow.

*Visualization and Action*

Close your eyes and allow your mind to inhale your surroundings. What do you touch, hear, feel, smell, and taste? Offer reverence and attention to the background of your environment, allowing it to move forward with each breath.

# HUMMINGBIRD

 Done era of my life had hummingbirds showing up everywhere I looked, as if they were special messengers sent just for me. This period of time found me wrestling with normal daily issues that left me feeling deflated and anything but joyful. I am a firm believer that life is a journey to be lived rather than endured, but some days the realities of life still send me running for the covers. I'm also a proponent of taking time to rest, quit processing, and letting things just be for a while, but I realize that sometimes it can get a little too comfy down there under the "woe is me" blanket and I need a nudge to ease off the covers.

Enter the hummingbird. After several days of these charming creatures popping around other people's houses, one finally showed up in my backyard. Standing at the kitchen window, watching this hummingbird enjoy my garden, I was spellbound. With further study, I learned that the hummingbird reminds us to find joy in what we do (no matter what that might be). They are also a symbol for accomplishing things that seem impossible (like crawling out from underneath our cozy covers). This tiny bird's swiftness is also a cue to grab for happiness as often and quickly as we can, because our moments are fleeting.

Keeping my eyes open, I was able to receive these wonderful and rich promptings packed within this minuscule creation. My attitude took a shift and life seemed less drudgery-filled. It was one more reminder that paying attention is priceless as we see and hear the messengers of the world.

*Visualization and Action*

 Consider where your life may feel drudgery-filled today. Name this area and imagine placing it outside yourself where you can be an observer. With your imagination, watch a hummingbird zip and sing around this drudgery, sprinkling it with joy and creating space for happiness or contentment to enter the situation. Offer gratitude for this present moment.

# FREEDOM

Freedom, pleasure, and ritual. What are mine? Stretching before I arise. Steaming hot coffee, fresh in the moment. A burning candle to awaken my senses. Music for ears and soul. Gentle pleasures. A desire to live in France or at least embrace the joie de vivre. To not fear dying. To not fear living. Awakening to everything. Pleasure. Desire. Wellness.

Freedom to speak my mind and share my magic. To spread my arms and soar like an eagle or a graceful pelican along the Sonoran sea. Pleasure to walk on the beach and feel the sand between my toes. To climb a rock wall and feel the strength of my body. To witness the lean and toned muscles in my arms that share the same body with crepe-paper thighs. To knowingly love the signs and tokens of where I've been and who I am.

*Pondering*

 What brings you freedom and pleasure? What is the ritual that awakens your senses?

# REFLECTIONS FROM
# MABEL DODGE HOUSE

What do I want? Today I want to sit in this glorious Adirondack chair and dream of the people who have sat here before me—Georgia O'Keefe, Ansel Adams, Dennis Hopper, Natalie Goldberg, and countless others. If they did not place their actual buttocks on these specific planks, perhaps they stepped across the uneven stones where my flip-flopped sandals now rest. I want to believe and know that the spirit of their creativity infuses this earth and that it has been passed along to me.

What do I want? I want to feel the gentle breeze on my skin and taste the crisp apple between my teeth and on my tongue. I want to know there is no moment other than this. I want to hear the birds trill in the branches of the spring green trees and acknowledge the bells pealing from the church in town. I want to inhale the dry warm air and exhale gratitude for all that is. I want to inhabit every sense of my being with the knowledge that I am here now.

*Ponder and Apply*

What do you want in this moment right now? Name it and claim it as yours.

# MEETING AT THE CROSS

There is an abandoned morada above Taos—a place at the foot of the Stations of the Cross where Penitentes used to reside and watch over the desolate land. The adobe building contrasts its ruddy color against the cornflower sky and sits like a sentinel above the valley. The blackened cross—one of Georgia O'Keefe's capturings—rises above the barren dirt, looking like a leftover reminder of a horrid Ku Klux Klan ritual. A shiver runs up my spine even as I shake off the image that flashes through my mind.

As if matching my shiver, there begins a rustling in the overgrown grass nestled against the old building. A waving plume arises, makes itself seen, and begins to move stealthily alongside the wall. I stand fascinated and mesmerized. Cat? Raccoon? The feathery flag, grayish and white, zigzags through the grass until it makes its way into an open space. A slight aroma spritzes the air. Skunk.

My first instinct is to pull away and escape in fear. Not a wise decision. Fear breeds fear. Breathe. Gather calm. Be at peace. I'm not here to harm this little creature. Nor does she want anything to do with me. And then I notice the second plume waving and weaving in synchrony with the first. A mother and child are making their way across my path. Do they see me? Can they smell my aroma as I inhale theirs? Fear breeds fear. Slowly, I move along the road, steering out of their way and hoping they have no desire to shower me, that they understand I have no ill will toward them.

Fear breeds fear. One quick move—a sprint toward my own safety—could set off an unwelcome spray. There is no reason for emission weapons here. We are just two mothers out for a morning stroll. I send my best vibes of goodwill toward the little mammals. I hold my breath slightly and search deep for the place of love and compassion. Can she sense I am no threat? Do I notice a glance my way? In mere moments our meeting is over. With a wave of her plume, she whispers *"Bonjour"* as the two synchronized tails disappear into the swaying grass as silently as they arrived.

*Journal Meditation*

Bring to mind a situation where you may currently be experiencing fear. How is your situation like an encounter with a skunk? Spend a few moments journaling your response. Now imagine approaching your condition gently and with compassion rather than swift movements and knee-jerk reactions. Breathe deeply into the place of fear, open to another way of being, and whisper a sweet *"bonjour."*

# OASIS

Like an oasis in the desert, the garden pond materializes in the midst of the arid landscape. The colors of azure and green, contours of flora and fauna, and sounds of trickling water refresh my senses. I stop and ponder. How do you capture running water with a Bic pen? Or illuminate a flash of koi glimmering amid the lily pads? What is true and resplendent for me in this moment? As if on cue, noise erupts and my thoughts are shredded as an edge trimmer bursts its clanging voice into the silent reverie. The distraction is joined by my inner critic. *What the heck are you doing? You can't write here. There's no way to capture with words what even the eye has a challenge to hold.*

Stop. Breathe. Listen. Pause. I welcome this old friend who offers me much, and so begin again.

What do I see? What do I notice? The earth has provided a chair for me. Will this basin of rock hold my form? It takes a small risk to know, so I gingerly settle onto the lava throne, perfectly and randomly constructed. The strap on my tank top pesters me with its looseness. Can I be loose too? Another koi dances under the pond's surface. Water bugs flit and chase across the murky wildness. Water's flow and the *vroom* of a mower surround me. Chaos and serenity combine to create yet another oasis in my midst. Gratitude swells. The critic drifts away as I lean back and let the earth hold me in this moment—welcoming what may come and all that is.

*Body Practice*

 Do a quick scan of your body, beginning at your toes and moving to the top of your head. Where do you feel tightness? Notice any spaciousness that resides within you. Breathe deeply into all areas of openness and tension, welcoming all that is.

# GLOW, BABY, GLOW

There are myths and legends around the world relating to what happens in the days surrounding the full moon, many of them pertaining to bizarre happenings or behaviors. Vacationing in Bermuda one year, we arrived two days before the month's lunar fullness, and our hosts were reminded of something they witnessed several years earlier. The story goes that for three nights following the full moon in Bermuda at exactly fifty-six minutes past sunset, the waters begin to illuminate with the mating ritual of glowworms. This frenzy lasts for approximately ten minutes each night and then subsides until the next full moon.

This sounds entirely too precise to believe. Fifty-six minutes after sunset? Not wanting to be gullible, we decided to seek out the luminous worms. At the appointed time, we ventured to a nearby ferry landing following the big storm of the day. At precisely fifty-six minutes after sunset, we witnessed one lonely chartreuse worm glowing in the water, although he appeared to be swimming circles inside a transparent jellyfish. (I posed that he warned the others not to come out, lest they meet the same fate.) While we were disappointed in the lack of numbers, it did not deter us from trying again. What better way to track a potential myth down than through the locals?

We found a Bermudian comrade who declared a friend of hers had one of the definitive glowworm sighting spots. This time the whole entourage went (including the teenagers who were probably hoping to prove their crazy parents wrong). Ten of us lined up around the dock waiting for the magic time. My husband was our official timekeeper. Five Minutes. Four. Three. Two. One. Blast off! I kid you not—at exactly fifty-six minutes past sunset, two days after the full moon, the water started glowing and the frenzy began. Amidst clouds of love potion, the fluorescent green worms did their thing. We oohed, ahhhed, shouted, "Look, Look, Look," and were amazed at the miraculous offering.

Random? Precise? A fluke? Creator? All I know is, I will sing, "Shine little glowworm, glimmer, glimmer" with a whole new appreciation.

*Pondering*

 Spend several moments pondering the miracles of nature.

# WHAT MAKES THE DIFFERENCE?

"Remember always that you have not only the right to be
an individual; you have an obligation to be one."
*Eleanor Roosevelt*

One of my favorite things to ponder is the topic of small things in life. Is there really such a thing as something too small or insignificant? I have the privilege of living in a beautiful part of the country and often travel to other places deemed paradisiacal in nature. It may be easy to enjoy things when you are surrounded by phenomenal beauty and caring friends. I also recall dark and challenging moments in these same locales. So what makes the difference?

I believe that if we fulfill our "obligation" as Eleanor suggests, we move right out of ordinary and into extraordinary. This magical movement manifests in a connection that permeates through life's layers and touches us deep within while spreading outward to others.

One of the most sacred things I recall doing while on vacation one year was to lovingly set the table for those with whom I was going to dine. As I rolled the napkins and silverware and placed the paper plates on the simple table, I considered each person and viewed my gesture as an act of love toward them. While I did not verbally share this with anyone, it was a vision that stayed with me. This seemingly small gesture was sandwiched amidst many other events that could have been viewed as much more extraordinary. Does setting a table become more sacred in paradise? Is there anything called ordinary? Only if we allow it to be so.

*Action Invitation*

Today as you go about your ordinary tasks, offer presence and gratitude during the process. Take note of any changes in your witness during these times.

# CRYSTAL CLEAR

It is not in the doing that we meet others well, but rather in our being.

What might it mean for our eyes and ears to become like crystal—to be able to see and hear with such beauty and clarity that healing light could be generated by the mere act of presence? What if we asked for a daily, moment-by-moment practice of being clean and clear while moving throughout the day?

What I've noticed when I intentionally make this request for myself is that the energy becomes magically fluid when I sit with others. Very little is required as I simply offer presence with eyes and ears like crystal. Our time together is what it is. Nothing more and nothing less. I leave these encounters feeling energized versus drained, satisfied instead of self-important. When I grasp and strive or believe I can make things happen, the crystal-like quality gets cloudy. My should's and must's get in the way.

I realize it's counterintuitive to focus on being. Focus isn't even the best word—it's more invitation and making space for this clean energy to arise. When I offer an intention of being clean and clear, the next imperative step is to let go of any expectations. If busy thoughts begin to cloud the air, I can release expectancies once again. Like breath when it starts to get raspy—rather than panicking, I can slow down and gently inhale until I find myself back at being rather than doing.

We've heard it before, but have we really listened? We are human beings, not human doings.

*Visualization and Action*

Today, imagine yourself as a beautiful, clear crystal—perhaps a magnificent diamond—as you move throughout the day.

# PASSIONATE LOESS

"Don't ask yourself what the world needs. Ask yourself what
makes you come alive, and go do that, because what
the world needs is people who have come alive."
*Howard Thurman*

Have you ever watched a grown man turn into an excited
little boy right before your eyes? Or witness a woman so filled
with energy that she glows like a kid at the circus? Those
transformational moments are Passion with a capital P. They are
life-giving, not only for the participant, but also for the lucky
bystanders.

We can find passion in the most ordinary of things. I can only
imagine the delight and playfulness that God has for creation.
On a trip to Washington's wine country, I had the pleasure of
witnessing a renowned geologist share his passion—in this case,
basalt and loess (a fancy word for dirt).

Standing on the side of a miniature Grand Canyon, he warned
us to steer clear of the rim that has been known to "spontaneously
disintegrate." With a "what the heck," he charged off the side
of the cliff and became a young spirit romping through the tall,
probably rattlesnake-infested grass to show us what he wanted to
communicate. Before us lay centuries of organic history, commonly
missed by an ordinary observer, yet extraordinary in the eye of this
impassioned explorer. While we gasped from our safe viewpoint
and muttered, "Oh, I wish he hadn't done that," the earth, like
magic, converted from dirt and the man transformed beyond a
middle-aged person into a passionate being who made even the

most inert objects (rocks and dirt) become exciting for all of us. It was truly a gift to behold and experience. We had just received a lesson in how passion begets passion.

*Journal Meditation*

 What brings you alive? Sit quietly and allow the moments you've felt most alive come to mind. Make a list and vow to do one item on your list today. The world will thank you for it!

# CYCLES OF SHEDDING

*"The wise ones who journey with me remind me that there are cycles of shedding before there is conception, that birthing is painful and messy and loud, and that we find it so hard to let go, to open so that new life can emerge."*
*Jan L. Richardson*

Before me lies a table full of photos of a young girl. Me. I see my second birthday; my fifth; another one or two. I think I look dorky, sullen, and goofy. I also witness a face that is brilliant, wise, and beautiful. Inside all these photos are both joy for the life I've lived and pain for areas that could have been better. Feeling the pain in messy and loud ways has been essential to arrive at the place of birth and new life. I've come through a painful journey and have fought to find what is true for me. Cycles of shedding have been my constant companions throughout recent years.

My childhood was one of imperfection—perhaps everyone's is. I know I was cared for, although not always in the ways I desired. Most of the pictures before me are studio portraits with perfect hair and carefully selected clothing. One photo, however, rises to the forefront. I am eight years old and only a few weeks before the picture, I fell off my bicycle and broke my front teeth. My lip was split so badly it would droop for several years before being surgically corrected. Ironically, it is this slightly disheveled picture that engages me as most authentic. It is the only picture that bears my signature, both literally and figuratively. My gratitude swells as I see my young handwriting testifying to the spunk I had even in my brokenness.

I am grateful for the table full of pictures I did not think existed.

They show me someone took care to document my life, however perfectly and imprecisely. These photos bear witness to my life. They allow me to see the cycles of growth, including the spaces of sullenness, beauty, brilliance, brokenness, and spunk. Each phase led to a new space. Each year and memory gave way for new life to emerge.

*Artistic Meditation*

Take a piece of fruit or vegetable that can be peeled and set it where you can examine it closely. Notice any imperfections while also taking in the beauty and uniqueness of this creation. Consider what might need to be peeled away before you could enjoy its full flavor. What needs to be shed from your life to experience personal wholeness?

# WAKING DREAMS

Waking dreams step into my day as my long-deceased father kisses me on the brow. The roots of my ancestry grab hold and pull at me like the long winding tendrils of the floating lily pads. Their shiny surface beckons and calls, saying, *Step into the deep. We will hold you.* But they lie. The path is deceiving. The shine will dull and the river of baptism is not a promise but a curse.

The tendrils pull me deeper, threatening to take me under. The struggle only wraps the vines tighter around my limbs. My throat closes as I am pulled down into the muck. "Help, Help," I gasp. A shining knight drifts past the surface—slow, easy, gentle. "That is the way," he whispers through gills that breathe beneath the heavy surface. "Follow me. Hold me and I will give you life."

The baptism is deep and it is true. Only the story of just one way is a lie. We are one. We are entwined like the hidden tendrils. It is time to open my eyes and witness the blossom. Yellow like shining sun. Resplendent like the golden crown. The tendrils in the muck lead to this beautiful blossom. As I open my eyes, they bloom and spread. A white one here. A golden there. Awaking, I sense the imprint of a kiss on my brow.

*Pondering*

 Find a quiet place and allow yourself a few moments of breathing deeply. Notice what holds you or tugs at your heart in this space and time.

# Dance or Die

"Rejoice with those who rejoice, and weep with those who weep."
*Romans 12:15*

And dance like there is no tomorrow.

What are we to make of this life we are offered? Daily we are faced with choice. Get up or stay in bed? Smile at the sunshine or decide it is too bright and close the blinds? Are the birds singing a joyful song or is it noise that hinders my sleep? Each minute is a choice. Will I choose to rejoice with gratitude for all I have or will I weep from pity at what I think I deserve and do not possess?

Choice. It faces us every minute of every day and often we are pushed to our limits. The point where it feels like we can take no more. The edge of life where a choice must be made. Dance or die.

Today there is a choice to be made. Dance or die.

Which will it be?

*Action Invitation*

Close your eyes and listen to the music in your heart. Find the song that makes you want to dance. Play the song. (If you don't own it, you may want to consider it as a gift for yourself.) See how choosing to dance affects your state of mind.

# GENEROUS ANTS

There is an inspired line from a Billy Collins poem that speaks of devoted ants following him home from the woods on one memorable occasion. Sitting down with my own pen and paper, I began to ponder what had followed me home this day. It was a morning rife with unremarkable markedness. A glorious hike in the crisp morning air. Two stealth skunks crossing my path, their odorous aroma transmuting into flora. A sparkling sprinkler delightfully catching me by surprise. Engaging in the practice of getting lost and being found. Amazement and awe at the summer colors bursting and blooming. The ineffable beauty of compatriots surrounding me.

A stream of images continued with ramshackle headstones adorned in garish flowers, surreal and everlasting. Simple rocks formed into crosses, nearly invisible yet ever so present by the side of my path. A scar unveiled. Winged magpie. Parade of cooing rooftop pigeons. An unidentified flock swooping across the cotton-sprinkled azure sky.

While walking today, Heaven surrounded me through my senses, then followed me home like a trail of generous ants marching across the page.

*Action Meditation*

Step outside into the big-hearted fresh air. Take a sojourn around your block or neighborhood, inhaling deeply along the way. Allow all of your senses to engage. Upon your return, pause and notice what followed you home.

JULY 16

# GROWING PAINS ... MINE OR HERS?

Raising a teenage daughter, I often ask questions like these: How do you protect someone who is spreading her wings? When is it time for the mother bird to push her baby from the nest? What happens when the baby jumps before the mother is ready? Are they lost to each other forever? Does the mother try to push the baby back into the nest or does she come alongside her young and help them learn to fly?

The natural world is brutal. So is the human world. Can I live with myself if I do not protect her? Can I even protect her? Nothing is in my control, especially this bright, spirited young woman. "You have raised an amazing daughter," she once said to me. "You gave birth to a great person." She is absolutely right, so when will I trust her? When does she stand up and walk on her own two feet? She was so cautious as a baby, waiting until she was sure she could walk, watching to see that no one knocked her over. Is she still so cautious? She has learned to walk and now she says she is ready to fly. Will I smother her inside the nest to keep her safe? Or will I let her leap, knowing she may fall?

*Visualization and Action*

Bring to mind a cozy nest filled with open-beaked birds. Imagine each little mouth as a personal hunger or longing. Listen quietly to yourself and name each longing. Consider what it would take to risk leaving the nest and reaching for this dream.

# HEARTBEAT

Whew we listen to our hearts and find God's voice and connection through prayer and stillness, we cannot help being moved to action. When we move in kindness and with our whole heart, the act becomes a form of holiness and prayer.

It is a beautiful circle of life. Spirit arising within me through prayer. Taking love into the world where Christ walks beside me and in front of me. Listening to the Father. Seeing the world beating around me and feeling it move within me.

*Visualization and Meditation*

 Center yourself and begin to breathe deeply. Allow the heartbeat of your spirit to arise and move within you. In your mind's eye, see the world beating around you.

# TWINKLE TWINKLE

Standing in an open field in the high desert of New Mexico, it feels like we are inside a massive planetarium—only better. The sky envelops us like a colossal bowl that's been dropped over the earth. From the lofty desert peak, the stars float above and wrap around our sides as they dip into the horizon.

What would it mean to be wrapped in starlight? To shimmer like a million stars? To glisten and glow and burst with full life? And at the end, to shoot across the ebony night like the flame of a skyrocket? Oh, to be a star. Twinkle, twinkle little star. When I ponder the stars, I don't really wonder about their origin or think about organic composition, but rather I view them as guides and compass.

The North Star leading me home. Big Dipper, open and ready to be filled. Orion, the hunter, searching on my behalf. Each unique and yet connected. Twinkle, twinkle little star. How I wonder who you are? I offer the same question with the passing faces I see each day. I wonder who you are and what constellations we shall build as we live together inside our giant planetarium.

*Pondering*

Twinkle, twinkle little star, ponder which one you are.

# CRY OF THE HEART

What is the cry of the heart? Anguish and joy. Yin and yang. Contrast. Paradox. Coming home while leaving home. It sounds cliché, but home is where the heart is. Home is with me. How can I be true to myself no matter where I am? In a room full of strangers, students, friends, colleagues, family, or alone—how can I be me? The heart of me?

The cry of my heart is to see and be seen. To be me. Lovely, kind, free. Full of joy while often threatened on the edges by my own malice and humanity.

My heart breaks open with both anguish and joy. One would not hold the same tenor without the other. The swing of the pendulum. Feeling sorrow. Despair. Weakness and pain. Letting go. Returning home. Listening to the cry of the heart.

*Meditation*

What is the cry of your heart? Sit quietly for a moment and rest your hand over your heart. Feel the beating as you follow your breath. Listen to its fullness.

# LOVE ME OR HATE ME, BUT PLEASE DON'T BE INDIFFERENT

We live in a world that likes to define whatever we do. Being productive is valued. When we find ourselves in that in-between space where movement isn't apparent, it can be daunting, or at a minimum confusing.

With so many choices to be made, I can drift into questions that ponder my state of being. Am I waiting or wasting time? Blocked or resting? Dabbling or mastering? As a writer, when motivation won't come, I'm reminded of the Nike slogan "Just do it." This tactic encourages me to put pen to paper or type a few lines into my laptop whether I feel inspired or not. Sometimes this works and presses me over the hump, and other days I am dry as toast, my thoughts scattered like confetti in the wind. My creativity feels wrung out and hung to dry. It would be easy to berate myself at this point.

My contemplative side considers it to be counterproductive to move through questions and try to make sense of where I am. Perhaps it would be better to patiently wait for answers to come. Maybe, but sometimes waiting just doesn't cut it. Paying attention, however, is crucial to staying connected to wholeness. So when I turn to the questions, I'm present to my state of being and not operating from a place of disconnect and numbness. Asking the questions allows me to show love for myself by engaging current circumstances.

*Visualization and Meditation*

What are the questions you need to ask today? Does your body beg for rest as you push through your days? Is there a longing for something to bring you out of a stuck place? Close your eyes and imagine yourself as a fresh, clean sheet floating on a clothesline under blue skies. Breathe deeply and allow the questions to simply drift with you in the breeze.

# Refusal of Silence

"Being a Silent Woman (or Man) is not about being quiet and reticent, it's about stifling our truth. Our real truth."
*Sue Monk Kidd*

There are places and times in our lives that resonate deeply and profoundly throughout the years like ripples moving out from a stone dropped in the center of a pond. The moments can be about specific faces, times, and places, but as they move through the years, they grow wider and broader, capturing a parade of companion events along the way. Throughout my story, I recall the simmering faces that attempted to silence me. My adult story has matured into one that holds much beauty, because this woman and that little girl (one and the same) refused to be silenced.

Once while creating a collage, I began with a portrait of myself as the base. When I started, my vision included layers of color ranging from dark to light with an emphasis more on the darkness I felt surrounding me. As I worked, however, the darkness began to recede and colors of life and light arose. A lioness emerged with her power and courage. Jewels began to cover the page. The process was remarkable, because even as I selected dark rows of background, I found myself covering them with flowers and diamonds and kisses, with sweetness and bubbles and butterflies. Something very real emerged. Even in the midst of darkness, my true essence would not be silenced or stifled.

*Artistic Meditation*

Select a portrait of yourself that you can copy and / or distort. Begin by tearing the image into strips, triangles, or squares. Next select magazine images that complement and/or capture your true essence. Gently reassemble your portrait with the added images and notice what emerges.

# THE LISTENER

Here I sit on my lava throne—balanced and true. A pointed edge tweaks my right buttock as the shadow of my hand follows me across the page. Tendrils of freshly washed hair curl and mix with dark and light. Turquoise blue caresses my body and my skin glows with the exuberance of fresh air and sunshine. My soul has been wrapped too long in a cocoon of gray. The element of air beckons to be acknowledged. Earth and stone cradle my body. The heat of the sun warms my skin as hungry eyes feast on the gift of water. Lily pads and water bugs dance lightly across the surface, reminding me of play and rest. Waterfalls feed the pond, offering the gift of movement that wards off stagnation, similar to that of air within a home closed up too long.

A statue mirrors my body from across the nearby lawn. She, too, is an artist, her form forever captured in bronze patina. Here we sit together—woman of flesh and bone and muse, immobile and bronze. We both glisten in the golden light and tune our ears toward heaven. My name today is gratitude. The bronze has been dubbed "The Listener."

*Visualization*

 Imagine yourself as a bronze muse with ear tilted toward your human heart. What does she hear as she listens deeply to your soul?

## JULY 23

# RE-GATHERING

Some mornings my thoughts are fleeting. I want to write to capture my essence, my soul, and the world reflected in my eyes and mirrored in my heart. Life throws hard balls and curves. I duck and dodge like a ninja, feet firmly planted while body bends and turns. I want to stay grounded—to be like the ancient Irish tree, reaching into the earth and stretching toward the heavens. The light in my eyes flickers when I open the door to an unwelcome message; when I rush around and feel cranky with my family; when I jump up from bed and hurry to the next thing; when I charge out the door to yoga. Something feels very wrong.

And so, I settle into my cozy cocoon in the light of morning and dream I am at the beach with an ocean breeze blowing across my skin. I am centered and calm—a prayerful stance—floating above the ground yet still fully connected to the Universe. God is with me, around me, within me. Earth uncovered. Soul recovered and reclaimed. It only takes a moment to connect, re-find, and re-gather.

We each need soul nourishment. God. Silence. Gratitude. Slowing down. What can I give up for ten minutes each day? Sleep. Email. A rigid schedule. And you? Where do you find nourishment? What might you have forgotten? Is there a piece of you you'd like to reclaim or re-gather? It only takes a moment.

*Action Invitation*

 Spend ten minutes nourishing yourself today. You get to choose what that looks like.

# Hearts Aching with Joy

"We are ignored even though we are well known. We live close to death, but we are still alive. We have been beaten, but we have not been killed. Our hearts ache, but we always have joy. We are poor, but we give spiritual riches to others. We own nothing, and yet we have everything."

*II Corinthians 6:9–10*

To breathe in all that God offers is to live an embodied life. There are times being feels more like the whirl of a hurricane than a peaceful morning. To be drawn to the wonder of the simple things like breath and waiting is to live in awe of this existence. Gratitude expressed for life can be clouded with thoughts of whether or not guilt should replace happiness. Let the clouds drift on by.

In God's graciousness, we are reminded of the times (present and past) when our hearts have ached and broken. Somehow, there is rest in remembering the suffering. There is release in realizing that, through grace and compassion, we can find calm in the midst of the storm and know it is okay to experience joy.

*Body Practice*

 Check in with how you're feeling today. Notice whether you lean toward worry, peace, or balance. Offer gratitude for wherever you are in this moment.

# REMEMBRANCE TOWARD FREEDOM

Why is it such a challenge to be the people we are created to be? It is my belief that we each innately hold the knowledge and truth of who we are deep inside our hearts. What we know to be true is always there whispering to us. Often, however, the whisper needs prompting to move the truth out of storage and toward remembrance and life.

We are well aware when the truth shows up. It is the moment our heart sings with recognition—a smell, a sight, a voice. You know you are home. You know you are safe. There is intimacy in memory. It sustains us and nurtures us here and now so we can remain rooted in the midst of this crazy life, knowing we are whole and pure.

We spend more time than necessary wallowing in the mud and muck of life. The truth, however, remains rooted inside us like an everlasting friend whose voice is always a welcome sound. It is a song for our hearts beckoning us to remember who we are. To walk daily in freedom, we must remember our past stories of both tragedy and redemption. We must dream of future hopes and we must choose to love God, our neighbors, and ourselves in the present moment.

We are anchored through our humanity and the magnificence of the Universe. There is a great knowing of something that we can't quite seem to remember yet know is ancient, everlasting, and true. This knowing holds me above the waves of life, buoyant as a bird in flight, cradled in the embrace of a friend.

It is my desire to remember the anchors of my life. The smells, the tastes, the sounds, and the sights that draw me toward becoming the person I was created to be. It is through remembrance that each one of us can walk in freedom.

*Body Practice*

Plant your feet solidly on the ground. Gently rise onto your toes and rock back to your heels. Inhale and exhale deeply while continuing this motion of lifting and grounding. Acknowledge your connection to the earth and remember we are anchored through the magnificence of the universe.

# SLOW DOWN

Take a walk and really notice what is around you.
Ride the bus. Smell the smells. Feel the life.
Encounter God in the midst.

I met Faith at a bus stop.
So beautiful. So memorable. Was she real?
A stranger in the scene? An angel?

Take time to smell the coffee. Feel its warmth.
Be soothed by it rather than jolted and injected. Breathe.
Listen to the sounds of silence.
A whispering fan. A chirping bird. A passing car. Notes of a
strumming guitar.
Sounds of silence. Sounds of quiet. A pause in the new day.

Consider things to be done slowly.
The start of the new day. The evening's close. Prayer. Peace.
Patience.

*Meditation*

 Choose your own simple meditation for today. Slow
down. Embrace and enjoy.

# THANK HEAVEN FOR LITTLE GIRLS

Giggling little girls, full of joy and eager to greet the world. "Come on. Come on," they say. "Come play with us." The years fade away—the hurts, the sorrows, the weight of life. We are girls—skipping, laughing, tumbling. Full of joy. Generations cascading together. Somersaulting like acrobats. Walking a tightwire without fear. Taking each other's hands and holding, caressing. We raise each other upright with our laughter—lightness and light. A puddle of puppies, but we are giggling girls. All of us. Grandmas. Aunties. Mothers. Nieces. Daughters. Tumbling together on beds of feathers, light as air. Pure goodness. All else dissolves into fits of laughter.

Those who have gone before and those who come after share in the joy. Let it out of the box for all to see. Little girls. Aunts. Cousins. Daughters. Mothers. Grandmas. Sisters. Blond. Raven-haired. Straight and curly. Giggling girls. Our laughter and compassion will save the world. Little girls, come dance with me. Little girls of wonder for all the world to see. Communion white and taffeta red, pink, yellow, golden girls. All tumbling into giggle pie.

Little girls skip and scuff their shoes. Giggling precious girls. Generations and generations. Our blood flows through from Eve. Transformed girls. How can anyone be angry with them? Look through the wrinkles of gray and death, into the eyes of laughing girls. Full of hope and compassion and joy! Blessed be the little girls.

*Visualization and Meditation*

Imagine a feather carried lightly through the air. Witness it touching today's generations as well as those who have gone before and those yet to come. Send a prayer of compassion and joy with the feather as it floats through the atmosphere.

# THREADS. CRUMBS. ROCKS.

Standing in the darkness
reaching for something to hold, to grasp and touch.
Can a thread be a lifeline?
A crumb, a meal?
A rock, a source of safety and comfort?

Holding on by a thread, the smallest thread of hope.
Thin and fine, fragile as a spider's web.
The tiniest thread waiting, hoping to be woven
into something strong and beautiful.

Being present to life allows hope to arise in the most unexpected ways. Although I penned the above words many years ago, my mind now turns to a time I spent traveling in the Sinai desert of Egypt. The threads remind me of my fellow pilgrims. There were days when I couldn't carry my own hope—the road seemed too arduous, the heat too stifling, the surroundings unfamiliar—and then a friend would notice something in a life-giving way. Each person brought their unique thread of hope into our midst and our threads, while separate, were woven collectively in a luscious tapestry.

On the same trip, we encountered Bedouin people who, by Western standards, were living in poverty—on mere crumbs compared to our lavishness. Their hospitality, however, exceeded any I've known elsewhere, for it was shared in abundance, and the meager offerings became a banquet to my soul.

And the rocks? Well, the soaring rocks became our friends. They provided much-needed shade in the heat of day and served as windbreak in the breeze of night. One formation even held the shape of a giant heart at its center. Hope sprang from the most unusual places and threads were woven into something strong and everlasting.

*Visualization and Action*

Look around and find something that is made up of threads—clothing, carpet, a tapestry. Focus on the tiniest thread you can find. Breathe in and out imagining threads of hope and community. Slowly move outward and consider the wonder of each tiny thread creating this object. Consider what each thread might represent and how they are woven into your world.

# TO BE OR NOT TO BE

Focus. The word seems to arise for me with its own sense of humor. As I pore over my journal pages, they often show little focus. They appear abrupt and interrupted—unfocused. Can they be enough? Can I be enough? Can simply "being" be enough?

The focus of Being. I see it as the tension between allowing things to bubble up, percolate, be what they will be in the moment and putting a course into action—following what wants to arise with more steps, through more effort.

For example, I've wanted to write a book for years and the thought terrified me. I used to ask myself questions like, Will it simply bubble up? Might someone just say, "Here, let me put those unfocused journals into a book for you?" Progress takes effort, focus. Will my body get healthy if I just sit around "being" all the time? No, it takes at least a small push to get out and walk, take a class, stretch on my yoga mat.

Simply being doesn't always cut it. Sometimes you have to focus.

*Action Invitation*

Select one task you've been avoiding. Imagine the absolute smallest step you can take toward completing the task. Quoting a famous ad campaign, just do it. Congratulations! You're one step closer to your goal.

# TOURING YOUR OWN TOWN

Have you ever considered what it's like to be a tourist in your own town? The territory may be familiar, but it calls for some new guidelines to get the full benefit of the journey. Being a local tourist means letting go of preconceived notions of what's corny (or undignified), and visiting places normally avoided at all costs. It requires using your street smarts to navigate pathways, but also surrendering and entering into the dreaded crowds while on the lookout for life-giving experiences. Being a tourist in your own town allows freedom of movement and new insight into what it means to play on your own turf.

Once, I was touring a young relative around town and had many opportunities for play. At the local science center there is a bicycle on a rail set about thirty feet above the ground. It is circular and weighted for balance with a trampoline-sized net below for extra measure. My charge decided we were going to experience this and when it was my turn, I felt a strong inner resistance that begged for some understanding. Why was I resisting, since part of me really wanted to do it? Fear of heights? No. Fear of falling? Not really. Fear of looking foolish? Oh, yes . . . that nasty fright.

My inner critic said things like *You're too old to do this. What will other people think?* While my playful inner child pleaded, *Let's do it. Please. Go for it!* Since I'm rarely happy when fear wins, I claimed my place in line, strapped myself onto the seat, and toured around the high-wire for one of the greatest delights of the day. I can't imagine having missed that feeling of exhilaration and accomplishment, one I would have bypassed had my inner critic won and had I not cleared the space to be a tourist and say yes!

*Ponder and Apply*

Consider a time you said no when your heart's desire was to say yes. Who or what was your censor? Imagine what it would look and feel like to say yes instead of no. Breathe this feeling in and carry it with you throughout your day.

# Traveling Muse

Often when I am at home, my golden fluffy cat, Aslan, serves as my creative muse. With luscious silken fur and confident humming purr, he offers me serenity and calm. When I leave home for days at a time, I imagine tucking him in my carry-on bag and inviting his grounding presence to journey with me.

Once, on a trip to Taos, I was stunned as I walked down a gravel road one evening and Aslan met me on the lane. While the land in this locale is famous for its magical qualities, I was nonetheless taken aback to see my little king strolling in the twilight. How in the world had my golden muse come to be here? The similarity was uncanny, although the sparkle in this kitty's eye could not match my golden boy's brilliance. Stopping in my tracks, I took a deep breath and shook my head clear as I realized it was merely a feline twin. Or was it? Perhaps we need only invite our muses to come along wherever we go.

*Active Meditation*

Ponder how you could use a muse right now. Through imagination or intentionality, invite your chosen muse along for the day.

# ORIGINAL MEDICINE

"We are all 'original medicine,' born to this earth with gifts
and talents that are ours and ours alone. If we do not
bring those gifts and talents forward, they are
lost to the world for all time."
*Gail Larsen*

How freely do you share your "original medicine"? Is it easy to recognize the places where your gifts and talents make an impact in your world? Or to paraphrase an often-quoted scripture, do you hide your light under a bushel?

We live in a world where conformity can seem the most reasonable road to follow. Sticking with the status quo and doing what is practical keeps us safe, but is it fulfilling? If you're anything like me, there's probably a bit of rebel inside just waiting to burst out and spread his or her special "medicine" in the world. While you might not pinpoint this desire, you may experience it with the tug of your heart, a lump in the throat, tears in your eyes, or an empty feeling in your body. These signals are the body's way of getting your attention and pointing out the direction toward your deepest yearnings.

Can you sense there's something more you long to do? Remember, if you don't bring out your unique talents, "they are lost to the world for all time."

*Body Practice*

Slowly read the beginning quote, paying close attention to your senses. Notice if there's a tug of your heart, a stirring in your belly, or any other sensation. Focus on this area of your body as you ponder your "original medicine."

# YOUNG AT HEART

"Age is an issue of mind over matter.
If you don't mind, it doesn't matter."
*Mark Twain*

One of my favorite memories occurred not so long ago while at a family reunion when a young cousin asked if I would like to go for a paddleboat ride. His sweet voice and big blue eyes were persuasion enough, and it was a glorious day, so I leapt at the opportunity. Soon, my nephews decided they should come along, too. Three of us struck out in the paddleboat while the fourth followed in a rubber rowboat. Our destination was the floating trampoline near the center of the small lake.

Once we arrived at our target, we tied up and all clambered onto the trampoline. "What now?" I asked.

"Huh?" my young comrades responded with puzzled looks.

"This is *it*?" I said somewhat dismayed. I was anticipating a greater adventure than sitting on a trampoline.

"Well, we could jump in the lake," one of them said tentatively.

"Sounds good to me."

They wondered if I was bluffing. "We'll go if you go first."

And that was all I needed. With a hearty "Okay!" I stood up and dove into the lake—clothes, jewelry, contact lenses, and all.

On the shore, rumors stirred. Someone thought I had been pushed in. Another believed I lost my balance and fell. Rescue plans and worried parents headed toward the shore. My husband zoomed in with his giant camera and quickly realized all was well with the world. His wife was gaily laughing as she cavorted in the water with her playmates.

There's nothing like a spontaneous and joyful move by an adult to stir the curiosity of children. For a moment in time, we were all the same age, laughing and playing in the water without a care for the world of adults. Who says you can't be young again?

*Action Invitation*

Close your eyes and imagine for a moment that it's a brilliant summer day and you are a content and happy child. Notice what you're doing. See what activities enhance your contentment and joy. Write them down. Now, pick one and go do it!

# SUMMER SOUL SINGING

Returning home after several weeks of travel, I am aware of the moments I most enjoyed, the seemingly small and slow ones I could savor, like waking up to sunshine and savoring my morning latte. Watching snails move along the tidepool. A mid-afternoon nap. Coming face-to-face with a bunny in a field. Watching my children surf. Rubbing a dog's ears. Strolling through Central Park. Feeling my husband's caress around my shoulder. Entering the cool of the Cloisters with the rush of the world drifting away. Singing "How Great Thou Art." Sharing a glass of wine with my niece. Watching the sunset over the Olympic Mountains on our return ride from the airport. Unlocking the door to our house. Sleeping in my own bed. Delighting in a slow morning at home.

*Ponder and Apply*

How is your summer pace? Are things frantic and rushed or are you allowing yourself time to see and savor each precious moment? Can you name the moments when your soul sings?

# August 4
## Living on Retreat

One of my greatest joys in life is going on retreat—setting aside time in this busy life and unplugging from daily distractions and obligations. Upon returning from one luxurious week, a dear friend inquired as to how I re-enter life after being away. It's a provocative question and one I can only answer for myself. I imagine others may ponder this same thought. I've consistently noticed that few people choose to take time for themselves and even fewer know how to integrate the gift once they return. Some find it impossible and others don't even try. Wouldn't it be wonderful to engage in a life where each day felt as comfortable as a retreat?

Staying on retreat, like most valuable things in life, is a practice. It's not unlike engaging in studies at school or learning to stay on the yoga mat. It can be likened to running a marathon and training never-ending miles on the road. Have you ever seen the face of someone who's just finished a 26.2-mile race? While their body may be aching with sore joints and blistered feet, the sense of accomplishment, joy, and well-being resonates around them as the exhilaration far outweighs the pain.

As my friend asked the question, "How do you re-enter?" I quickly heard my answer. "I actually live on retreat." My life is filled with delight of my own making and all I have to do is remember that. Does it mean life is easy? Heck no! I still have laundry to do, groceries to buy, and relationships to navigate, but even as I write those words, I realize how grateful I am to have clothes to wash, food to buy, and people to love. As I remember the idea that life is my retreat, the notion of how to re-enter gently drifts away.

*Action Invitation*

Name five delicious ways you find retreat either at home or away. Treat yourself to a retreat today by practicing one of your ways. Repeat each day.

# TRANSPORTED IN TIME

W hen I was sixteen, I drove a 1969 pale-yellow, black-top VW convertible Beetle. That era and little bug hold some of the most carefree memories of my life. How perfect to be old enough to experience freedom but young enough to not carry many responsibilities.

One summer evening almost four decades later, I was driving home in my 2007 cream-on-cream VW convertible. (Who says you can't go back?) It was chilly outside, but the sky was beautiful as I headed across Lake Washington toward home. I cranked up the heater and the stereo and soaked it all in. My iPod was doing its shuffle thing and *wham*—I was transported in time. Bachman-Turner Overdrive's "Takin' Care of Business" came zooming toward me like a wild karaoke host who put a make-believe microphone in my hand and shouted, "Sing it, girlfriend!" Well, all I can say is that for a few brief moments, any pressure, stress, or worry that comes with being a "responsible" adult drifted right out of my car into the night air. I gave myself over to the moment and was ageless. I sang like a diva. I dreamed like a child. I felt every sense of my body like the woman I am. Oh, it was great.

Perhaps I am easily amused. Who cares? Those moments of being fully alive are really what count, right? Have you experienced any of those lately? Music is one of the things that can take me back in time (or out of time) faster than anything else. How about you?

*Artistic Mediation*

If you wanted to pop into another place or mood, what song would hit the top of your playlist? Where would it take you? What would it tell you? Play it now and see.

# What Color Is Your World?

Blue. I raise my eyes from the written page and I see blue. Water. Sky. Mountains, too. Dark. Light. Rippling. Still. Streaked with gentle white clouds and punctuated by fluffy balls of cotton.

Blue. Surrounded by sentries of green pines. Waves gently moving. In and out. Away and toward. The motion churns my stomach until we become one. Molecules of water—all. Why should we be separate?

Blue. My jacket is blue. My heart, too. The sadness stirring deep within. Inside the depths. It starts as a ripple. Surface smooth. Deep inside I have all I need. A fish deep within the dark pool. Safe inside the womb. Free from the raging hurricane above.

*Journal Meditation*

With pen and paper, spend the next few moments describing the colors of your world.

# TAOS MOUNTAIN

They say the Taos Mountain is the guide to that region. Thousands have bowed to the ancient peak and asked if they might reside there. Legend says those who do not respect and honor the mountain's word may find they meet disaster or discomfort along their path. It seems that, for at least a brief period of time, the mountain has welcomed me. I sit, drawn to this place of creation, finding myself grounded by earth and air. I wholly believe there are hallowed places that draw us uniquely toward ourselves.

I never recognized this until I arrived in places where I felt truly at home. I didn't understand what had been missing until I found it. I am a woman of fire and heat. For some, the Taos air is too thin and they cannot breathe. Me? I want to sink into this land and fold into the landscape. To infuse my skin with the red soil and bottle the dry air to carry home as a talisman for moist days.

I am also a woman of water with flow and movement feeding my soul. It's no wonder one of my favorite activities is reclining on an air mattress in the middle of a warm summer lake. There I float while feeling the restoration of heat wash over me. Whereas the thought of rolling in sun-kissed grass or barreling down a blazing sand dune brings me immense delight, snow banks and ski slopes chill me to the bone.

But I am here now. I shall embrace this land that has welcomed me—offering heat, sun, arid air, and a deep connection to my native spirit. Thank you, Taos Mountain, for your heartfelt embrace.

*Visualization and Meditation*

Take yourself on a little "home" break right now. With eyes closed, follow your breath and allow yourself to enter the landscape in which you feel most at home (beach, desert, forest, etc.) Add a soundtrack, if you like, and be embraced in your welcoming land.

## AUGUST 8

# UNCONDITIONAL LOVE

Often we confuse unconditional love with unconditional acceptance. Nowhere is this more profoundly seen than in relationship, whether it be our relationship with God, others, or ourselves. The parent–child relationship is a powerful example. Are we not often like naughty children who treat each other poorly, test boundaries, and push hard to see if our "parent" will still love us no matter what we do? We test the boundaries of love to see if acceptance will still follow.

Being the parent of two strong-willed teenagers brings this truth to light daily for me. Do I love my children? Absolutely. Do I love and accept their choices and behaviors? Not always. I can, however, accept the choices are theirs to make just as we have free will to choose our own path.

Regardless of spiritual belief, the view of God as father and protector is a powerful archetypal image. Does this God love us without condition? My heart says yes. I also imagine the Universe weeping when I forget the beautiful core of my being and respond to the world in an unlovely manner. Whether I recognize it in the moment, the sorrow is carried within me because I am created to respond out of love rather than fear and hatred. The key is finding resonance between our actions and our soul.

*Action Invitation*

As you go about your day, I invite you to pay close attention to how you interact with others. Imagine responding to every person you meet with a heart of love. Notice the places of resonance and dissonance between your actions and feelings.

## AUGUST 9

# INDIFFERENCE

Someone near and dear to me once chose to label me indifferent. It started a squall of questions storming through my mind. Do indifferent people experience anger and hurt? Do they spend days or weeks (or months or years) considering how to repair someone else's hurt even though they know it is an impossible task? Do they awaken feeling unrested from a nighttime of grief? Do they consider ceasing to do what they love most to pacify someone else's needs? Do they measure their words and weigh the cost of speaking from their heart? Do they think about little else than the one who has been hurt by their "indifference"?

How does one adequately respond to such a claim? It feels like a bind, because to say, "No, I'm not indifferent" appears to dismiss the importance of the feelings of the other. It also feels like justifying or trying to excuse the indifference that did not exist in the first place. And to not respond only seems to indicate or prove that indifference does exist. It seems like indifference should be less exhausting than all this. I wonder if someone got the label wrong.

*Ponder and Apply*

 How do you define indifference? Notice what it feels like in your body. Consider if there's a situation where you've been indifferent that you'd like to remedy. If so, take a step today.

# Kingdom Come

Nestling into my throne of stone, I settle back and allow the earth to hold me. "Can you open and close the gate of heaven without clinging to earth?" the Tao Te Ching whispers in my ear. Here I rest, planted in an oasis where heaven meets earth. My self-proclaimed mermaid chair carved out of ebony rock graciously embraces my dreamlike form. Scottish trees wave and rise in the midst of this high-desert plateau. Dragonflies chase and tease across the cerulean-blue pond. They swoop and veer dangerously near the large-mouth bass that lurks beneath. If not planted in this solid seat, I too would magically arise and join the dragonflies in their dance. Or swim through the depths waving my mermaid tail. Painted on the same canvas, butterfly wings and buzzing bees beckon me to follow their lead. Be. Be still. Be beautiful. Be me.

Do I cling to this earth or am I opening the gates of heaven here in my repose? Are clinging and earthbound one in the same? Cannot the gates of heaven be seen through a dragonfly's wing? Is the bass's wide mouth a gateway, too? Is it possible to be on this earth and *not* be in heaven at the same time? Nestling into my majestic throne, I gratefully embrace this kingdom that has come.

*Pondering*

Ponder this magical place of heaven on earth.

# GOOD MORNING, SUNSHINE

Good morning, sunshine.
Smile. Rest. Pause in the day.
Take a slow start for
even goodness moves things along too quickly.
So pause.
Consider things slowly and thoughtfully.

Spend time with a friend. With God. Listen to the words of a
  song.
Take them in. Absorb them.
Stop to smell the roses.
Let their fragrance permeate your soul.

Watch the sunset. The sunrise. Embrace the seasons of life.
Touch a baby's skin. An aged person's wrinkles. Experience the
  beauty.

Look into another's eyes.
Eyes surrounded by a dirt-crusted face and filthy hair.
Look into the soul.
You may see Jesus there or you may see yourself—
hurting and longing for something more.

*Ponder and Apply*

Consider this momentary pause as a gift for your day.
Listen to the longing of your heart. Take one small step
to experience it more fully. The above suggestions offer
a place to begin.

# PONDERING SEA GLASS

Sea glass. My collection is meager, fitting into two ounces of crystal my mother used to serve Bailey's Irish Cream. The tiny assortment mesmerizes me, both in the meditative gathering along the beach, as well as here in captivity, nestled amidst my simple treasures.

Pieces of glass tossed into the sea. Like memories, some sink to the depths of unknowing. Others magically appear on the desolate beach—glimmering, waiting to be collected, taken home and treasured as something new.

Tiny bits of amber, azure, emerald, and smoky white. From where did they tumble? A humble beginning? Beer bottle in the hand of a local drunken boatman? Something more grand? The carrier of passionate script from a star-crossed lover? Ancient treasure tossing in the surf for centuries?

How began the journey to now? The essential breaking against an exotic piece of ebony coral? A fate more ordinary perhaps? Colliding with the hulk of a massive container ship or the speeding prop of a passing pleasure boat?

What seems most certain is no one noticed when the change began. Or how long the agitation cycle spun to achieve the smooth edges. Can one measure the length of metamorphosis from dangerous garbage on the beach into a treasure to collect? Oh, I wonder . . .

*Active Meditation*

 If you were sea glass, what color would you be? Why? What are the tumbles of life that smooth your rough edges?

# DANCING IN THE WATER OF LIFE

"For to cling to the past is to lose one's continuity with the past, since this means clinging to what is no longer there. My ideas are always changing, always moving around one center, and I am always seeing that center from somewhere else. Hence, I will always be accused of inconsistency. But I will no longer be there to hear the accusation."

*Thomas Merton*

With Merton's words, I am reminded of my personal life as well as seeing the connection with the therapeutic world of counseling. It is possible and often necessary to take a look at the past to see from where we have come, and I appreciate Merton's expression of futility: "clinging to what is no longer there." To cling is to be stuck without forward movement. Change is evidence of growth and maturity, and there is also a playfulness and freedom in Merton's words: "But I will no longer be there to hear the accusation."

Inconsistency or change? It is my belief that with each new day and encounter, we are called to change, to grow, to dance in the water of life.

*Artistic Meditation*

Fill a bowl with water and be present to the smoothness of the surface. Drop a coin and watch the surface shift. As the liquid calms again, imagine how the movement between tranquil and disrupted mirrors your dance in life.

# DARE I ASK?

Have you ever noticed how children around the age of three are full of the question why? Just like two-year-olds can't get enough of "no," these slightly older tots are blessed with inquisitiveness. As parents and adults, we often don't have the answers or the patience to respond. We may lack the courage or wisdom to say "I don't know" or answer truthfully. Another option is to offer fire hydrant responses or mumble answers with the force of a subtle drip. Somewhere along the way, kids stop asking if their questions haven't been met with candor—or met at all. As humans, we learn to project in our minds what the response will be if we do ask. Disappointment or silence are highly ranked replies.

What if not only with our children but with everyone, we answered honestly with kind hearts and internal wisdom? One of the most powerful moments of truth in my life came when my teenage son was rapidly accelerating through all established boundaries. He shouted how I was living in fear, which was most likely true. The greatest fear I carried during those excruciating times was that he would push too far and I wouldn't be able to love him anymore. As I agonizingly shared this with him, a fleeting moment of relief washed across his face, because he knew what I offered was true. There is respite in knowing someone is being honest even when it's hard to hear. We find solace as we understand we're not the only ones with questions or hard answers. There is wisdom in speaking the truth and honor in saying "I don't have the answer."

*Action Invitation*

 As you go through your day, notice what questions arise for you. Do you ask them or hold back? Pay attention to how others respond when inquiries are made of them. While being age appropriate, consider asking and answering questions today with the blessedness of a three-year-old.

# DANCING WITH THE JELLYFISH

Walking on the tropical shore, I found myself staring at transparent beauty, and beauty began to stare back at me. She silently cried out with each heave and gasp, "Help me. Save me. I'm dying here." The jellyfish pled to be rescued. She looked at me through her translucent form. "Water of life, I need you."

And so the dance began. Scooping her up with a sheet of plastic garbage left in the sand. Scooping and tossing. Over and over again. The currents and waves not cooperating. They refused to carry her out to sea.

Watching the rhythm, she landed in the ocean and began to swim, her tentacles spreading and floating, her form beautiful and deadly. I nearly forgot she could harm me, so mesmerized was I by the beauty.

Could she escape to the open sea? No. This day, she was destined to arrive on the shore and nothing I could do would save her. Did she understand how I fought for her? Scooping and tossing repeatedly until the futile game was over.

Sorrowfully, I left her by a rock, a small pool of water keeping her moist. For the moment, life-giving and sustaining. Maybe that shallow puddle was enough to nourish her. Perhaps the tide changed and pulled her back to sea. Nevertheless, her beauty stayed with me.

*Pondering*

Where have you been touched by the beauty of breathing creation?

# THE DARKEST NIGHT

How can black become even blacker? What is the color of darkness?

Who knows the color of water? The color of tears? The color of sorrow?

What is the taste of sorrow? Bitter and salty. Full of pain.

Too bitter. Too much. Too black.

What is there to do when the darkness feels like too much? I carry a multitude of memories from when I believed I would not survive. The loneliness of abandonment. The heartbreak of relationship. The arduous climb of life. And yet, I have survived and, dare I say it, even thrived.

We each hold our own pain and sorrows—there really is no escaping it. But what if instead of pushing against pain, we entered in and examined it? If we asked, What is the color of this place? How does it taste in my mouth? Where does it churn in my body?

We make choices everyday of whether or not we fondle pain, stuff it, or rage against it. What if we considered it a guidepost along our pathway and instead approached it with curiosity rather than trepidation? Will I really disappear or evaporate from loneliness? Has my broken heart rendered me useless forever? The climb will end when I reach my destination, won't it? Curiosity has saved my sanity and helped me laugh at myself when I thought only tears were possible. It has taught me to hold my pain gently and helped me understand that no situation has yet turned out to be too much.

*Body Practice*
Make a closed fist with one of your hands and imagine it is pain. Hold it as tightly as possible and begin to

examine it with curiosity. Allow yourself to see each line, freckle, scar, knuckle, and finger. Slowly allow your hand to open as you continue exploring the pain. Be curious about the difference in a tight closed fist and an open hand—both representing pain.

# HOLDING TIGHT

The young woman sat before me dressed in work clothes of tailored black pants and crisp white shirt. Her face clean of makeup. Her eyes tired beyond her years. Her long silky hair pulled away from her face in a ponytail that was a little messy but still very "together." She held onto herself with crossed arms, grasping her stomach tightly. Her face turned deeper shades of red as she tried to convince me she "operates best under stress." It was almost as if I could hear her saying, "If I just hold on tight enough, all of the emotions I feel inside will not spill out and fill this room. If I can just convince you, maybe I can convince myself that everything is all right and I don't need help." But she did not convince me.

I could see the terror on her youthful face. What was she running from? My gut told me if she were to slow down the motions, she might drown in her tears. Did she have that same sense? Nowhere to turn. No one to trust. A ticking time bomb waiting to explode. A waterfall held back by a fragile dam.

She hinted of betrayal. Friends she could not trust. A young love gone bad. The fighting in her house followed by the absence of family members. "They just leave," she said with a shrug. The themes were all over the place, but still she tried to convince me she did not need help. She could only trust herself, but there she sat betraying herself. Pushing her body. Exhausted and worn out. Driven. Holding tight. She saw herself as moving toward something. I saw it as running away. Her attempts at security slowly eating away at her soul.

*Body Practice*

Take a moment to check in with your body. Close your eyes and see where any tension might be residing.

Focus on the most prominent spot and see what comes to mind. (Are you holding tight? Carrying excess weight for yourself or another?) Breathe deeply into that place. If possible, gently move that part of your body, or massage it tenderly. As the tension releases, consider how you might hold a little less tightly today.

# August 18

## On the Lighter Side

Weighing what it means to be authentic in life feels exhausting when focused on too intensely. It can be heady stuff, and sometimes you just have to reach for some plain old mindless fun. Who better to model that than a couple of teenagers? In this case, they happened to be my own who were slowly coming to see we had more in common than they'd care to admit (and maybe we actually are from the same planet).

One evening, at the urging of my then nineteen-year-old son, we went to a 10:00 p.m. movie in the middle of the week. That in itself is pretty bold since generally I am cuddled into bed by that time. But with summer upon us and lightness hanging in the air, I couldn't resist when I heard him say, "Come on, Mom. Live a little." I could see his crooked grin through the phone, and quickly replied, "What the heck!" His charms prevailed even further as he managed to convince his sister to come along, too.

So that night, the three of us toddled off to a ridiculous and definitely not critically acclaimed teen action film. The movie was not my normal style; however, it was the perfect contrast for too much seriousness. Yes, this contemplative soul was laughing out loud at all sorts of inappropriateness while surrounded by an auditorium full of teens and twenty-somethings. Forget exhausting topics—sometimes you just have to let go and head for the lighter side of life!

*Ponder and Apply*

Where could you use some lightening up? Make a list of five or more things that make you laugh. Live a little and do at least one today.

# How or Why Don't Matter

I believe. I believe in God, magic, and a Universe that conspire on my behalf. I believe in my power to make things happen and I understand I have control over nothing—absolutely nothing. I believe each and every moment in time has the opportunity to be life changing. They are all worthy of being placed in the mosaic of our life. Some pieces shine a little brighter, but even within those shards are miniscule elements forming to create the whole.

When those shining moments arrive, there can be a tendency to ask when the elements began to form. Experiencing one such time, I recall my wise young son offering, "Mom, who knows how or why things aligned like they did, but they did." Magic happened. God showed up. The Universe did its thing and in a moment life changed forever. The how or why didn't matter.

*Visualization and Meditation*

Take a moment and recall a positive pivotal moment in your life. Allow yourself to feel the experience in your body here and now. Breathe deeply and hold the moment tenderly in your heart. Know this moment will always be with you.

# I STOPPED DREAMING WHEN . . .

How would you complete this statement: I stopped dreaming when . . . Have you recently considered what your dreams are or if you've stopped following them? Perhaps you live in a closed-off or fearful place where dreaming seems frivolous and unproductive. Do you consider that sharing your dreams might be met with ridicule and thus the dreams snatched out of your realm or buried deeper inside your psyche?

"I stopped dreaming when" is part of an exercise I have participated in dozens of times. The goal is to let the words flow and find their rhythm until you stop thinking about what you are saying. For many sessions, the things that popped out of my mouth were based on childhood experiences that gradually moved upward through my adult years. And then one instance, I was demonstrating this process and out popped, "I stopped dreaming when I couldn't dance."

These words came forth with a ferocity that surprised both the partner with whom I was working and especially me, because I had no clue where they came from. While I took some basic tap-dancing classes as a child and shuffled my way through proms and weddings, I don't really consider the actual act of dancing to be the essence of my exercise epiphany. It feels bigger than pirouetting and representative of something deep in my soul. It points toward a rhythm lost and a culmination of this loss. It does not feel despairing, but more like a mystery to be considered. My "dance" is waiting to be rediscovered as I ponder my current dreams.

*Journal Meditation*

 Close your eyes and follow your inhale and exhale for several moments. In your journal, allow yourself to start writing with the prompt: I stopped dreaming when . . . Continue writing nonstop for several minutes as you rediscover your dreams. Breathe deeply and decide what small step you could take today to revive one.

# HOPE

Now, where or in what lies your hope?

Hope lies in remembering how and where the Universe has met us in the past. Turning impossible situations into amazing outcomes far beyond anything humanly imaginable. Hope lies in the present moment, for it is all we have. Hope lies in the future, for we know there is more to come.

Paradoxical? Maybe. Complete? Absolutely! Hope lies in the past, the present, and the future.

*Pondering*

In what or where lies your hope?

## AUGUST 22
# MOMENT'S OFFERING

I offer myself to the moment and in return, the moment's magnificence unabashedly greets me. A dreamlike yet immensely present state surrounds me as I lie down in the summer grass and observe the dragonflies' exquisite dance through the guardian willow fronds. The ripple of beauty and delight flows out like a coin tossed into the silent pond. I listen to the alto voice of a bullfrog humming in the marsh. A crow adds his tentative "caw" to nature's symphony, then swoops deftly across the cerulean blue water. Industrious ants work their way across my path, weaving through the pattern of my yoga mat turned magic carpet. All worries and stress wash away with the flow of the waterfall near my side. This moment is a healer. This moment is all I need.

*Meditation*

 Set a timer for ten minutes. Simply follow your breath. Nothing else. Inhale. Exhale. Repeat.

# RIDING THE WAVE OF BREATH

Before daybreak and bleary-eyed from my night's sleep, I enter my studio. As I touch match to wick, the soft glow of candlelight enters the room and morning shadows dance across the walls. I curl myself into a comfortable cross-legged position, close my eyes ever so slightly, and offer myself to this new day.

Inhale. Exhale. I ride the wave of my breath. As I meditate, there are moments where my curiosity stirs, and I wonder from where this tranquility comes. I sit in silence and follow my breath. In. Out. One. Two. Three. Four. My body settles into a gentle rhythm. With the inhale, I hear the sound of wind through aspens. On the exhale, a storm is brewing in the Midwest. My thoughts float by like gentle clouds on a summer day. Grounded. Breathing. Simple. I am tranquil. Again, I wonder how I got to this place until even that thought drifts on by. In. Out. One. Two. Three. Four.

*Meditation*

Position yourself comfortably and rest your palms gently upon your thighs. With eyes slightly closed, find a place of focus within the room and begin to breathe. Simply ride the wave of your inhale and exhale, allowing thoughts to drift by as they come. Enjoy!

# RILEY

The little dog wiggled his way into their hearts with ears of bright pink and hair the color of an old woman or a young punk star—silvery with darkened roots and undertones. Teeth like Dracula's fangs, only more inclined to nuzzle rather than bite. Still, he is ready to pounce at the nearest squirrel or unassuming bird—standing stock still with four-inch tail on point. He stole their books (found shredded and buried in the garden), their draperies (heaped near the patio door, the casualty of a squirrel hunt gone bad), and their hearts (forever changed by his presence).

Typically, one thinks of the dog as offering love unbounded. While this may also be true for Riley, his rapscallion ways seem to have brought a new kind of unconditional love into their lives. "Love me. Love my dog."

Oh, that the world could look at the mistakes and misdoings of others and laugh with delight the way Riley's family does with him.

*Ponder and Apply*

Consider how you treat yourself when you make mistakes. Does your internal voice scold or do you offer laughter at your misdoings? Notice the difference in these two responses. Imagine treating yourself with Riley's unconditional love.

# RIPENING DREAMS

*"Remind me of the gifts that come from
the slow ripening of dreams."*
*Christine Valters Paintner*

Slowly, slowly we move into the desert of our hearts. Slowly, slowly we begin to emerge from the desolation. A dream arrives in a flash of unconsciousness. We witness it deeply within ourselves and though ethereal, it resonates as more profound than anything which has gone before. Without conscious tending, our night vision weakens and the dreams dissolve inside the daylight. Even though faded, true dreams are still present, waiting in the heavens until that moment when they are called to shine.

Their gifts are like bits of brilliance twinkling in the night sky. Arriving one by one in the darkened night, they sing of tiny, shiny presents waiting to be unwrapped, beckoning our consciousness to peel off the layers, announcing the time to hang our own ripened dreams in the night sky.

*Visualization and Meditation*

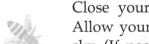

Close your eyes and begin to follow your breath. Allow your mind's eye to envision a darkened night sky. (If possible, step outside in the evening.) Allow the twinkling stars to arrive, and see if one shines a little brighter. Imagine this star as a dream or longing waiting to emerge. Breathe deeply and give this dream a name.

# TRANSITION

In his book *Transitions,* William Bridges says: "Every transition begins with an ending. We have to let go of the old thing before we can pick up the new one—not just outwardly, but inwardly." It feels like I am always letting go of something. Something forever ending. A new thing beginning. At times, the transition is joyful. Other times it's heartbreaking. Occasionally it goes unnoticed. Letting go of even the hard stuff is not easy. Welcoming in the new can be terrifying. Transition seems to be the way we move forward and grow. If nothing changes, our lives become stagnant.

Beginnings and endings are the way of life. Our lives begin at birth and end when we breathe our last breath on earth. The sun rises in the morning only to set in the evening. The hours of the day circle 'round the clock. We have to say hello before we can say good-bye. We have to let go before we can receive.

*Visualization and Action*

Select a small object and gently close your hand around it in a secured fist. Explore the precious object with your mind as you hold your hand in this closed position. Now slowly open your palm and notice what changes with this new movement. What is gained? What is lost?

# TRUE CONFESSIONS

Have you ever had one of those moments when you encountered someone you've never met and immediately don't like him or her? This happened to me while on a flight across the country. My negative reaction to my seatmate was intense, and I didn't want to be anywhere near her. I felt like I was back in college meeting the glamorous city girls and I was the unsophisticated hick from Podunk, USA. My desire to sum both of us up in an instant without reasonable cause was stirred. (It is a response I vehemently dislike.) Nonetheless, I clung to the discomfort of sitting next to this woman. I observed her peripherally while she incessantly texted on her phone long after the flight attendants had asked us to "please turn off all cellular devices." My response felt juvenile and I wanted to tattle on her. She was getting away with something and I wanted her caught. To what universe did my normally compassionate, curious self disappear?

In hindsight, lots of reasons came to mind, with exhaustion hitting the top of the list and anxiety a close second. Finally, I began to wonder what hurt or need might have had her frantically texting well past the stop time. My compassion and curiosity kicked in while considering she was probably a nice person outside of her airplane seat. My reaction most likely had nothing to do with her specifically, but rather it was about me. Perhaps it resulted from past hurts, a current lack of self-care, or the combination of both.

How about you? Ever have one of those moments? What sets it off for you? When does your tendency to judge kick in?

*Body Practice*

 Check in with yourself and consider the moments you judge yourself or others. Name the judgment. Breathe into the judgment for a few moments. Now imagine offering a new solution for the offending act. Notice how the two judgments feel in your body as you continue to breathe.

# August 28

# Turn Your Frown Upside Down

Change is something that was frowned upon in my family of origin. Growing up with parents who survived the Depression and valued hard work over touchy-feely explorations, I learned the importance of committing—and staying committed. Messages like "Get good grades," "Stand by your man," and "Buy a house and live there until you die" prevailed. Frivolous was a four-letter word. Loyalty was crucial and if you had a good job, for goodness' sake, keep it!

Not bad guidelines to aspire to, one might say. Commitment. Loyalty. Hard work. Who can argue with those things? But the problem with childhood messages is they come from someone else. As children, we may miss the point that grownups don't have all the answers. I was certain for a long time that if someone was older, they must be wiser. It's taken me over half a lifetime to sort through these messages and find personal clarity.

In the sorting, I've come to understand that change is essential for me to live fully. Growth fuels my passionate fire. Learning is an integral part of who I am. Movement is critical. I've lived through some pretty intense internal battles as my heart longed to expand, seek, and grow, and the old voices shouted, *Stay put. Don't be flighty or crazy or foolish.*

Gratefully, I've been up to the task and pushed through some mighty barriers. I've taken what my ancestors would call "frivolous" risks in order to reach a more stable place. Standing by a loved one has been best served through detachment. Commitments have held because the heart agrees, not because an ancient paradigm said I had to stay.

*Body Practice*

Sit quietly and place your hands gently over your mouth. Pucker your lips and scrunch your face into a frown. Hold this position and feel it for a moment. Release and come back to a neutral spot. With hands still gently over mouth, inhale deeply and lift the corners of your lips into a smile. Return to neutral. Ponder these three positions: Neutral, Frown, Smile. Consider which one best represents your life.

# UNEXPECTED WHOLENESS

There is a wholeness I feel that reaches beyond any book's pages. Contradictory as it might sound, it is a wholeness originated out of the brokenness of my life and includes the discovery of joy in unexpected places. It has been birthed out of tenacity and a curiosity to stretch past the boundaries of normalcy.

Exploring the world—all corners of it—is my pathway in life. Studying yoga, chakras, centering prayer. Praying with the elements, soul collage, drumming, dance. Laughter, tears, travel, silence. Creating art, writing poetry, doing nothing. These are the passageways where I have met the fullness of creation. Some are trails that have ventured outside my traditional Southern upbringing and ones that may cause consternation for those who have not traveled my unique journey.

If I were to give in to worry about what others think—if I let someone else dictate my way—then they would become the keepers of my growth and happiness. So, I must ask myself, What is my path? Which way will I choose to live?

My pathway is connected to the world, intertwined with God, grounded in the earth, reaching toward the heavens. It is the place where I seek wholeness in whatever shape it may come and pursue joy in the most unexpected places.

*Active Meditation*

 Explore a crack in a sidewalk or dinner plate. Ponder how this crack is part of the whole. How are the fractures in your life part of your wholeness?

# FAREWELL OR FAILURE?

Relationships are complex. Large doses of energy are spent considering relationships of multiple forms. I awoke one morning with these words running through my mind: It is in relationship that we are broken, and in relationship we are healed.

There's a theme of abandonment that runs through my personal narrative and—because I'm human—I can lean toward believing the ended relationships are failures on my part. If only I'd been a better friend, mother, daughter, fill in the blank, maybe then they wouldn't have left. If only I'd done something different.

And then there are those relationships where I know I was the one who threw down the gauntlet and said, "This isn't working and something needs to change." And the other party chose not to engage, so the relationship ended. Who failed then? Perhaps no one. Maybe everyone.

Regret is a miserable waste of energy and "if only's" go nowhere but straight to regret and wallowing. The truth is that some broken relationships need to end in order for healing to begin. It doesn't mean parting is easy, but it also doesn't signify failure when it's necessary to say good-bye. Sometimes a well-placed farewell is the ultimate definition of success.

*Pondering*

Notice if you recall any regret-filled relationships and find yourself wallowing in an "if only." Is it time to let go? Or is there one more effort you feel called to make? How might your perspective change if you saw the ending of a defunct relationship as a success rather than a failure?

# August 31

# Not Today

Forgetting he is gone, I arise in the morning and look out the door to see if Curry, my faithful companion, slept outside. I walk into the house at the end of the day expecting to be greeted. I look in the backyard over the fence and hope to see that slobbery smile. I miss my old yellow dog. It is too much and it is not.

I know it was time, I tell myself. The house will stay cleaner now. I slowly started to put away his things: bowls and medicine moved downstairs, but not totally disposed. I will remove a rug today that we used to keep him from slipping on the hardwood floors. My husband cannot bring himself to scoop the last bits of poop in the yard. An empty plastic bag sits stuffed in the Adirondack chair—waiting. "I don't want to do it," he says. It is not the complaining, an "I don't wanna," but one filled with sadness that this will be the last time.

So, no more poop scooping, no more balls of fur throughout the house, no more slobber on the walls. When will I clean the kitchen door? The brown smudge where Curry used his nose to push it open and let himself in? Not today. Maybe tomorrow. Maybe after I have looked for him on the rug or after I have noticed he is not on the back porch and my heart has stopped a little because I know he won't be there. It all happens in less than a second, maybe a couple of seconds. But the memory, the routine, the pattern of life is still there.

Oh, it is too much and, of course, it is not. I will go on living. Maybe someday I will allow another furry creature to enter my heart, but not today. Today I will allow myself to feel all the feelings. I will go about my routine. I will send my daughter off to her first day of tenth grade. I will enjoy the sunshine that is here. I will take my walk and go to my dance class. I will dance for Curry and for me.

*Ponder and Apply*

Is there a place in your life with lingering grief? What feelings or thoughts surround your memories? Today, allow yourself space to name and feel them. Express love and gratitude for where you are right now.

## September 1
# Everlasting Love

Many of my fondest childhood memories stem from the time I was in kindergarten. Those recollections hold images of skipping, playing, and having the freedom to just be me. Kindergarten was a time of living fully into my true self as a pint-sized person.

My most joyous memories came from being in Mrs. Peck's kindergarten class. The classroom was in a backyard cottage that resembled a story book house just around the corner from my home. I remember the independence of being free to skip around the block on my way to school. To this day, I can sense the embrace of Mrs. Peck when I hug women who feel like her. Her whole being resonated unconditional love. Many years later, I found a letter penned by this loving teacher in which she confirmed her fondness for me.

I had always known deep in my heart that she loved me, but I also questioned if I had built it up in my imagination. What a gift to find those words of confirmation almost fifty years after they were penned. The power of her unconditional love sustained me during times of trial and sorrow in ways I can't begin to fathom. I wonder if this teacher ever knew how far her love would reach.

*Visualization and Meditation*

 Center yourself and draw your attention to your heart center. Breathe deeply and focus on the power of unconditional love. Notice if there are faces or images that come to mind. Imagine times where you have either witnessed or received this kind of care. Offer gratitude for the places you receive love in small and large ways.

# START YOUR OWN DRUM CIRCLE

The sound of drums calls through the crystal blue sky. Beckoning. Singing. Saying, "Come play with us. All are welcome here." The message is clear. "Find a perch on the grassy knoll, soak up some sunshine, and live your own rhythm."

If you've never participated in a community drum circle, it's quite an experience. From out of the silence, a lone drummer begins. Soon another joins in, percussion instruments follow, and—if you're lucky—a bass carries the heartbeat. It's a magical experience as multifarious people of assorted talent levels come together to create music. Dancers step into the mix and uniquely sway to the emerging beats. All elements are essential to create this life-engaging experience.

One such time, a lone dancer who swayed on the outer perimeter of the circle. My curious self wondered why he steered clear of the middle and whether he longed to be center stage. Later as we had a brief conversation, I realized his perfect rhythm was to be exactly where he was—nothing more or less. Many of us don't listen that well. If everyone isn't doing it (whatever "it" is), we draw back because it might not be acceptable. We choose to listen to everyone else's rhythm and find ourselves out of sync, thus missing out on our unique part of life's harmony.

My part in this experience was to sit on the knoll and play my djembe. I didn't need to be the one to start or stop the circle. My role was to find harmony, and in that I was content. I was grateful for those who brilliantly began each round of music and less appreciative of those who exerted an odd power to bring the circle to an unnatural close. In practicing our personal rhythms, it's important to know when we must follow the beat of our own drum and when it feels best to play harmony. There's magic in listening to the pulse and finding the simpatico places both within and without.

*Visualization*

Take a moment and imagine leaning into your own grassy knoll and soaking up your personal rhythm. What instrument are you playing? What role is uniquely yours? Where do you dance in the circle? What beat will you choose to follow?

# SNAPSHOTS OF SPACIOUSNESS

Walking and SoulStrolling® are two of my favorite forms of meditation. Sometimes, I choose to listen to music or carry my camera, but most days it's just my solid walking shoes and me. There's a great scene in the movie *Elizabethtown* where the female lead fashions her fingers as though holding a camera and takes mental snapshots. One morning while walking, it felt important to record mental snapshots along the way, even though I was certain they'd be forgotten by the time I returned home. However, the images lingered long after my morning sojourn.

A tiny sign upon a fence said, "Please do not feed Riley. Doctor's orders." The sun gleaming on the steeple of a church previously unnoticed. White Fruit of the Looms flattened in the street. Lavender bikini undies at another spot along the way. (Had someone lost their laundry or had the world stripped off its clothes to dance naked in the moonlight?) A "No Trespassing" sign attached to a church door. Blue sky. Glistening sun. Tiny chickadees playing in bare tree branches. Red, freshly painted doors. Children frolicking at the park. People delighted to be out in the sunshine.

Taking snapshots without a camera reminded me how sweet it is to pay attention and what a delight it is to savor the world around me. There are abundant riches and joy in being fully present.

*Action Invitation*

 Set aside at least ten minutes to take a stroll around your neighborhood. Notice the world as though looking through the lens of a camera. Savor the abundance that surrounds you.

# MEETING LIBERTY

Walking through our neighborhood park one morning, I found myself strolling behind an older gentlemen and his golden retriever. My pace quickened to catch them, because I'm incapable of bypassing the opportunity to receive a little "golden" love, especially since the death of my beloved dog, Curry. My selfish tendencies were in high gear and I was intent on getting what I needed.

Catching up with them, I politely asked if I could love on his dog for a minute and then felt like I had come face-to-face with the reincarnation of my old sweet guy. "He's thirteen," the owner announced. With a lump in my throat, I confessed that we had just lost our thirteen-year-old golden. What ensued was a gentle and kind retelling of the last days and moments of Curry's life. The owner asked me questions like, "How did you know when it was time?" "Was it peaceful?" "Did he suffer?" Somewhere in the conversation, I realized that this moment was not just for me. Liberty's owner was entering his own process of letting go and needed reassurance that they would get through it.

There was something in this encounter that spoke deeply of emptying and filling. I have not decided yet how the process transpired. Who was filled and who was emptied? Does it even matter? What I do know is that I followed my heart, seeking what I needed in the moment, to help me with my own grieving process, and in the midst I met another person with his own sorrow to share. Both of us walked away comforted. I will remember Liberty and his owner for quite some time. At first site, Liberty appeared to be the ghost of Curry, but now I'm pretty sure he was an angel.

*Body Practice*

Notice if there is a secret grief you carry in your heart. Gently welcome it as a friend upon the path. Give yourself permission to experience this grief fully for the next ninety seconds (set a timer if you like). Upon completion, express gratitude for this encounter.

# IN PRAISE OF SUNSHINE

One afternoon, I was conversing with a dear friend on the topic of sunshine and convertibles and she said, "I don't like the feel of sun on my skin." My visceral response was noticeable as I wondered how that could possibly be. Where I live in the Pacific Northwest, even seconds of the day when the gray lifts momentarily have been named "sun breaks." Not like the feel of the sun? My mind quickly downloaded moments of summer bliss without warnings of skin cancer and age spots. Sitting on my deck in the sunshine, cool breeze blowing over me, surrounded by blooming flowers, the sky amazingly blue and clear above me, book in hand, iced tea by my side, old dog happily sniffing the breeze, feeling down to my core the embrace of sunlight.

Moments like this bring warmth deep into my soul. The joy of childhood, the tickle of sprinklers, and the splash of the ocean wash over me through the rays of the summer sun. I can't possibly imagine what could be better than that!

*Visualization*

As you read today's descriptions, see if there are images that bubble to the surface. What brings warmth to the depth of your soul? Breathe deeply and let it warm you today.

## September 6

# Do I Need a List to Get It Right?

During a season of my life, the theme of petitioning God continually came to my awareness. Petition seemed to arise in the form of what I call the laundry list of needs, and as I found myself resisting this impression, I became curious as to why. Pondering the notion, questions arose in my mind: Do I believe in a god who answers lists? Do I consider myself above petition? Or is it resistance to the notion of somehow needing a list to get it right? The first time this came up was while meeting with my spiritual director. I felt the resistance again one Sunday in a potentially self-righteous but curious kind of way. The priest was encouraging us to spend time with God without the need to bring "the list," i.e., to be grateful, to honor God, to be in God's presence. I felt affirmed at that moment because "being" is definitely more my style. I feel like every breath is prayer. I have thrown away my list.

So where is the balance? Is it in the moments when there is no need of list and I simply know God is? Where does that leave the notion of petition? The space of holding others in thought and prayer—safety for travel, healing of sick, hearts to be protected. It no longer feels like a list (or petition), but breath. One movement.

Do I need to be doing something different? Is it okay to simply be? Can I merely be in the presence of this God I cannot name and yet know throughout every cell of my bones? The paradox is huge. The faith is strong and the unknowing and questions run right alongside. I continue to seek even though I have already found. I continue to grow even though I am an adult. I continue forward—most days. Do I need a list to get it right? Do you?

*Visualization and Meditation*

Imagine your prayer life as a playground teeter-totter. Place prayer and petition on one side, and the act of simply being on the other. Where does the weight fall? From where does your balance come? Do you need a list to get it right?

# DIALOGUE WITH THE DESTROYER

The archetype of the destroyer ultimately calls us to relinquish anything that isn't necessary in our lives so we may encounter our deepest selves. While working with this archetype, I posed the question: Who are you?

I am the one who loves you best. The one who cuts through the muck and strips away the lies. I am the one who loves you enough to push and prod until your perfect shining self is revealed. I am one who brings grief to your hardened heart and allows it to soften, disintegrate, and be reborn. I am necessary for new life. The old must die to make way for the new.

Show gratitude for all of who you are and what I, the destroyer, offer. I am the one who burns away the dross, turns up the heat, and descends into the dark. Welcome me. Love me if you can. Have compassion as you enter the dark, because transformation is birthed out of darkness and pain, just as a new babe emerges from the womb. Birthing cannot be forced or the gift will not be fully formed. Remember, I only destroy what is no longer needed. I am the one who loves you unflinchingly.

*Journal Meditation*

Spend a few moments meditating on the destroyer. In your journal, have your destroyer respond beginning with "I am one who . . ." Free-write for at least five minutes. Ponder what needs to be destroyed for you to shine fully.

# Doing without Doing

"If you align yourself with your Stargazer (essential self),
the whole energy of reality will carry you along
like a raft on a river."
*Martha Beck*

One night I dreamed of a strong river flowing parallel to a sparsely wooded shore. Was I in the river or were we one? Indistinguishable. My presence was both calm and very aware of the powerful current. Going with the flow, there was no straining, panic, or attempts to break for solid ground. The experience resounded with a feeling of everything being exactly as it should be.

Awaking the next morning, I was reminded of the ancient Tao concept called *wu wei wu*, which translates "doing without doing." The words describe exactly what my dream conveyed as I allowed the river to carry me. Moments like this are not so different from times I truly experience God and connect with the Universe. Moments when the reality becomes bigger than words can explain. I am reminded that the only thing I need to do is float and be carried.

*Visualization and Meditation*

 Close your eyes and imagine a flowing river. As you deepen your breath, allow yourself to experience the rise and fall of the current. For a few moments simply breathe and be the river. Do without doing,

## September 9

## Off to the Races

Time fills up. Precious time. Treasurable space. Moments spent doing the things I cherish. Being with friends. Family. Clients. All worthy endeavors in my mind. As someone who values solitude and is energized by work, I seek ongoing balance between the two. It can be humbling to hear myself say, "I don't have time for solitude, writing, play . . ." Fill in the blank. Yet here I sit with my heart pounding and my mind racing because my list is full.

The new day sits before me and I pause to smile, because the Universe is paying attention. I've opened up my morning devotional and the day's title shimmers at me: *Too Full*. The frantic pace takes a step back and I remember I've experienced this racing before. For the moment, I breathe deeply, make a list of things that must be done and attempt to enjoy this season rather than just get through it.

I am grateful and my gratitude is boundless. I've received a gift and stepped into a single moment of solitude and it is enough. This tiny awareness has reintroduced me to peace and momentarily stopped the racing. Now, if I can just keep my mind from firing the starter gun again.

*Active Meditation*

Pause for a moment and consider the things on your list. Make a mental note of which things must be done right now. Write them down to help ease your racing mind. Let them go and breathe deeply for five full rounds of breath. Offer gratitude for right now.

# A GLIMPSE OF AN EMPRESS

While offering a workshop on the archetypal energy of the empress, our group engaged in conversation about what it means to embrace one's inner sovereign. A sticking point that arose time and again was the idea of how it is easy to claim sovereignty, power, health, and privilege when they are readily available. But what would happen if you were poor?

When this question was posed during our discussions, one empress ascended in my mind. It wasn't Queen Elizabeth or Michelle Obama or the latest super star, but rather a lady I met in Egypt. By most standards this woman would be considered poor, even poverty stricken. But I had to wonder. Did she think she was poor?

I encountered her as our small group was leaving the Sinai desert and dropping our Bedouin comrade off at his home. My jeep arrived behind the others and we were asked not to disembark due to time constraints. The draw to leap from the car and mingle with the children and goats was strong. Only our leader's firm request that we stay seated kept me in the car. In the brief moments we waited, this woman—indefinable in age; fifty? Eighty? A hundred?—approached our vehicle and extended her hand to each pilgrim. Language was unnecessary as she took my palm in hers and offered wisdom and hospitality with her eyes. This woman is an empress—one who stands solidly in who she is, invites others into her realm and does not know the meaning of scarcity. She is sovereign over her world and makes sure that those within her kingdom are welcomed.

This role model has given me much pause to consider what things I value most. Certainly not jewels and extravagance in the traditional sense. The jewels I treasure in this moment are a few stones, a fossil and a piece of coral. Extravagance is resting under a billion stars with only a sleeping bag to shelter my body. And my kingdom lies in a castle that looks quite different from the land of fairy tales.

*Pondering*

Ponder one or all of these questions: Where does your sovereign reside? What are the jewels that shine for your inner empress/emperor? How do you define wealth?

# INNER POET

My inner poet is French.

Tipped beret and Mona Lisa smile. Her voice rings out with playful laughter, her arms wide open, leaping into darkness and light. She is beautiful and earnest. Seductive and serious.

She was born on the wings of angels and birthed out of pain and suffering.

I recognize her in the first morning light by the gentle shores of the sea. She is bathed in God's fragrance and surrounded by belief.

What does this inner poet know for sure?

She is light. She is dark. Complete and unfinished. A creature of God. A glorious paradox.

This poet lives hidden from sight. Covered in blue scarves and white. Peeking through the window and knocking on the door. She lives at home inviting others to come and sit by her fire.

Her imagination is infinite. She dreams of knowing and being known, of embracing and being embraced. She desires community, fellowship, peace and solitude. She must speak of everything. The resonant and the dissonant. The beauty and the depravity. The joy and the sorrow. The fullness of life and the darkness of death.

She sits on the sidewalks of life, holding a thin cigarette and dreaming her dreams.

Her voice speaks in a beautiful accent. Tipped beret and all-knowing smile.

My inner poet is a romantic. She is French.

*Poetry Ponder*
What does your inner poet look like?

# TABLE OF TRUTH

If I simply told my truth without caring if it's been told before or wondering whether it was special enough or too dark to reveal, I would write it all. The words would flow uncensored as I cherished and exposed the beauty, the broken, and the unseemly. I would offer both heartbreak and joy. I would not hold back, nor would I overly embellish. The prose would be raw, revealing, and revelational. My truth would weave this brilliantly unique tapestry that is only me.

I would not compare or judge and wonder if every mother were critical or if other offspring had experienced tragedy. I would reveal my own ugliness without apology and my beauty and pain without permission. I would share the whole journey. I would speak of becoming an enraged woman who screeched into the face of a child. I would become the little child, muted with the crook of a finger and silenced by a commanding nod. I would write of mythical experiences and struggles with spirituality. I would acknowledge my deep faith and abolish the voice of tyranny. All tales would have their place. Each thread of color and strand of reality would be welcomed at the table of my truth.

*Journal Meditation*

Freewrite for five minutes with the prompt: If I told my truth without restraint . . .

## September 13

# Flowing Truth

When truth begins to flow from my pen, I recognize it because my heart breaks into song. I get lost in the words and found in my soul. Deep wells of inner grounding saturate my bones. Truth screams of vulnerability and honesty. It feels primal and pours from deep within. It has not formed from that head place where I worry about what others think or want to know. I do not worry, because this belief has arrived specifically for me in this perfect moment. The truth is mine and it feels universal. It's also okay if no one agrees.

Tears form in my eyes and a lump rises in my throat. Sometimes my breath comes to a near standstill as my inner voice declares itself heard. Goose bumps rise while my heart pounds with excitement or reaches a level of calm and peace that only comes from knowing this flowing truth.

*Action Invitation*

 Read the words on truth you free-wrote yesterday. As you read, notice what truth feels like for you and name how you recognize it.

# THE FACE OF A CHILD

What do I see when I look into this face? I see wisdom. The perfection of a beautiful young spirit full of knowing. She is wrapped in a patchwork jacket that is warming her with memories from the centuries, surrounded by the green of growth and layers of shadows in the earth. I see a face half-covered by shadow, hinting of mystery and stories untold. Her other side is resilient with light and invitation. I see me. I see you. I see the world in the eyes of this child.

Her skin is fresh and smooth to the touch. It is not like velvet or silk, but perhaps the texture of a seal's moist skin. Her eyelashes speak of butterfly kisses and her brow, a fuzzy caterpillar beneath my caressing fingers. On her head is perched a man's fedora, aslant at the perfect provocative tilt. She beckons me to see her—to caress the gentle softness of her flowing hair. She invites me to come near and lets me know she is strong on her own. She wants to be seen yet is confident in what she needs. No one can take her brilliant light away. I see wisdom in the face of this child-woman. I see light, shadow, love, and life. I see the world in the face of a child.

*Artistic Meditation*

Select a photo of a child of any age. It can be from a magazine or perhaps someone you know. Write for five minutes, beginning with the prompt: When I look in this face I see . . .

# DOSES OF DELIGHT

Some days you just need a big dose of delight. One such dosage came to me while visiting a dear friend along the Hood Canal of Washington State. Dressed in wading boots and snuggly coats, shoulder to shoulder we walked along the rugged shore for several hours. We found ourselves crawling over logs, steering around oyster beds, stepping lightly through hundreds of sand dollars, and watching my friend's ten-year-old Weimaraner, with her keen sense of smell, search out crab shells for her morning snack. The walk was full of conversation on esoteric topics like good and evil as well as moments pausing in awe of the majestic heron fishing in the shallows.

Our biggest dose of delight came in surprise form (as surprises are prone to do) when without warning, my friend's foot vanished ankle-deep into the wet sand. Just as quickly, her other foot disappeared. Poof! As I reached out to give her a helping hand, both my feet were simultaneously swallowed by the beach, too. My balance not being as good as hers, I soon tilted backwards and plopped down in the sodden sand. Bursting into raucous fits of laughter, we were literally "stuck" in time for several moments. Rather than panicking or complaining of muddy clothes and soggy socks, we relinquished ourselves to the moment as the delight cleansed our hearts deeply and fully.

Some say laughter is the best medicine—others describe it as carbonated holiness. It can't be manufactured, but it can be imagined. When was the last time you received a huge dose of delight?

*Visualization*

I invite you to spend the next few moments thinking of your own silly memory. Let the laughter lift your heart and consider where in your day you can let go and sink into delight.

## September 16

# Trust for the Day

W hat would it be like to invite trust into my day? To pose the question? To ponder what it means to trust and then to offer myself a response? Because I trust myself and the story that wants to carry me, today I will choose to live freely, without hindrance. I will be still when silence calls, and when thoughts and details threaten with their hectic pace. I will be bold in paying attention and asking for what I need. I will not live in the shadow of others' expectations. I commit this day to feeling and believing what is true for me. I will remember the moments that make no sense to anyone else, like the encounter with the skywalker or my father coming to visit with a touch and a tear.

I will let sorrow, joy, and difficult discourse flow from and through me. When I begin to think too much or perform for others, I will pause and breathe. I will come back to my center—the place where I am balanced, enlivened, and focused on what simply is. When life threatens to overwhelm and chaos creeps in, I will remember it is time to trust, pause, and reclaim my day.

*Pondering*

 What does it look like to invite trust into your day?

# IMAGINE

Imagine if any single day of your life had not been lived. How different would you be? Less whole or more so? Some days have torn holes in my heart and others have penned indelible images into my soul. If any one moment had been skipped over or passed by, would I still be who I am today? Do we need all of the moments? I might guess no, but some are so defining they could not be missed.

It is kind of like the word "whole." Without a single letter, the word becomes "hole" and indicates something empty, lacking, or possibly waiting to be filled. Our life is filled with moments built and woven together like a fine tapestry comprised of death, divorce, marriage, birth, rebirth, life—repeated over and over in seemingly random patterns.

A moment. When does it become defining? When does the weight of an instant become irreversible? What times do children choose to remember? What are the memories I have chosen to hang onto? Why do some seemingly disappear from recollection? Are they always with us? Lingering? Waiting? Forming? Shaping? Making up the wholeness of who we are?

So, what is wholeness? I see it as being fully and completely who we are as best we can at any given moment. Knowing that a moment in time can change a life forever, because the tapestry is always growing thread by thread.

*Pondering*

What are the moments that have shaped you? What will you choose to do with the coming moments of your life—beginning right now?

# IMPACT AND LOSS

Have you ever considered the lasting impact others have in your life, both those you know and share life with, as well as strangers and people you encounter for brief moments? If we have even a momentary connection with someone, there is potential for loss, while the memory can last a lifetime.

Some losses are profound, like the sudden death of a parent or the lingering breakup of a relationship. Other losses come from unforeseen places, like the loss of people you know for only a fleeting moment in time. I can picture several seemingly insignificant encounters that left an impact on my heart: a student who battled hard against me and then quit school suddenly and silently; a man on the bus who sleepily nodded off against my shoulder; another stranger I knew for an hour before we shared a prayer, never to see each other again. Each encounter touched me deeply by its presence and I can feel the absence along with the significant impact on my life.

Loss is indeed intense in our lives, especially when we permit ourselves to acknowledge and experience it. Feeling deeply leads to an emptying, which then allows us to be refilled with joy and other emotions of life. If we refuse to empty ourselves, grief fills us to the brim and we find ourselves immobilized and waiting to overflow or explode. A balanced life cycle includes both emptying and filling. It is a cycle repeated over and over again.

There is something magnificent in accepting what we are offered each day. Some days request emptying—others offer filling. Not expecting grand results, we are open to surprise and then can see where we have been touched and filled after allowing ourselves to be emptied of held-in emotions. Will you allow yourself to be impacted today by first emptying yourself? Can you recall the moments when you felt the inflow of life?

*Active Meditation*

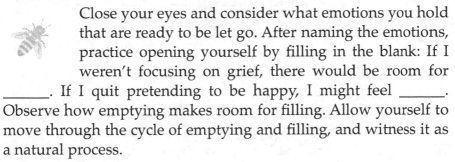

Close your eyes and consider what emotions you hold that are ready to be let go. After naming the emotions, practice opening yourself by filling in the blank: If I weren't focusing on grief, there would be room for _____. If I quit pretending to be happy, I might feel _____. Observe how emptying makes room for filling. Allow yourself to move through the cycle of emptying and filling, and witness it as a natural process.

# SELF-INDULGENCE

What are the boundaries of self-indulgence? Are personal actions overly indulgent if they inspire others to live more fully? What are your criteria for taking care of self, going on retreat, saying no to stifling obligations, or responding yes to life-giving opportunities? What inspires you? Consider the movies, books, or stories that tug at your heart or bring tears to your eyes. Do you long to be the bold singer on stage or a cloistered monk living in Tibet? Can you see yourself as a renowned chef or perhaps the lead cyclist on the Tour de France? Might you consider that these tugs of heart could lead you to your best life?

*Pondering*

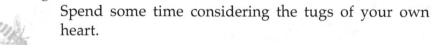

Spend some time considering the tugs of your own heart.

# ROOM FOR DOUBT

My faith foundation was born out of a conservative Christian base. The Bible was preached as the inerrant truth, and there was very little wiggle room for my own interpretation. My adult years have seen me wrestling with this inerrancy and figuring out how to reconcile the Bible I believe to be God-inspired against a text that was assembled according to humanity's rigid interpretation and fallibility.

It was in graduate school that I was first introduced to the concept of hermeneutics. Much discussion was made of our personal hermeneutic and what we bring to the text, as well as historical considerations, context, etc. In my religious upbringing, I always considered that others had studied this in depth and they, therefore, knew the "right" interpretation of what I was reading. There was minimal allowance for doubt or opinions that differed from the "correct" interpretation. Today I ask, Whose right is it to say that one man or woman's interpretation is more correct than another's?

Don't we each have the right to choose our own convictions rather than press ourselves into a box someone else created? I have found great hope in knowing it's okay to question the Bible (or any personal text of choice) while still holding it at the center and core of my spiritual beliefs. I believe God wants us to live with a sense of dignity and freedom rather than oppression and fear.

Wouldn't it be magnificent to consider that the God who inspires you and me today also inspired the Old Testament prophets and New Testament writers? That the same voice who spoke to the Buddha or Mohammed still whispers to us? Consider the possibilities for life and freedom if the texts are fluid versus stagnant. What if the way to ultimate truth isn't rigid and unforgiving?

*Active Meditation*

 Consider what you are convinced of. Do you leave room for doubt? Meditate on the properties of fluidity versus rigidity as you ponder your beliefs.

## September 21

# Incarnational Spark

I once had the privilege to share a relationship with a woman raised in a very different culture from my own. She was one of several daughters in a family that valued boys. She had been raised to believe she was nothing. In her humble story, she spoke of many years of emotional abuse—first at the hands of her parents, then followed by decades with a narcissistic husband. Somewhere deep inside this woman, however, there was a spark that kept her alive and reaching for the love she knew was available but didn't yet have access to.

Other stories similar to this resonate with me and lead me to wonder what it is that keeps us searching for love even when we are led to believe we're unworthy of it. What are the moments that give us hope in the midst of chaos and hurt? What is the impact of a simple hug or cradling in the arms? What is the power that lets us know love exists?

The woman of this story believes she is searching for God's love. She knows it is there. She believes it to be true in her head but hasn't quite connected it to her heart. She wants to experience it in humankind so she can believe it in spiritual form. Can the two be separated? Is that not what being incarnational means? In the Christian story, Jesus was God incarnate. Do we not share incarnationally when we give unconditional love to ourselves and others? Is that perhaps the spark that keeps us reaching?

*Body Practice*

Rest comfortably where you are and softly wrap your arms across your chest. Pat each arm gently for a moment or two and then rub your arms up and down with tenderness. Allow yourself to be comforted. During this time you may become aware of other people who comforted you in your life, or those to whom you have offered care. Release a prayer of gratitude for these moments of care and love.

# CHANGING SEASONS

As days grow shorter and summer draws to a close, there is a quietness and stillness that catches in the air. Entering fall. Saying goodbye to summertime's longer days. Preparing a nest for winter. Commencing an uncharted journey into the next season. Welcoming newness. Recognizing the leaves must die to prepare this new way. Anticipation. Holiness. Stillness. Excitement. What will autumn bring? The Universe whispers the answers when we are still, if we are willing to listen. There is a quietness and tranquility that lingers as summer draws to a close. May we be willing to listen for the newness that awaits.

*Action Invitation*

Venture outside today or spend time at a window. Observe the changing season. Notice how nature prepares the way for something new. Are squirrels filling their coffers? Are the last of the flowers relinquishing their blooms? See what begs for your attention. Is there something calling you to prepare for a new season?

## September 23

## Sacred

Some solitary days revolve around curious conversations with myself. One day I woke pondering what it means to name something sacred. Are there any particular requirements for the word? The thought that landed first in my mind was "connected." This resonates with me. It's simple without too many words or fuss.

My mind then turned to the evening before and how it defined sacred for me. The night had been about finding connection on a warm evening, far away from the walls of any institution. Feeling the life force around me while driving along the beach and soaking up the urban culture. The magnificence of the city spread before us. My friend and I tempted by the call of lapping waves. Dipping our toes into the cold ocean while conversing with a waif of a girl and her scraggly old dog puppy. Fresh sea air mixed with the warm heat of the day. Friendship. Bread. Wine. Communion. Being seen in the eyes of another. Flowing conversation—not how to "save" the world, but how to "be" in the world. Inspired and inspiring. Sacred? Yes.

*Artistic Meditation*

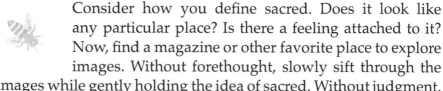

Consider how you define sacred. Does it look like any particular place? Is there a feeling attached to it? Now, find a magazine or other favorite place to explore images. Without forethought, slowly sift through the images while gently holding the idea of sacred. Without judgment, gather those images that cause you to pause. When you've made your selections, lay them out before you and see how sacred resonates with you.

# September 24

# Saturated

Like a sponge . . .
Soaking up the luscious green of Ireland
Feeling the presence of ancestors
Creating poetry with addicts and alcoholics
Holding space for compassionate listeners

Snuggling with my kitty
Listening to the thunderstorm of night
Stretching my weary body
Birthing the dreams of my soul

. . . I am saturated.

*Active Meditation*

Stand at your sink with a sponge or washcloth. Allow the water to run and saturate the sponge. Imagine each drop as a portion of your life. Notice if the saturation feels satisfying or suffocating. Ponder how you could wring out any excess. Follow through by twisting the sponge as necessary.

## September 25

# Are You an Ascetic?

A few years ago, experimenting with a new daily rhythm, I engaged in an early-morning boot camp. My body discovered new muscles and screamed in pain following the strenuous exercise, and I found myself wondering what I was trying to prove. As camp began at 5:30 a.m., I also began to embody new strength, endurance, and vitality as I pushed through bicep curls and ran obstacle courses. It was a surreal experience to gather in the dark and fog, do my thing, and return home before sunrise.

Exhausted and exhilarated at the same time, I discovered my brain unwilling to engage once I returned home. Focusing on spiritual matters when muscles beg to be the center of attention is a bit distracting. I thought about the ascetics, particularly those who practice self-mortification. It seemed counterintuitive that bringing more pain to the body could bring one closer to God—I found it extremely difficult to center myself when my body was yelling, "Take care of me." I realize, of course, that a strenuous exercise program is not necessarily the same as a strict ascetic practice. Nonetheless, I pondered how bodies influence spiritual practice since both mind and matter share space in our human state. How do you consider matters such as this? Do you follow the logic of "no pain, no gain" when it comes to spiritual practice? Do you see your body as separate or part of a whole? Does it make a difference?

*Body Practice*

Close your eyes and begin to follow your breath. See if there's a place in your body calling for attention. Gently begin to breathe into that area. Take your time and allow yourself to mindfully share oxygen with each area that says, "Take care of me." Consider how you feel after a few moments of breathing into the pain with compassion rather than fighting the discomfort and wishing it would dissipate. Notice how your body and spirit work together.

# AESTHETICALLY PLEASING

Yesterday, I mentioned an ascetic way of being, but today I ask, when was the last time you allowed yourself to be compellingly moved by the aesthetic beauty of nature?

This is the time of year I find myself physically drawn toward gigantic sunflowers. They beckon me from the side of the road, and I gravitate toward them as if under a magical spell. They gleam with splendor from neighborhood gardens, bringing their full brilliance into summer's end. Looking closely, I see some have started to bow their heads prayerfully, while others lift their faces toward the lowering sun. Their countenance is a reminder of the new place we enter as seasons change. They invite us to consider our personal rhythms and how we will choose to live as days grow shorter in the Northern Hemisphere or longer in the southern. Will I choose to raise my face toward the sun as if in worship, or gently bow my head and rest from a season well-lived?

What are your rhythms as the seasons begin to change? Are you drawn to ascetic or aesthetic thoughts? Eugene Peterson speaks of the ascetic and aesthetic movements as being the "no and the yes that work together at the heart of spiritual theology."

*Visualization and Action*

Close your eyes and imagine the face of a giant sunflower (unless you're fortunate enough to have the real thing nearby). Consider each petal as a moment from the past season. Let your mind linger on both the blooming and withering times. Now, focus in the center of the flower and envision each seed as the promise of new growth for the coming season. Allow yourself to name any dreams or hopes that arise in the seeds. Carefully plant them in the soil of your heart and carry their aesthetic beauty into your day(s).

# SAFE LANDING

Sometimes the pendulum of life swings us back and forth until it becomes necessary to audaciously let go and fling ourselves into the unknown. This space reminds me of my skydiving adventure. While stepping out of the plane, I clung to the door and bowed my head in frenzied prayer.

The place just before you let go is terrifying. You know it's coming. You know you have to release or you will forever regret it. Standing on that tiny platform I had no choice, really, but to unclench my fingers and surrender into the unknown. It seems that in order for life to keep moving forward, that is exactly what must happen: let go, trust the unknown, and pray for a safe landing.

*Visualization*

Bring to mind something in your life that feels risky to let go. Imagine standing at the door of an airplane or soaring through the air via trapeze. How might things be different if you let go and released yourself into the unknown? Do you expect a safe landing or do you assume you will crash and burn?

## September 28

# Unfinished

Process versus product. Do those words resonate with you? How about journey versus destination?

As a person who spends time listening to others wrestle with life and faith journeys, I have witnessed that one of the most repetitive struggles people have is not having everything (life, faith, ourselves) all figured out. As I listen to others, I often wonder if they realize that no one has it all figured out. No one. And if someone tries to tell you they do, well, that's a whole other topic.

When I consider my own pattern in similar struggles, I often return to the idea of being "unfinished." There may be a final product for which I strive, but it is in the process that all the meaty stuff really happens. If I am "finished," then what? This is a concept that has helped me throughout my journey, especially when I find myself in places where I feel like the process may never stop. When I allow myself to be present and feel my emotions—to wrestle with the issues or enjoy the value of a gray day—figuring "it" out doesn't seem quite so important.

Today, I invite you to consider how you spend your days. Do you strive for product or are you awake to the beauty of process? Are you so focused on the destination that you miss the intricacies of the journey? Does it have to be one or the other? Could it be both? How about keeping an eye on the destination while enjoying the music of the ride?

*Visualization*

 Close your eyes wherever you are and picture a gray-covered sky. Allow yourself to be wrapped in the blanket of clouds and feel the cool against your skin. Imagine what it's like to be in the midst of the darkness and not able to see any further. Now, envision the same sky holding the orb of the sun. Remember the sun (or moon) still shines even though the clouds cover it in the moment. Consider how this might make a difference when wrestling with the unknown.

# THE "UNGODLY" HOUR

Depending upon the time of year, each hour of the day takes on distinct qualities. Midnight, for example, may be experienced as the darkest hour. High noon evokes images of brilliant and blinding sunlight. Sunset and sunrise have been honored in many a painting and photograph. When I tell people I rise around 5:30 a.m., the response is often, "Ugh, what an ungodly hour!"

Perspective colors how we view things, and there are definitely days I find the early morn less desirable. However, the "ungodly hour" offers gifts I rarely find at midnight or high noon. There is something pure, sweet, and unblemished about the early dawn hours. For me, it's like God is anxiously waiting to offer me a blessing for the day. All I have to do is wake up and receive it.

*Action Invitation*

Commit to waking up in the early dawn at least one day this week. Allow no less than five or ten minutes to simply sit in the new morning. Quietly receive the blessings of a fresh and unblemished day.

# UNMERITED FAVOR

Grace. The definitions abound. Unmerited favor. Seemingly effortless beauty. Charm of movement, form, or proportion. The sovereign favor of God for humankind. Disposition to be generous or helpful. Goodwill. A prayer of blessing. And more . . .

Grace comes in many shapes and forms and out of a multitude of belief systems. My intent is neither to defend or dispute anyone's definition, but rather to share what I see as grace and how every definition encompasses it in its own gracious way. In the beauty of the world, as well as in its seeming distortions, grace is present. When I look upon a sunrise or sunset, have I done anything to merit that beauty? When I see a squirrel playing amid the splendor of autumn leaves, am I not witnessing grace of movement and form?

As I consider grace in one of its most general definitions—unmerited favor—I am amazed at the audacity of what greets me when I awaken to a new day. The notion that my heart continues to beat and my lungs fill and expel air . . . Simply put, it takes my breath away. And all of that can happen before I even open my eyes. If favor is considered to be overgenerous and preferential treatment, then truly the feast that awaits us each day is unmerited indeed.

*Pondering*

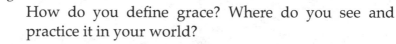 How do you define grace? Where do you see and practice it in your world?

# OCTOBER 1

# HOME

In the fall of 2010, I had the privilege of traveling to the Sinai desert and spending several days with sky and sand as my home. The earth pulses in the desert. It speaks of ancient times while holding only now. I have drunk from the truth of the desert—tasted the painted landscape and witnessed the dying acacia, crumbling rock, shade-seeking lizard, wise camels, and their Bedouin leaders. I have been washed in the silence of the early morning and the brilliance of a billion stars—the grit of sand reaching into every nook and cranny. I have felt the freedom of standing naked in a barren landscape and blending into it until I resembled finely chiseled stone.

The desert mirrored beauty back to me—even as my skin grew gritty, mosquito bites on my face blossomed into epic plague, and my hair took on new designs of its own unwashed creation. I was the lizard seeking the cool shade, the camel gently rocking across uneven sand, the mother bird fiercely protecting her nest, and the painted desert floor swirling with patterns few paintbrushes would dare create.

Returning home, I pondered what that even meant—to return home. Home is in the here and now. Somewhere along the way, I learned to take home with me like an authentic pilgrim—one who carries my heart wherever I go. I am home and the Sinai is a part of my soul, imprinted in my heart and every fiber of my being. I am home.

*Meditation*

Where do you find home? Follow your breath and sink into your surroundings. Hold the theme of home gently and place your hand over your heart center. Continue breathing for several moments. Be still and allow "home" to find you.

## October 2

# Quilt of Life

Our days are filled with a glorious patchwork of experiences. Full. Slow. Balanced. Sunny. Crisp. Gray. Colors of purple and gold with a little aqua bringing a quilt together. Like pieces of life. Each slice essential. Each with its own distinction. Some bold and brilliant, saying, *Play with me. Laugh with me.* Others muted and dark. Purple in every hue. Bits of black punctuating the surface. Brilliant and shining golden moments tucked into an afternoon. Glorious moments of life.

The clock moves 'round like sun shifting across a green field. Crisp autumn leaves blow into the sunset as lovers stroll arm in arm into the dark night. Dawn rises again with excitement for a new day. The morning cloaked in darkness waits to burst forth into color once again.

Memory-filled snapshots like pieces of a quilt. Dark spots that grab for attention and golden moments that shine like new morning light. Muted tones filling in the background. We need them all to make the full blanket—the quilt that covers our heart and keeps us warm and protected. The thread that brings us comfort and binds us together to make us who we are. Ours are technicolor lives. Full of golden moments, blue skies and, yes, even dark patches to punctuate our existence.

*Visualization*

 Close your eyes and imagine your life as a quilt. What colors rise to the front? Which ones blend together? What is the thread that holds together the quilt of your life?

# LIFE THROUGH A CAMERA LENS

One could easily consider the morning sunrise or stars of the night as miracles beyond words. In our busy existence, however, we often do not even take the time to look up or around us as we make our way through hectic days. We miss the big things, so—needless to say—the small things naturally go unnoticed. In my most thoughtful mind, there is no big or small. Everything is magnificent and beautiful in its own right. Everything has been poured out for us with unmerited and generous favor. The world itself is filled with this thing called grace, if only we choose to open our eyes.

*Action Invitation*

Imagine viewing life as through a camera lens. Allow yourself to focus on the beauty of small things that might otherwise be overlooked, as well as big things like a child's smile or the cloud-filled sky. Open your eyes to the grace around you.

## OCTOBER 4

# THE JOURNEY HAS ALREADY BEGUN

I am the one who sits and waits. Waiting for what? Today? Tomorrow? The Holy? The Sacred is already here. I sit in the shadows—in the space of waiting. The already and the not yet. My heart has turned to the days ahead. The journey has begun.

A few days before leaving on pilgrimage, I woke up wondering, *What is wrong with me? Is something the matter?* I was leaving for Egypt in two days and all I wanted to do was immerse myself in mindless videos. It was almost a compulsion and I pondered. *Am I avoiding, or waiting, or something entirely different?*

I couldn't motivate myself to read the history of St. Anthony whose footsteps we would be following. Instead, I read the current Vanity Fair and the sad adventures of a wayward starlet. My heart was breaking for the world around me and I felt wrapped inside my own little cocoon. The journey had already begun.

*Pondering*

 How do you prepare for the pilgrimage of life each day? Do you wait? Avoid? Jump in? What is your longing for contact with the Sacred?

## October 5

# Sacraments and Flowing Water

---

"We are asked to pour ourselves out, trusting
that in this act we will be refilled."
*Christine Valters Paintner*

---

"The universal call to holiness is an invitation to be
ourselves. It's also an invitation to remember
the sacramentality of everyday life."
*James Martin, SJ*

---

Pouring out. Seeing all things as sacrament. These themes challenge me to continue considering how I spend my days. I don't always know what will fill me, but I do know that in order to be refilled, I must make space by pouring out. Pausing, I consider the times I've spent emptying out of obligation rather than love. When giving has been experienced as duty rather than sacrament. The "filling" looks quite different—resentment and loneliness flooding out peace and sanctity.

Where are the places I impede my flow of love? Where do I allow old hurts to get in the way and feel myself building dams rather than letting springs gush? When did I become so self-sufficient and forget the "sacramentality of everyday life"?

Sacraments and flowing water. The Universe calls me to be more fluid. Effortless with acts of self, allowing love to fill in the cracks and crevasses rather than patching them with illusions of fulfillment. I am called to relish the sacraments of daily life.

*Action Invitation*

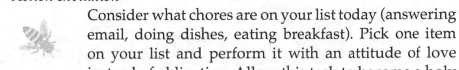

Consider what chores are on your list today (answering email, doing dishes, eating breakfast). Pick one item on your list and perform it with an attitude of love instead of obligation. Allow this task to become a holy sacrament in your day. Notice if this allows space for something new inside you.

## October 6

# Soulful Travel

---

*"If we truly want to know the secret of soulful travel,
we need to believe that there is something sacred waiting
to be discovered in virtually every journey."*
*Phil Cousineau*

---

As fall enters the air in the Northern Hemisphere, my mind shows an increasing propensity to dream of the journeys that lie ahead. While this may seem an odd perspective because the traditional season of summer vacation has ended, journeying speaks to me of something further-realized than literal trips.

Traditional travel offers a unique opportunity to explore outside our usual surroundings. It is both exhilarating and a bit frightening to step into unknown mysteries of faraway or unfamiliar lands. However, it is no more exciting to me than what lies ahead as the seasons change—or even as I awaken each new day. Every moment offers an opportunity to step into soulful travel while exploring the depths of one's unique presence.

*Action Invitation*

What will your journey be today? Consider your day as uncharted territory with no map to follow. Listen to the tug of your heart throughout the day and explore your world as though it's brand new. Journey with a pilgrim's eyes and heart.

# THE SKY IS ON FIRE

What if the sky were on fire this morning? Can you imagine? The orange ball exploded, spreading a palette of salmon, ginger, scarlet, and gold across the fall sky. Uncapturable with a camera. So ethereal, it slips through the crevices of my mind. I want to hold it, touch it, capture it, roll around and lavishly bathe in it until I find myself washed with the colors of roses. Fragrant and sweet. A pleasing aroma.

The image of the sky brings me alive. Washes away the pain in my aching body. I find myself slipping away and floating with the pink-tinted clouds. For a moment or two, I leave this place. My being is one with the sky. The pen and paper. The world. The Universe. More me than the moment before and the moment after. Glimpses of heaven. Shout of purity. Paradox. Both/and. Beauty.

The sky is on fire this morning and, of course, it is not.

*Body Practice*

Quietly move to where you can look out a window. While gazing at the sky, gently begin to follow your breath in and out. See if there is a response your body wants to offer. Perhaps a gesture or a word comes to mind. Allow yourself to sink into this word or gesture as you continue to follow your breath. When complete, offer a gift of gratitude for these brief moments.

## OCTOBER 8

# INHALE LOVE AND LIGHT

Today I'm grateful for birth and life. My family. My flawed self. Forgiveness and peace. I'm grateful for miracles and turnarounds and wise words of wisdom from within and without. I'm grateful for light and warmth. For my cozy corner, my caring heart, my siblings and friends. Life and death. A new day to begin again. I'm grateful for a God who holds the whole world's misery and my ability to hold my own while you hold yours. I am grateful for doing the work and making time to play. Today I am grateful to simply be.

*Meditation*

 Center yourself wherever you are. For the next few moments, inhale deeply, breathing in love and light. Exhale misery and fear. Allow yourself this time to simply be.

# JE COMPRENDE

By covering the fields of unexplored territory through outward travel, I have consistently come upon fresh elucidations of my inward self. One truth I have discovered is that I am more pilgrim than tourist. My desire is to be infused with the world's culture and make each place home, if only for a hiccup in time. My journeys are not about checklists and frantic tours, but rather allowing everlasting moments through surprising simplicity.

While traveling with my family through the cultural and architectural wonders of Paris and Barcelona, I found it was often the simple moments rather than the world-renowned wonders that infused my soul. Napping on a Sunday afternoon with the street noise of the El Borne district drifting through my consciousness and the Mediterranean breeze tickling my sore and weary feet. Being astounded by a thirteenth-century Gothic church that pulled me into a pew and held me captive with music and mystery. The chaos of a world market filled with enchantments that both lured and repulsed. Slipping into a hole-in-the-wall restaurant and being served one of the finest meals of our trip. Chatting with a whacky, over-the-top, bold, brash, and charming French taxi driver. Risking my faulty language skills (and potentially my dignity) to perform earnest pantomime in order to find the most enchanting restaurant in the French village of Vienne.

In hindsight, many of the greatest moments came out of risk. Walking into a church even though we weren't sure it was open to the public. Asking questions in French while realizing I probably couldn't keep up with a fluent answer. Miraculously finding my language when someone was rude to me and firmly letting her know, "*Je comprende*" (I understand). Stepping into a sketchy café and leaving sated and celebrated with newfound friends. Pointing on the destination-rich map and saying, "Let's stop here." Following my heart into each new day and committing to do the same when my body returned home.

*Ponder and Apply*

 What do you understand? Think about the places where you have taken risks only to ultimately discover you feel more free. Where are you being called to risk and follow your heart today?

# DROPS OF EMOTION

At times life hits so hard and fast that the oxygen in which we live can scarcely fill our tightened lungs as we rise and fall like the endless rhythms of the ocean. The waves appear in changing form—some rock us gently so we float as if on an air mattress in the middle of a serene lake. Other moments, it feels like we've been slammed by a giant tsunami, shaking and gasping for air from the force of the hit.

As complex human beings, we have a capacity to present many faces to the world. The waves that follow us throughout our days are mystifying. We may simultaneously experience both the gentle rocking of comfort as well as motion sickness. The water that washes our spirit clean and gently holds the floating raft is the same element that threatens to drown and take away our breath. The two cannot be separated, for they flow in and out of each other like waves moving against the shore, both gentle and wild.

Periods of loneliness can accompany the quiet and rocky moments, but to the outside world they may appear the same. So I ponder. If you knew the size of the wave within someone's soul, would it make a difference? How often do we settle for the pat answer when someone responds with a standard "I'm fine"? Would you make more of an effort to engage if you knew they might be gasping for air? Would you stop and speak to a coworker or a child or a stranger if you thought your comfort would make a difference?

*Active Meditation*

 Fill a glass of water and place it in front of you. Imagine the glass as a person and each drop of liquid an emotion within them. Notice how the drops can't be separated without reaching into the glass. Ponder how your interactions might change if you were curious about the fullness of emotion residing in each person you meet.

# Up and Down Serious

Sometimes I wonder what it would be like to let go of the seriousness that keeps me stuck and instead jump fully into life and play. I could pretend all memories of should and shouldn't have been erased, and my notions of what is good and bad or right and wrong present themselves on a clean, blank slate. My rational mind wants to fight this idea, says I must be serious if I want change to occur. "Pooh pooh," says my playful self. Serious is boring. Fighting is more apt to invite problems, while play draws me toward delight, like a bird trilling in the trees just because. But one person's play is another's fight. I see the battle within myself. I truly desire to let go of seriousness, but even as I make that statement, the censoring voices say, "Get real. You must be serious to get anything of value done."

What do you want? What do I want? I want to change the world *my* way. It is the only way I can do it. Just like the beetle only knows how to be a beetle or the ladybug who is resplendent with her distinct spots can be nothing else, I can only offer who I am. Some days it looks like seriousness. Other days it looks like play, and the ability to play is serious business. Today I will choose to play like a child.

Perhaps it will only be in my imagination that the world is saved. Perhaps it will seep into the stratosphere and accomplish something greater. Today I will choose to be me as I ride the waves of wisdom up and down the serious road of play.

*Pondering*

What is your own notion of serious play?

# OCTOBER 12

## RESTLESS

There are days I slow down to a snail's pace and view my movements through the lens of a laboratory experiment. I step outside and begin to observe what is happening as though peering through a telescope. What is this subject doing? She seems to be searching for something but can't quite land on what it is. She says she wants to write yet decides to offer her distracted self the prize of a nap following a short period of dedicated writing.

She twitches and shifts and changes positions. Wanders around looking for the perfect place to land and take up her pen and pad. She moans and whines and makes herself all-important about how others need her. By sitting down to write, she will be taking something away from them. She quickly switches to the notion that she might be missing out on something elsewhere and begins to feel the loneliness of isolation. She keeps padding around the area searching for who knows what.

The time monsters keep her seeking that next shiny object. She tries to become useful as she clicks through the Internet or calls up a friend, seeking someone to help—anyone but herself. Awareness dawns and this slight realization leaves her feeling icky and sad. She ponders and probes and becomes curious about what she's avoiding. Sadness and grief seep into the landscape. Only a gossamer veil of protection sits between her and the gaping wound that dares to break open. She is exhausted and wants to rest. She longs for sleep so the hurt will drift away. Dancing around what begs to be noticed is like trying to avoid the creaking planks in an ancient floor. Slowly, she settles into a spot, picks up her pad, and begins to put voice to the moan.

*Active Meditation*

Imagine your day as an experiment observed through compassion and curiosity. View your own movements through the lens of a gentle witness. What do you notice? How are you moving? Where can you pause?

## OCTOBER 13

# RACING THE GARBAGE

O ne brilliant fall Seattle morning, I had a wonderful encounter that left me giggling and pondering for quite a while. Taking full advantage of an Indian summer day, I hopped on my pistachio green scooter and headed down the four-lane road toward work. Due to traffic and the not-so-timed lights, I found myself incessantly stopping and starting along with the other cars and, in particular, a giant garbage truck to my left.

Imagine this: a pint-sized scooter next to a colossal malodorous garbage truck. Now close your eyes and take a big whiff. Can you smell it? What do you think my instinct was? To get away from the garbage, of course! And so we played this cat and mouse game for a couple of stoplights until I found myself giggling to realize the imagery (and reality) that I was racing the garbage.

Oh, what a metaphor for life. Isn't that what we do all of the time? Race around trying to get away from the garbage? Sometimes we feel as tiny as a scooter next to a mammoth pile of you-know-what and we go to great lengths to get away from it rather than consider "smelling" things in a new way. Other times we wallow in the grime and lose our entire sense of smell for what is refreshing and preferable. And my giggles? Well, I decided to enjoy the sunshine and laugh at the ridiculousness of the situation rather than putting myself in harm's way or letting the "smell" ruin my day.

*Active Meditation*

 What garbage are you racing today? How will you choose to smell it? Plug your nose? Inhale deeply? Laugh?

# OCTOBER 14

# NOBLE SILENCE

A reflection from Ireland:

Through days and miles, I close my eyes and see the wondrous faces of Noble Silence.

Dim lit room. Candles flickering. Features softened. Some faces weary from a day of feasting on the senses—others radiant upon reflection of the ancestors and saints gone by.

Silently, we form a circle. Entering meditative prayer through reading and ritual. We bow our heads with soft-focused eyes until the words of the first person bubble to the surface.

Palms together. Gentle nod. The words flow. Some brief—others a longer story. They wash over me, absorbing me in the soft light—the dark of night surrounding us beyond.

A bow to finish and the silence rests upon us again.

The ancient practice of Noble Silence is a timeless and wise tradition that helps us begin the process of listening in a new way. By practicing silence and attending to all of our senses, we learn to hear with fresh ears.

*Meditation*

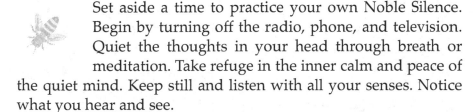

Set aside a time to practice your own Noble Silence. Begin by turning off the radio, phone, and television. Quiet the thoughts in your head through breath or meditation. Take refuge in the inner calm and peace of the quiet mind. Keep still and listen with all your senses. Notice what you hear and see.

# DOUBT AS FRIEND

Doubting Thomas is a label often attached to people who refuse to believe anything without incontrovertible proof and are thus lacking in faith. Yet doubt and skepticism defy the narrowness found in absolute certainty and leave room for mystery. The Doubter archetype opens space for new vision and finds possibility through questions and atypical responses. It exhibits bravery and boldness to probe what others put out as certitude. History is filled with imaginative souls who questioned the status quo, embarked on worldly adventures, and developed phenomenal creations by courageously asking why or why not.

Often we limit ourselves—become stuck living lies our parents, the media, or someone else has convinced us are true—simply because we aren't bold enough to doubt. We don't question statements like Professional people are more valuable than artists. If you don't make X dollars, you aren't successful. The more material possessions you own, the higher quality your life.

"Why" is a powerful and simple question that doubt invites us to engage. Through questions and inquiry, we are better able to refine and clarify what we truly value. Doubt pushes us to believe more fully, or at least to understand the magnitude of what we do not or cannot know. It doesn't mean we throw our faith out the window if we can't grasp a finite definition of God, or that we cease to create art because we don't know the ultimate impact. Even Epicurus, known as one of the great religious skeptics, said, "You know, it feels good to pray. You might as well."

*Visualization and Action*

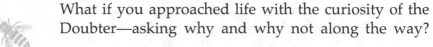 What if you approached life with the curiosity of the Doubter—asking why and why not along the way?

Imagine letting the spaciousness of the Doubter guide you by challenging what you need or don't need in each moment. What holds you back from living fully and why? Invite the Doubter to dance alongside you as you refine and define what it means to be alive.

# WHAT DO YOU WANT
# TO LIE ABOUT?

Wandering through a rustic bookshop, I flipped open a book on writing. On the page before me was the prompt "What do you want to lie about?" This question sat with me for several days as I played with the responses in my mind. There are times when I want to lie about my privileged story and say I am an orphan who grew up with only bread and water to eat. There are times I want to scream from the rooftops that I was raised with my voice being silenced day after day. Which is the lie and which is the truth? Are they not possibly the same experience? One is literally true and the other not, yet I believe they are not so radically different.

I want to lie when parents begin the competition of "What does your child do?" or begin to rattle off accomplishments as though the parent were the achiever. My children have never followed the status quo, so it's interesting deciding how candid to be. Through years of observing faces presented with difficult situations, I've encountered people time and again who have a hard time receiving truths that fall out of the norm. The average person at a cocktail party doesn't want to know that your child is in prison. A friend once offered me a great gift when she shared with honesty that if it could happen to me then it could happen to her, and that was terrifying.

Sometimes I want to lie and shock the ostriches out of their complacency. To say my child is on death row and I've taken up prostitution to support my resulting drug habit. I want to shake things up and swim a different stroke. To be noticed and not dismissed. Other times, I want to crawl into the woodwork or make up a heroic story about my family inventing a naturopathic cure to AIDS. Most of the time, I want to boldly tell the truth, because I'm sick and tired of lies. The truth heals, and in my experience, lies rarely offer much of anything positive . . . except perhaps a little mischievousness and perhaps a dose of shock value to an otherwise boring conversation.

*Pondering*

What do you want to lie about?

# LECTIO DIVINA

As I began to read a book on the ancient prayer practice of Lectio Divina (which translates as "holy reading"), I found an air of familiarity surrounded me. "This is what I do," my internal voice whispered. And then the ego piped in to say, "Oh, you think you know everything. Don't you see how that closes the door to possibility?" It is a wonder I can even get past the first page as my inner dialogue carries on a full-blown conversation. And then I read the words "hold this lightly." Ahhh, I can feel a sense of peace come over me, and then I am reminded of the opposite of holding lightly. It is grasping.

Buddhism speaks of the grasping mind and how it keeps us from peace and serenity. When we grasp our desires strongly, there is a driven quality that arises. Anxiety, jealousy, rigidity, and insecurity all become stronger. So, as I consider Lectio Divina, I wonder how I can hold lightly to the structure. How can I keep myself free of the arrogant sense of knowing and therefore leave myself open to new possibilities?

I read. Contemplate. Meditate. Act. It flows. I move. I listen. I find myself open to possibility. Open to hearing. Do I express my gratitude? Do I allow myself to sit, resting in holy presence? The piece that has been missing for me recently is Scripture. I have chosen to use other texts: music, nature, blogs, poetry, and sacred readings. Do I attend them with holy listening? Am I open to what they say? I am formed and informed through the listening. I often do not remember details, but rather have an overall sense of what I have taken in. I have breathed the experience (the text) in and let it permeate my being.

*Action Invitation*

Allow yourself to read the following questions as if they were holy. Notice which one shimmers and invites you to open and explore more deeply. What are the battles of your own mind? How does your ego strive to overcome your stillness? Where do you find yourself grasping? Where do you need to let go or show gratitude?

# WOODS OF SPLENDOR

The journey winds through woods of splendor. Darkness and exposure reach from barren limbs intertwined with delight and holiness. Bending boughs offer protection from the storm and their purpose is filled with love and fullness.

It is perfect and whole.

The path is wet and wild, brilliant in its darkness.

The sensual and luscious step out of hiding to become known—enriching the journey in blazing splendor.

*Poetry Ponder*

Pause and ponder your own woods and branches—literal or metaphorical.

# PAUCITY OF LISTENING

*Poverty: the state of being inferior in quality
or insufficient in amount.*

Where do you experience poverty in your life? Do you listen closely to those around you? Do you feel that others listen to you? Do you operate on autopilot, hurrying from one place to the next? Do you wonder what a day focused on poverty has to do with you?

Consider this: When we are not fully present to the lives that cohabit our world, we close off the possibility that there is something new to be heard or discovered. We close our minds and our hearts to the possibility that we have something in common with the child in Africa, the mother in Harlem, the senator in Congress, the homeless man on the corner, our next-door neighbor, and even the people who sleep in our own warm house.

On this day of poverty awareness, I would like to pose that we experience a paucity of listening. How might our world be different if we fought the poverty within our own cold hearts of stone? What if we started listening more deeply today? How would the world change? How would you? If only for today, I hope you will choose to listen a little more closely to the world around you.

*Action Invitation*

Spend time today with these ideas of poverty and paucity.

# INJUSTICE

"Being true to who we are means carrying our spirit
like a candle in the center of our darkness."
*Mark Nepo*

A teenager at a county fair is beaten because of the color of his skin. Girls walking to school in Afghanistan have acid thrown in their faces for wanting an education. Sickening. Emotions of shame and anger arise at these injustices. My own heart shudders with temptation to turn away from this violence. Yet I cannot flee, because once I've seen it or read it or heard it, it is imprinted on my heart.

Every day I sit with people and hear stories of hurt and rejection. Parents who refuse to hug their children. Others who use demeaning words and shame to control. Men and women who are beaten or sexually abused. No one is immune.

How will I use my voice to battle injustice? How will I live out of the gifts God has given me? How will I carry my candle into the darkness? Some days it feels like enough to listen to one person at a time and help them see their own gifts so they may go into the world slightly more equipped. Sometimes I feel like I'm living into my full self. And other times, I feel at a loss. I wonder what will ever be enough, yet even this small acknowledgement of injustice feels like a step forward. May this be a candle glimmering in the darkness.

*Action Invitation*

 Consider an injustice you desire to see righted. Imagine one small step you could make toward this (e.g., if you want world peace, you can begin by seeking peace within yourself). Name your step and take it today. Allow that to be enough. Repeat again tomorrow.

# INSIDE OUT

have a friend who is absolutely the most gorgeous woman I've ever known. She has a face and body that many would consider "perfect." She's been described as "better than anything that's stepped out of Hollywood." For all outward appearances, she lives a charmed life—handsome husband, beautiful house, successful child . . . the list goes on. And she is miserable, lost, and floundering in her life.

As we caught up about old times and what's been happening in our lives for the past few decades, she listened compassionately to the story of my journey and looked at me with her gentle eyes to offer, "Your life hasn't been easy." True. It hasn't. And I wouldn't trade the hard times, because they have brought me here. Her "hard times" are very different from mine, but in many ways they seem even trickier—they are subtle and keep her trapped in a place of confusion because she "shouldn't be complaining." The outside world sees perfection while inside she desperately yearns for something different.

What if perfection was defined from the inside out and beauty included wrinkles and gray hair? What if should's were erased from the world and happiness ceased to be measured in dollars and possessions? Imagine.

*Body Practice*

Look in the mirror and take a good inventory. Examine each wrinkle, freckle, eyelash, or hair and name them beautiful. Draw your gaze to your eyes and look deeply within. Close with the statement, "I am perfect just as I am." Practice this each day until you believe it from the inside out.

## OCTOBER 22

# INTENTION

Allow me to see the face of this day
Let me enter into each space with intention
Crossing the holy thresholds
Touching the ancient stones

Let me enter into each space with intention
Do not allow me to cloud my own vision
Touching the ancient stones
I will be the face of this day

Do not allow me to cloud my own vision
Crossing the holy thresholds
I will be the face of this day
Allow me to see the precious face of this day

*Active Meditation*

Slowly read aloud the above prayer. Notice which word or phrase invites you to stop. Spend time savoring this word, phrase, or image. Notice if an emotion or response is stirred.

# ROOTED IN DANCE

First, allow me to disclose that I've never considered myself much of a dancer. But when I think of being rooted and dancing, I have little movies that play across the screen of my mind. I recall the first time I placed my head onto the ground resembling a Muslim form of worship. It was during a class on creativity, and though I did not recognize it as worship at the time, there was something akin to an electrical charge that went through my body. I felt like I could stay in that bowed position forever. This movement has carried over with me as I have become more active in my yoga practice. Whenever I have the opportunity to go into child's pose, I always noticeably relax. I've considered whether or not this is just a relief from the more strenuous poses and agree that is part of it. However, there is something intrinsic that recognizes the groundedness and connection with the earth, the Universe, and life when I am in this position.

On my internal movie screen, I notice trees swaying in the wind as they dance with grace and beauty. I am reminded of a woman I saw in the park while walking one day. She was standing very still next to a huge tree. I didn't want to stop and stare, but to this day I cannot get the image out of my head. It was like she and the tree were one. I sensed a gentle swaying in her alongside the mammoth oak. It was as if they were dancing and praying together even though their movement was almost unrecognizable. They were both grounded and dancing.

In my playful movement class, we are advised to dance without shoes because this provides us a greater ability to ground and feel the earth beneath our feet. Near the end of class one day when we were invited to move about the room unchoreographed, I felt extremely light, flowing, and beautiful for a few brief moments. It was as if I were floating inches above the ground. I was dancing to the rhythm of my own soul and, paradoxically, even in this "floating" there was a strong sense of connection to everything. I was grounded.

To be rooted in dance is to feel the rhythm of the Universe. Planted. Grounded. Connected.

*Visualization*

 Where are the places you feel most grounded? When are the times you want to dance? What connection do the two hold for you?

# OCTOBER 24

# SAND DOLLARS

S and dollars. Whole. Broken. Covered with bugs and barnacles. Green hats of seaweed finery. Perfect on the outside. What is on the inside? Decorated. Plain. Upside down. Right side up. Holes all the way through. Broken in half. Waiting to be taken back to sea or carried home by a passerby.

Dollars and people—are they really so different?

One fall, I strolled on a shell-laden beach and contemplated an upcoming workshop where I was entrusted to be a facilitator. The images I saw in the pebbled sand became an apt metaphor for the resulting experience where words seemed inadequate and insufficient.

Like the sand dollars, some participants appeared whole, while finery and beauty kept their companions at bay. Others broke wide open and remained hidden behind tears and confusion (bugs and barnacles). Boldness said, "Get away!" Caretaker, mother, protector—looking out for others while slowly letting their "control" cover them like tiny bugs invading the shells. Holes in the middle. Some broken in two. Torn between two sides with a gaping space filled with nothing. Nearly invisible, buried deep in the sand on the edge, slightly away from the others. Will this one be noticed?

Journeying together, we gently pick up the shells. Change doesn't allow us to return to original form. Each experience marks that we will never be the same and yet desire moves us toward being whole. The beauty is that we get to redefine what wholeness looks like. Maybe it looks like glorious, magical, flawed and broken, pure and true sand dollars on the beach.

Sand dollars and people—are they really so different?

*Visualization*

 Imagine yourself as a sand dollar on the beach. Are you whole? Broken? Covered with bugs and barnacles? How will you cherish yourself as shell?

# VESSELS

Our heart is an amazing vessel that often lives in its shadow side. (Think of the Tinman in *The Wizard of Oz* and his wish for a heart.) The physical heart is filled with blood vessels. Yes, vessels . . . carrying the lifeblood that runs through our veins. The blood that comes from our ancestors. Parents. Grandparents. "Greats" we never knew.

Vessels of life. Petals of red. Crimson roses. Scarlet poppies. Claret wine. Sacrificial blood. Dying so that we might live. Opening up space. A field of flowers—open and wild. Making room for forgiveness. Creating spaciousness for compassion. Only when I love myself deeply can I hold the same for another. Only then can I become a vessel.

Vessels of crystal and glass. Of wood and earth. All fragile. They break. They crack. So tenderly care for your vessel. Be a holy carrier of Spirit. Hollowed, so you may hold. Filing away the rough edges to be saturated with love. May the lifeblood flow freely through the vessels of our hearts.

*Visualization and Meditation*

Sit quietly and bring your attention to the heart center. Close your eyes and breathe deeply while imagining the blood flowing through every vein of your heart. With each inhale feel the expansion of the vessel in the center of your chest. With each exhale imagine love and compassion flowing through you and out into the world.

# MORE VESSELS

Vessels. Mother as vessel. Woman as vessel. Man, too. Broken. Cracked. Whole. Sacred vessels. Pregnant with hope and life.

If a vessel is closed, it cannot be fed. If it is poured to overfilling, it may crack. Some days our vessels feel empty. Other days full and rich. The process of emptying and filling isn't easy. We want to hang tightly to sweet nectar or let it seep out at our preferred pace. Our choices can feel limited and out of our control. As we open ourselves just a bit, it's like a fire hydrant suddenly opens and pours into our tiny jar. How can the fragile vessel not be tossed around, cracked, or broken?

At times like this, the choice becomes how to be in the brokenness. How to become a vessel that is open—to let in the feelings—while also narrowing the opening so vapid thoughts don't fill us to the top. How do we learn to receive the clean pain that is ours to carry and not hold the guilt over things not in our control?

Daily we are called to make choices and tend our vessels. Be gentle with the cracks while not ignoring them. Mend the breaks we can. Remain open. See ourselves as whole. Sacred vessels. Pregnant with hope and life.

*Pondering*

How are you called to tend the cracks of life? Have you ever considered yourself as a vessel? What will help you stay open to life rather than cause you to close or obstruct your own pathway?

# VINES, ROOTS, AND SERENDIPITY

Today I'm pondering the serendipity of life. Is it something the Universe sets in motion? Is it random energy or merely coincidence? Or is it something I make up in my brain to make sense of things that otherwise might make no sense at all?

Once, over coffee, a friend began to relay an experience of her own. This friend had been undergoing a sense of flightiness and floating away, feelings that were causing her some anxiety. As she sought counsel, her adviser asked her to try and imagine herself as rooted to the ground with strong vines holding her in place. She was curious about this imagery and wanted to know my thoughts on the topic.

My heart jumped when she shared the imagery of the vines because just a few days earlier I had participated in an exercise called dynamic meditation where the goal is to exhaust the body and active thoughts to clear space to hear our stillness within. Part of the exercise froze us in an immobile position for fifteen minutes. It was physically strenuous and all my brain could do was try to figure out how much longer it would last. I didn't feel clear of thought at all. However, when the music changed and we were given the opportunity to move again, I found my feet planted to the ground. I could not move and actually had no desire to do the very thing I had been focusing on for the past fifteen minutes.

As I stood there, a vision came into my mind of vines coming out of the ground and wrapping themselves around my right leg. They were beautiful like ivy and felt more akin to security than something binding or frightening. I stood and allowed myself to let the imagery sink in before physically reaching down and gently unwinding the vines so I could move my legs and participate in the next part of the exercise. It was a powerful experience on its own, and then to have my friend share virtually the same visual before hearing about mine was truly amazing. While pondering what to make of it, we both agreed our grounding feels as though things are exactly as they should be—rooted and draped in beautiful, strong vines.

*Visualization*

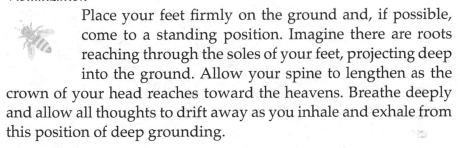

Place your feet firmly on the ground and, if possible, come to a standing position. Imagine there are roots reaching through the soles of your feet, projecting deep into the ground. Allow your spine to lengthen as the crown of your head reaches toward the heavens. Breathe deeply and allow all thoughts to drift away as you inhale and exhale from this position of deep grounding.

# Freeze-Frame

A moment in time. Sunday with my son. Beautiful. Slow. Steady. His glorious smile lighting the day. But first, a sharing of his heart. His fears. His struggles. Authentic and true. There is a humility about him. A realness. A maturity.

We talk over eggs and sausage. I smile. He is my son. We are so much alike and we are different. We spend the day driving together. He, practicing to get his license. Me, learning to let go. He, becoming more relaxed and, consequently, me too. (I wonder if the relaxation is with the car or with each other?) The day goes on. A stop by Sunset Hill. "Mom, will you take my picture?" We pick up his sister and drop her off at soccer and then it happens. The icing on the cake of an already perfect day.

He starts to sing along with the stereo. The Beatles. "Let it be." He sings aloud. Playfully. Not really in tune. We are so much alike. He is performing. No, he is singing to me—to us. I am holding my closed hand as microphone to his mouth. We laugh. I sing a little myself. Time stops. I want to freeze-frame this moment. This day. Let it be. It has been a long time coming. It has been well worth the wait, if only for this moment.

*Ponder and Apply*

 What are the moments in your life you'd like to freeze-frame? Allow them to wash over your soul as they well up from deep within.

# VOICE MODERATIONS

Seasons and themes of life flow in and out like tides upon a beach. One theme that continues to return to me over and over is the focus around finding my voice. Finding it and losing it. Experience tells me my personal beach is not the only shore this theme lands upon. One of the amazing and terrifying things about encouraging others to grow and become more authentic is that I am called to do the same thing for myself. Over and over again. Growth is a great thing and sometimes I am stunned by how much there still is for me to do. It can be disheartening, but mostly it is exciting. As long as I am growing and changing, then I am alive. Once I know everything—game over!

Early in my counseling career while working with a supervisor, I bravely asked how she thought I was doing. She responded with quick accolades that are always great to hear but not necessarily helpful. Then she paused and said, "Do you really want to know what I see?"

"Yes," I responded. *No!* I thought.

"Well there is this thing you do when you have something really great to say. You start out strong and then you let your voice slow down and trail off so that you end up losing the impact of what you are offering."

Damn! I had heard this before but not quite as concisely as this.

We continued the conversation and she said, "You're like a little kid who is passionate about something."

*Wham!* That's it. I am a child stopped by a withering stare or a "Hush, not now." My voice not welcomed. Passion and excitement squelched. My voice trails off and gets quieter until I speak no more. While I am familiar with this, it still makes me sad to know how the deep waters manage to linger on the shore. And the beautiful thing about awareness is now something can be done as I learn to catch my voice before it drifts back out to sea.

*Pondering*

Where do you get stuck in old patterns? What do you think about the thought "Once I know everything—game over"? Do you have your own voice moderations?

# BLESSEDNESS

Blessed are you who meets me where I am, in the quiet moments and hectic days.

Blessed are you who comes like a whisper in my breath and spreads images of majesty before me.

Blessed are you who comes incarnate through the smile of another, the touch of a hand, a kind word.

Blessed are you who shines in the light of the candle and sings through the song of the sparrow.

Blessed are you who meets me where I am—wretched, unholy, empty, and longing to be filled.

Blessed are you who greets me with a belly full of laughter under a starlit sky.

Blessed are you who remains faithful through my questions and storms.

Blessed are you who stands as sentinel in the night throughout my slumbering dreams or restless tossing.

Blessed are you I could name for an eternity and never be complete.

Blessed are you who simply says *I am*, and this is enough.

*Journal Meditation*

Using the prompt, "Blessed are you," write for five minutes and receive your daily blessing.

# CHANGING SEASONS

D rawn to fire. Bursting color—red and yellow. Texture. Shape. Bounty. Creativity. Drawn to the messy versus the neat and tidy. The composting leaves playing in water together.

The occasional blue leftover from summer—tranquil and calm.

The red is alive saying, "See me. Look at me."

The branches of trees providing shelter. The knobby trunks, gnarled with age.

The freshness of water. The cleansing of rain. The saturation of ground.

A pathway of color—neat and tidy—messy and disintegrating.

Earthy browns. Spring greens. Changing autumn. Waiting for winter. Welcoming the darkness.

Saying farewell to the brilliant light for a season.

*Poetry Ponder*
>        Ponder the changing of the seasons.

## November 1

# WAITING

*"When all we have relied upon has fallen away, there is nothing to do but wait without faith or hope. To choose life we have to be willing to wait, open to life and love at a time when opening seems impossible and we are sure that no one and nothing will ever be able to find us."*
*Oriah*

The theme of waiting pervades my mind until it seems like all I may ever do is wait. Hope inspires images of breathing more deeply without a tightening of the chest or short gasps for air. Opening to life offers an expansiveness that is neither breath-holding nor waiting anxiously for what may come next. Instead, it offers a full-bodied, lung-filling, life-enhancing intake of oxygen.

Wisdom would say life is a series of transitions and, because of this, we are always waiting for something. My life has taught me to be patient, and presence keeps me grounded in the here and now. A friend once reminded me that the practice of waiting without being overcome by anxiety is mandatory in my life. Choosing to live deeply speaks of new breath.

Today, I know this breath is the Spirit of God. My choice is to acknowledge both the inward and outward residence of this simple truth.

*Pondering*

Allow your mind to roll this around: The past is gone. The future will never arrive. All we have is now.

## NOVEMBER 2

# RESISTANT NESTLING

Nestled in this holy land. Consecrated by Pueblo history and artists' paint. Ritual and repose. Rest and relaxation. Resistance. What do I need? What do I want? Voices linger and move alongside the road. Here on this old balcony made of adobe and wood, gravel crunches beneath my feet. The rising sun peeks through a scraggly tree as the day begins to warm. Resist or rest? Which will it be? I want to sink into this land. To rub my skin with the red soil of my youth and bottle the crisp fresh air for my lungs.

As I close my eyes, shadows form and linger in my vision. The ancient mountain rises to my left. A ragged fence guides the way across the desert. My eyes lift slightly and I'm aware of a misshapen line of evergreens standing like sentries atop the mountain ridge. What do I need? What do I want? Ritual and repose. Rest and relaxation. Why do I resist?

*Visualization and Meditation*

 With eyes open, scan your surroundings while breathing deeply. Close your eyes and notice what lingers with you. Continue inhaling and exhaling fully, simply bringing attention to this moment.

# TENDER SPACE

The crisp fall air calls to me. I need space to breathe. I've come out of the womb of a solid night's sleep and rushed to meet a late client. She is distressed and weary. Her alarm didn't go off and now she's driven across town for a fifteen-minute session. Pausing, I invite her to breathe. It is all I have to offer, and exactly what she needs. The tears come as she weeps, "I'm so tired of failing." The sobs continue as she names herself a failure and lists the ways she does not meet others' expectations. Tender and vulnerable, her heart is exposed, and I pray I will not fail her in these fleeting moments.

When she leaves, I grab my coat and step outside. My lungs yearn for spaciousness and clean fresh air, not the stale forced heat of my studio. A slow walk around the block brings an unexpected gift as I spy a nest tucked high within the branches of an aged tree. It is hidden during spring and summer by lush leaves, but vulnerable now in this barren time. Still, the branches tenderly hold it, keeping the space until its occupants return. Keeping the space. Breathing deeply, I offer gratitude for this majestic tree so full of wisdom and grace.

*Body Practice*

Take a moment and check in with your body. Notice if there is a tender or tight space. With intention, move your breath into this area. Offer spaciousness and gentle care to this part of you. Continue breathing and close your time with an expression of gratitude.

# I REACH AND . . .

"I stretch out my hands to you; my soul thirsts for you
like a parched land."
*Psalm 143:6*

Rolling waves of parched land spread out before me.
Dry. Thirsty. Barren. My soul connects.
Spirit is present in the midst of my own desert. Thirst and longing.
I stretch my hand. I lift my eyes.
I feel your presence.

I see it through the window of a plane. The photo of a tree.
Creating a collage. Quieting my heart.
I engage with the mystery. Perhaps only I can name it. Perhaps.
Still, I know I am connected.
Blue sky.
Clouds drifting over.
Those who have gone before? Yes, I am connected,
even in my desolation.

I close my eyes and see the barren landscape. It is magnificent in
its beauty.
I hear your name in the sky and see it written across the lands.
I am created in your image. Earth. Fire. Water. Air.
All right here.
Beside me and around me. The fullness of your majesty. The
fullness of my life.
I stretch out my hands for you; my soul thirsts for you like a
parched land.

I reach . . .
. . . and you are there.

*Poetry Ponder*

Notice what bubbles up for you when you read this poem.

# EBB AND FLOW

Dreams, thoughts, and feelings flow through my being. My days are punctuated by a sense of contentment, until my old nature presses in saying, "Do something. You can't just sit around being content!" And so the tides of life continue to ebb and flow.

Often the messages for our contentment are right in front of us. Mine often show up in long forgotten journal entries. My friend's path arises in music she's written over the years. Another discovers answers in art purchased without known rhyme or reason. And so it is that I believe the answers are often right before our eyes. We toggle between the times we are open to seeing them and the times we are not. Occasionally it is simply not the right time to see.

Still, I ponder where the balance is between hyper-focusing and/or waiting for things to happen. What is my responsibility to move things along and/or when do I need to get out of the way? Am I willing to risk appearing foolish or suffering failure by putting myself out there? Or will I be like my encouraging friend who says we must celebrate the rejection letters because that means we made one more step toward our art?

So the question for me today is, what am I willing to risk? Time? Energy? Ego? Failure? If my dream is to share my gifts with the world, how can I move toward the fulfillment of that dream if I sequester myself behind a wall of fear?

*Pondering*

What are you willing to risk today?

## November 6

## Seeking Permission

Permission (or lack thereof) gets in our way of living our truest existence. When we believe we need permission before we can make our own decisions, we wait for some unknown authority to choose for us. This is different than intentionally reaching out to a friend and saying, "Please help me because I'm not strong enough today." For example, I have a wonderful buddy who supports me in amazing ways. While I was learning to care for myself, sometimes I would call her up and say, "I'd really like to take a nap this afternoon, but I can't seem to convince myself it's okay to do." Gently and firmly, she would respond, "I give you permission to go take a nap." My sense of relief was so tangible that even now when I hear those words, I feel drowsy and comforted.

Until we learn to quit listening to the messages that counterbalance our true desires and be our own providers of permission, it can be helpful to have someone supportive offer it on our behalf. With new and loving voices, we begin to forge better ways to care for ourselves. If your exhausted friend asked for permission to rest, can you imagine denying her? Would you tell a child he shouldn't be happy? Or a starving person seated at your table she couldn't eat?

*Action Invitation*

 Make a list of five things you won't normally do for yourself, but want to do. Pick one and say with firm kindness, "Today I give myself permission to . . ." Follow through.

# EVERYONE IS AN ARTIST

Each new day we are greeted with the energy of the Creator as morning unfurls a blank canvas of possibilities that await us. With each movement of our body—from the opening of our eyes to the way we lift and rise out of bed—we are creating our path in the world. This is the energy of the Artist. The one who takes what is at hand and forms something anew. In this way, we are daily involved in creativity through the construction of our lives.

Consider how you make choices throughout your day. Do you give thought to what kind of moment or experience you want to create? Perhaps you sink into autopilot and paint by numbers rather than reaching into the palette of your own unique colors. Do you operate from a place of fear that limits your creativity? Or does your love flow freely and abundantly for yourself and those you encounter? One of the essential pathways to becoming an artist comes from learning to accept yourself and follow your own voice. How will you create this day?

*Ponder and Apply*

 Bring special attention to how you create the moments of your day. What would it feel like to let artistry rise in your life? What gets in the way of accepting yourself and following your creative voice? Sit quietly for a few moments and ponder these questions.

# INTIMATE ALLIES

"To feel abandoned is to deny the intimacy
of your surroundings."
*David Whyte*

To feel abandoned is to forget you were once loved and still are. To disregard the warmth of sun and embrace the damp closeness of fog. To deny the intimacy of the stranger who passes along the walk. To forget the whisper of a secret when you were seven and let go of the palm that once held your hand.

To deny the intimacy of your surroundings is to say you are unequivocally alone, yet how can that be true when birds sing, candles flicker, and music plays? When breath rushes in and out of your lungs in moist particles of new air? Air that has reached across the world, or at least around the room. Air that has touched the bedpost, the coffee cup, your socked foot, and everything else in between.

To feel abandoned is to deny a source greater than imagination. To forget the one who has answered prayers and welcomed dreams. To let go of all those who have gone before and will come after. To feel abandoned is to turn our backs upon our lineage—the long line of ancestors who share our DNA. To abandon what has gone before and forget what is yet to come. It removes us from here and now as it sadly denies the intimacy of our surroundings.

*Visualization and Action*

Bring to mind a time or way you have felt abandoned and alone. See if there is a place in your body where this memory is held. Following your breath, begin to open the conversation with your surroundings. Focus on one or two nearby items and breathe them into the space where you feel alone. Consider your surroundings as intimate allies, as you allow your aloneness to soften.

# IS GOD A GIANT OUIJA BOARD?

What are the questions I'm most often curious about? Career. Time. Money. Relationship. God. Not always in that order. Is this for me? Am I on the right path? Was that a good decision? Did I do a caring thing? Am I okay? Oh my, it feels like I'm ten years old again and playing with a Ouija board.

Ouija boards and Magic 8-Balls—maybe they do hold all the answers. Will I be rich? Absolutely. Will I be famous? You bet. Does God exist? Ask again. Do we ever get past that fascination with wanting the answers? By asking questions, do we treat the Universe/Higher Power/God like a giant Ouija board? Asking for an answer and anticipating the answer we want to hear. Manipulating the planchette and acting like we're not. Pretending we've let go of control when, in fact, there is no way we'll remove our last finger from the game.

What might it take to release and let go? What is our role in the grand plan? I remember a friend telling me a story I'll never forget. Her college roommate had a big exam coming up. She didn't bother to study, then wondered why she failed the exam even though she'd prayed really hard. Is God our Magic 8-Ball? Are the answers right in front of us? Again, what's our role? I know if I sit around and eat chocolate all day I'm going to gain weight. Do I know if I work really hard it will pay off? It depends on how I define "pay off." If I already have the answer planned, then I may be disappointed. But if I let go of the Ouija board, I might be delightfully surprised by what happens.

What are your burning questions today? Do you need a speedy

answer or are you willing to wait for the surprise? Will you study for your exam, sit back and eat chocolates, or jump in the game?

*Action Invitation*

Consider a question that currently holds your curiosity. Now take a piece of paper and divide it in two. On one side, list what you already think the answers are. On the other side, record potential possibilities if you let go of what you think.

## NOVEMBER 10

# THE TIME IS NOW

There is a passage in the book of Revelation that speaks of a woman escaping into the desert until her time. The words leave me pondering: When will it be my time? An internal voice responds emphatically, "Now. Now is your time. It's time to bloom and shine and spread your brilliance in the world."

Continuing through my day, I muse about the boundaries and edges that support or confine me in this endeavor. I ventured out into the glistening sunshine to see what images wanted to be framed with my camera. My first stop was a playground where I couldn't take my eyes off the joyful elementary students at recess. Their energy was captivating. Full of brilliant colors and images of movement and exuberance. Flying and leaping and raising their arms in the air. A little girl with her face down on the ground captivated my gaze. Her position was not one of defeat, but rather a holy movement. Onward, fresh colors drew me throughout the walk, and even my own brilliant reflection called out to be photographed.

Now is the time to come out of the desert. Will I choose to believe this truth? My roots are planted in the ground. Deep and solid. Lovable and unshakable. Heaven knows I've tried to uproot myself. I've swayed with the winds—bent even. Still, I continue to flow with the breeze rather than break in the storm. This is beauty. Wonderful and blooming. Yes, it is my time to come out of the desert.

*Action Invitation*

Invite yourself on a mini-journey. With camera in hand, stroll through your neighborhood or home and see what images want to be framed. Allow them to create their own story and then read it back to you. Complete the phrase, "Now is my time to . . . "

## November 11

# Waiting for Ruach

"Feel the wind. The wind blows hard. The wind is blowing us
in a new direction. Guide the sails through Spirit."
*Kayce Stevens Hughlett*

Followers of my work cannot help noticing the importance of breath to the practice of pondering. Synchronicity and serendipity also play an important role in bringing new awareness to potentially overlooked connections.

My selective memory once displaced the wisdom that breath and spirit are both translations of the Hebrew word *Ruach* (also interpreted as wind). A period of time arose in my spiritual journey when it became clear I was being called to a new way of viewing the Holy Spirit. While I didn't know exactly what this meant, it felt delicious and liberating—like new breath, a sweet wind blowing, and the spirit of my heart lifting high. The feeling manifested as whole, connected, and embodied. To embody something is to provide a spirit with physical form. There is a fullness that takes over, like lungs filled with fresh air, when we allow our natural spirit to inhabit our being.

One of the most beautiful embodiments of spirit is the dolphin at play. Early Christians viewed this delightful mammal as a symbol of salvation. Breath. Spirit. New life. Salvation.

*Visualization and Action*

 How will you choose to view Spirit? Take a moment and allow your lungs to inhale deeply and embody that which brings you life. Play with this way of breath through experiencing the wind, feeling the spirit.

# WAITING ISN'T A GAME

"How tempting it is to turn waiting into a game of Clue—
hurrying as fast as you can through the corridors, searching
for clues that will give you the answers you need."
*Sue Monk Kidd*

Sometimes waiting needs to be just that . . . waiting.

A bud forced to bloom too soon turns into a broken blossom, not a flower.

A cocoon cut open before its time produces a butterfly with weak wings.

Telling God what we think is going to happen probably results in a chuckle or possibly even a belly laugh in the hallways of heaven.

Sometimes waiting needs to be just that . . . waiting.

*Meditation*

Allow the words of this poem to wash over you today. If you find yourself impatient, breathe deeply and release impatience. If you find yourself restless, fill your lungs and inhale contentment. Keep breathing— exhaling whatever you need to release and inhaling that which will help you wait more gently.

## November 13

# Boundaries

To live lives of authenticity, it is important to understand the role boundaries play between keeping us safe and holding us hostage. Setting and protecting our personal boundaries requires a certain level of internal awareness. The part of our self ruled by others sets up tidy boundaries and advises us that in order to remain safe we must stay within certain confines. It's not unlike the wicked stepmother who keeps a heroine trapped in a tower with exaggerated lies about the dangers outside the castle walls. In the fairytale, the heroine knows within her heart when it's necessary to break the spell and step outside the limits to find the life-giving treasure she seeks.

Much of my life was lived in a tiny space of safety and confinement. My inner self began to whisper things like, "Speak up, girl" until it finally started shouting, "Preach it, sister. It's time for you to live *big!*" There came a time when I had no choice but to listen and break the boundaries of limiting roles and acknowledge the ways I wasn't following my heart. My societal "name" was that of accountant, homemaker, and wife. While I still value those roles, my heart's desire called me to be a muse, an alchemist, and a weaver of dreams. I am one who listens to hear the call for others and myself. My joy is making gold out of metal, often by turning up the heat and stepping into seriously uncomfortable places.

*Visualization*

Imagine yourself confined to a high tower with no chance of escape. With eyes closed, notice what messages keep you trapped. Become the hero(ine) of your story as you envision doing what it takes to release yourself.

# MORE BOUNDARIES

Healthy boundaries acknowledge necessary limits while also fighting for what truly matters in life. Boundary setting is not a selfish action and doesn't function for personal gain. Clarity is a win-win situation as we stand up to injustice within (and without) and operate from a place of pure love. The courage to confront our inner battles is what ultimately allows us to confront outer situations with wisdom, self-discipline, and skill. It doesn't mean confrontation isn't scary or there is no risk, but there's a sense of peace in this way of movement. When you follow the path truly called for you, a sense of relative calm will settle over each decision. When we don't follow our essential selves, we remain locked up inside, which is anything but peaceful. It might appear safe, but turmoil exists. Only you and I have the key to our own best answers.

*Pondering*

 What has been your relationship with boundaries? Do you set them for yourself or allow others to do it for you? What keys are necessary to break free from your confining tower? Spend a few moments breathing deeply alongside these questions.

# NOVEMBER 15

# THE WATCHERS

Have you ever experienced the paranoia of "the watchers"—the fear that everyone is watching you, or worse, that no one is? I spent years shedding the notion that people were observing me and expecting me to fail or not live up to their standards. I learned that often people don't really care what you're up to as long as you don't get in their way. However, growing up under a highly critical eye helped me become finely attuned to those times when the watchers do show up.

I can't always name it, but I know when something's amiss. I begin to feel it in my gut. Sometimes it starts elsewhere—a prickle of the skin, a twinge of the heart. I know something is going on, but I can't exactly put it in words. I want to shrug it off—to deny the watchers are there, to hope for the goodness of others and deny the potential overreaction of myself. In many traditions, God is known as watcher and protector. It is comforting to know others are watching on our behalf. But what about the unwelcome watchers—those who watch through fear-clouded orbs instead of eyes of the heart? At times, I am guilty of this clouded vision. If an issue is someone else's fault, then I am absolved. It is much easier to blame our problems on others than to take personal responsibility. It seems that those watching for evil in others will find what they are looking for. My hope is that by opening our eyes to goodness, it will also be found.

*Journal Meditation*

 Bring to mind a situation or person in your life that you think needs watching. Letting your imagination flow freely, write down all the reasons why you think you need to keep an eye on this. Shift your attention and list all the reasons you should stop watching. Add one final list detailing what it would be like to watch with compassion and eyes of goodness.

# WE'VE ALL BEEN BIRTHED

Each morning as I finish my meditation, I offer the practice's merit back to the Universe. Today I acknowledge the appeal to dedicate my practice to all those who have been birthed into the world. I am called to remember those who came gently into life, as well as those who were ripped from wombs. Let us consider those arriving in the clean pristine loveliness of a birthing center or the dusty ground of a varmint-infested hut. The open air of a cotton field or the needle-filled nest of an addict. Planned births or accidental arrivals. We've all been born—there's no questioning that point. Our births come hard and easy. It's no coincidence the process is called labor.

Birth. What arises in you when you read the word? What might it be like to consider each person you meet carries his or her own story of arrival in the world?

*Active Meditation*

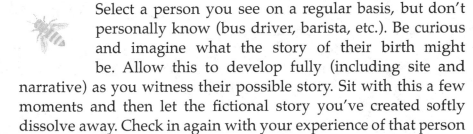

Select a person you see on a regular basis, but don't personally know (bus driver, barista, etc.). Be curious and imagine what the story of their birth might be. Allow this to develop fully (including site and narrative) as you witness their possible story. Sit with this a few moments and then let the fictional story you've created softly dissolve away. Check in again with your experience of that person and notice if or how it's shifted.

# WEB OF LIFE

I adore how we ingest and spread little pieces of matter here and there, never knowing when or how they may manifest in the world. Today's science continues to confirm the concept that nothing is separate. We live in a giant energy field that links everything. With each action and thought, the entire pulsating web of life is impacted. This notion is both sobering and exhilarating to ponder, because in it there is power to both harm and heal.

Imagine how a word offered in passing has the power to change someone's life on the other side of the world. For example, I once wrote a blog post about "annealing"—a process using heat to alter a material and cause changes in its properties. Several weeks later, I received word from a woman in Australia who was inspired to write a story about a glass blower. She was well into the tale before she remembered the word she first saw at my site. My words had rippled across the world to inspire another's creative process. Sobering and exhilarating. This potential power reminds me to choose my words judiciously and offer them from a place of love and positive intention toward others.

Buddhist tradition manifests this in the loving-kindness meditation, which begins with loving oneself and ultimately encompassing the universe with love and warmth. If indeed the world is one connected web, then our daily intentions matter greatly. We can change the world. As our capacity for love and compassion increases, so does the world's.

*Meditation*

Center yourself and focus on the area around your heart center. Bring a feeling of warmth and love to this area, allowing it to permeate your whole body. Imagine yourself at the center of an intricate web. With intention, spread this warmth and love outward to the edges of the universal web encompassing all that is.

## NOVEMBER 18

# WHAT IF LOVE IS *IT*?

In the world of spirituality and religion, much talk is made of the pathway of love. Divine powers are equated with and declared to be love. In my personal journey, I have come to believe that Jesus is love—pure and simple. So, what if that's true? What if Jesus and God and Buddha and fill-in-your-own personal favorite are *love*? Period. Love. That's it. If everyone believed in and practiced love, could that be enough to change the world?

If we could consistently operate from a place of love instead of fear, would it make a difference? What if we could show up with kindness and do our best each day? Accepting rather than expecting—not in a wishy-washy, no responsibility kind of way. What if we took responsibility for ourselves and called each other to a higher place in love—pure love, not the condemning, you-have-to-do-this-or-that-or-you're-going-to-hell kind of love? Would it be enough? What if God is love, period? Would it change your world?

*Visualization and Action*

Think of one situation in your life where you operate out of a place of fear. Now, envision dropping a small stone into the center of a smooth pond. Imagine your fear is the stone and by letting it go, love ripples out. Watch this ripple effect and consider how your world would look if you exchanged fear for love.

## November 19

## What Is Our Work?

Many of my morning ponderings are around this theme: What is my work? What am I called here to do ("here" being the world of this space and time)? I am inimitably created, just as each of us is. Part of my unique journey is to test, to ponder, to find my own path, often by pushing the boundaries of convention.
To ask the questions of myself for myself, and sometimes to share a bit of what I discover with others.

What is my work? What can I do?

How do I create a picture of a thousand words?

How do I put onto paper what no one before me has done?

How do I what?

Bless this space—my hearth—my home how do I live here? Now?

Being present to the life I have. Feeling my home. Tending my hearth. Blessing this space.

Offering a place of beauty.

*Pondering*

 What is your work? What are you uniquely created to do as no other before you has done? How will you tend your hearth and offer a place of beauty to your world?

# TANGIBLE OR INTANGIBLE?

It has taken me a long time, considerable practice, and intention to come to the place where I believe my spirituality and ability to be myself encircles everything I do. Still, there are times when I feel pulled or torn between being a go-with-the-flow, follow-my-heart, don't-worry-about-time-or-money kind of woman and the get-'er-done, make-a-list, be-productive, earn-a-living-while-tangibly-using-my-gifts person that dictates my mind. When these two clash, I discover myself caught between the tangible (product) and intangible (process).

In my experience, tangible output receives praise, financial reward, and acknowledgement and results in physical product—most often concerning others. It is the part that is outside myself. This approach glorifies product over process. It is the voice that often drives us away from our essential way of being. If not wisely monitored, we can allow our art to be dictated by what we think others expect. When I start to write exclusively for other people, my fluidity becomes rigid or I totally quit writing because I convince myself it's no good and they won't like it. In art, as in life, there are situations when balance is critical. We must find ways to follow our own process as we move toward a desired product. There are also times when we don't need to take things so seriously and can simply play and enjoy the process.

Process (or the intangible) comes from the times I'm able curl up on my sofa with music playing and candle lit simply allowing myself to be. Ineffable moments not limited by time or space. Yet, even this sacred time can be subjected to productivity results when I allow myself to judge the quality by how many pages I pen or the number of minutes my meditation lasts. The challenge and journey continue to be the movement toward finding how to simply be.

It all comes back to this for me. Greater wholeness and integration call me to this place where tangible and intangible meet and dissolve into one. Where product and process find their perfect balance. Where prayer becomes a way of being and being becomes a way of prayer.

*Pondering*

Ponder your own space of tangible versus intangible. Where do you strive to please others and allow output to drive your movements? How do you find ineffable moments without trying?

# WHAT STATION ARE YOU TUNED TO?

I once heard prayer described as setting a tuning fork to receive that which is always present and broadcasting. The trick is remembering we have a personal tuning fork as near as our conscious thought. It's easy to get going on our own frequencies and allow this intuitive instrument to appear obsolete.

Filling our heads with expectations of things we need to accomplish or how we should perform puts lots of static into the air, making it hard to either send or receive the messages that may serve us best. In these moments, it's critical to find a way to hit the reset button and come back to the present moment. Once we consciously choose to do this, the broadcasting of a greater power resonates within us. Sometimes, the signal is loud and clear. Other times, it's tinged with static. Nonetheless, our tuning fork reminds us we can slow down at any moment and receive this sustainable frequency.

*Visualization and Action*

Tune into all your senses. Breathe deeply while noticing what you taste, hear, see, smell, and touch. Imagine each sense as a different frequency that is sending and receiving. What is the message you need to hear or send today?

# WHAT'S YOUR BEST?

The process of living and loving well can be exhausting. Should it be? What is the cost of living well? Or thinking you must always do your best? From where does the pressure come? If I was brilliant yesterday, does that mean I must be dazzling again today or I risk being a failure? Can you hear your mother or father saying, "Always do your best"? Have you ever considered what "the best" even is? Does it change from moment to moment? Some days "best" means pulling the covers over my head and staying in bed.

Let's declare today Do Your Best Day. Who knows what that may look like? Maybe it's some ramblings on a page. Perhaps a few completed tasks. Or even pulling the covers back over your head. Life is exhausting . . . and it is an amazing and wonderful adventure. Maybe it's worth peeking through the covers to see what's out there. Maybe it's worth doing your best . . . whatever that may look like today.

*Active Meditation*

Take a moment and ponder your upcoming day. Decide what you'd like or need to do and determine what "the best" might look like. Can you accomplish that today? Or call a slightly more attainable result your best? Spend the day considering whatever you accomplish is your best.

## NOVEMBER 23

# WHERE CREATIVITY AND SPIRITUALITY MEET

In my life, creating art is where the world slips away and comes more fully into focus. It is where I get out of my own way. To disappear in one sense, but in another, to become more visible and alive.

The wind and I become one. The flame burns within my heart and I am consumed, yet not consumed at all. The words flow freely like water through a babbling spring or rushing like a powerful torrent over the edge of a mighty waterfall.

I am firmly rooted in the ground. My feet blending into the earth as I spring forth tall and majestic like the mighty oak reaching toward the heavens. I am the gentle breeze softly whispering words of love and care. The wind and I become one. And so the circle continues.

Timeless, beautiful, power-filled, and unique.

Whole. Complete. Perfect. Me.

*Action Invitation*

Where does your life come more fully into focus? Consider engaging in some form of art-making—visual, musical, movement—today. Or, step outside and allow your feet to connect with the ground, raise your face to the sky, feel the breeze on your skin, or let the rain wash over you as you breathe deeply. What does it feel (or look) like to be whole, complete, perfect you?

# MORE THAN ENOUGH

God smells like cinnamon. Baby's breath. Fresh-baked bread. Warm cookies. Sewer swamp. Compost. Earthen clay.

God tastes like sweet mint. Red wine. Honey on scones. The lips of a lover. Mother's breast milk.

God sounds like thunder. Silence. A bird's call. An infant's cry. My heart beating. Laughter and tears.

God feels like safety. Warm arms wrapped around me. Snug. Gentle. Distant. Knowing. Unknown. Filling every sense of my body.

God looks like the wind. The smile of a child. Weather-worn face. Toothless grin. Rock. Sand. Feather. Life. Death. New birth. Bloody war.

My sixth sense says, "Ahhhhh. Awe. Stop asking questions. Just be. Just be, my dear one."

*Journal Meditation*

With pen and paper in hand, explore God through your senses: smell, taste, sound, touch, vision.

## November 25

# Gratitude and Grief

This time of year offers blessings, and gratitude abounds in myriad ways. Brilliant sun and frosty roof. Family gathering to celebrate Thanksgiving. A familiar scent of pumpkin pie wafts through the house with the aroma of childhood traditions. Memories of coming home from school to the smell of baking pies offer a little taste of heaven.

Preparations abound while awaiting the arrival of modern-day pilgrims. It is a glorious time, and I am keenly aware there are people who do not have enough food, will not share their day with anyone, and may not even have a roof over their heads. My heart grieves and I realize that if I surrender to my grief and become melancholy or paralyzed, then I fail to acknowledge the moments for which I am so very grateful. It is a hard balance to follow. My hope is that I will be able to do both—grieve and remember and celebrate with gratitude.

*Meditation*

Begin to notice your breath and gently bring grief and gratitude to mind. Inhale grief and exhale gratitude. Do this for three rounds of breath. Reverse as you inhale gratitude and exhale grief. Repeat for three full rounds of breath.

# WHISPERS

how do you photograph a star in the dark night? how can you capture the wind?

where does day end and night begin?

how do you hold the hand of a long-lost friend?

god whispers the answers when we are still enough to listen— calm enough to hear.

*Action Invitation*

Make a date to step outside into the night air. With eyes open, bring your arms into a soft T-shape with palms spread. Breathing deeply, allow your senses to imagine capturing a star or lassoing the wind. Inhale possibility. Exhale expectations. Listen to the gentle whispers that surround you.

# FIERCE WARRIOR

How are you called to be fierce in your commitment?

I am a fierce warrior. This I know to be true. Still, I have a hard time understanding how other people see me because of conflicting messages. Shy—the label of my childhood. Bitchy—the critical murmurs that follow me as I learn to stand up for myself and set appropriate boundaries. Peaceful. Contemplative. Mean. Brilliant. Crazy.

There have been times in life when making a controversial decision has taken all the strength and courage I could muster. It was terrifying and it was absolutely the right thing to do. To walk away from someone or something you love is the hardest thing in the world. Agonizing. Painful. True. Even harder is to step back in when your heart's been broken. Rewards beyond our wildest imagination beckon us forward. Risk of rejection looms with infinite magnitude.

We reject ourselves all the time out of fear. *I can't do that. I could never.* When we hear those words coming out of our mouths— beware! Especially when they sound like "My child would never . . ." "I'll never allow . . ." "This is just the way it is." Absolutes get us into trouble most of the time. Words like "I can't" or "I won't" are rigid and stifle our growth and creative movement. They also push us away from what we are authentically called to do and be. They leave us passive and without choice or responsibility.

I choose to step into the places that scare me. I'm not afraid to do the hard or unpopular things, especially if it will benefit another's growth (or my own). There is a Hindu mudra called Abhaya. It is a gesture asserting power and giving peace at the same time. The Buddha is said to have quelled a rampaging elephant with this simple gesture. In it I see both compassion and fight. In this way, I am called to be fierce in my commitment to compassion for myself and the world. Finding compassion in the fight, and fight in the compassion. Yes, I am a fierce warrior.

*Action Invitation*

Where are you called to be fierce in your commitment? Today, challenge yourself to do one scary thing that supports this commitment.

# DESERT LESSONS ON SELF-CARE

My perfect self-care mentor showed up in the form of a majestic and sultry camel named Bella. She would be my wisdom guide for a day, and she lingers with me now as I reside over six thousand miles across the globe. Bella was truly a desert queen and knew exactly how to find her essential blossoms in the desert. She bloomed by following her own rhythm, and in these things we have much in common. Bella and I started our day with a Bedouin boy holding the ropes. Slowly we built trust until I received the reins. Nonetheless, it was Bella who led.

This glorious creature had an uncanny way of spotting the smallest shade of green hundreds of feet ahead. She would subtly pull away from the crowd and with precision-like focus make her way to the nourishing acacia bush. She knew exactly what she needed and wanted. After dining, Bella and I would take our time wandering and pondering through the dry land. At times we moved slowly and walked along the edges of our tribe. Sometimes the pace was brisk and we bumped up alongside other pilgrims. Other moments we pulled away from the herd to reach an unknown destination. As I remember Bella and write these words, it becomes clear she taught me the essentials of self-care—a life woven with times of rest, nourishment, and activity.

*Pondering*

Pause and ponder who your self-care mentors are. What are the attributes you admire? Notice how you can make them yours to achieve soul nourishment.

## NOVEMBER 29

# FAITHFUL TO LIFE

I have faith in the night—the place where dreams awaken, a flowing stream of insight, love, and consciousness drifts within and without me. I relish this near-sleep state that rests between slumber and wakefulness. The place where writing verse and prose, speaking of protection and protest, following dreams and daring, make their vision known throughout the darkest hours.

I have faith in this daily life that sometimes moves at a snail's sluggish pace until it surges forward with leaps of bravado and boldness. I have faith that life is happening—throughout the night and within the day—one step at a time . . . just as it should . . . could . . . would . . . is.

Yes, just as it is.

*Journal Meditation*

Complete this invitation: My faith lies in _____.

# November 30

# Sister, Sister

As a little girl, I remember peeking from behind a hallway door at my sister as she prepared to go to the prom or some equally glamorous event. Her date handsome in his tuxedo, and she with her crinoline dress, fluffy and ethereal. Me in my nylon pajamas and lopsided ponytail yearning to be part of the opulence. She was my idol. The beautiful princess. Outgoing cheerleader. Fairytale bride. Youthful mother. World traveler. New York City chic. (As seen through my younger romantic eyes, of course.)

My sister was my hero, a more grown-up and self-assured version of me. While we did not "know" each other for much of our lives, she is now one of my best friends. The years between us have shrunk. We are pals and playmates. Confidantes. I could tell her anything and she would still love me. It's a wonderful thing to know at this time in life with so much still ahead. It's a true delight to have this idol and hero off the pedestal where we can play and laugh and be real together.

*Journal Meditation*

Who is your hero? It could be anyone living or deceased, known or idolized. Today write a letter to this hero through freestyle journaling. Notice what you have to say, what attributes you observe, what qualities you admire. Consider how you mirror those same attributes and qualities.

# December 1
# Drafty Window:
# Part 1

"Other people's pain is the wind on our house(s)."
*Betsy Pearson*

The favorite room in my home is my studio/office. It is painted a brilliant color that brightens my day every time I see it. The walls are adorned with art and artifacts I've intentionally collected, and each piece holds special meaning. My studio is a place I can get messy, play, and also work hard. It's a place of comfort and rest, so it's ironic that it also encompasses one of my least favorite things—a drafty window.

Pondering this window with a friend, it came to represent a powerful metaphor in my life. The window has its special qualities which make it hard to replace. It folds gently in the middle, thus allowing fresh air to pour in during the warm months while also buffering the wind that can be too chilly in a northwest climate. There is a certain amount of protection and control from the weather. In the winter, however, the north wind blows stridently and seeps through the broken seals. Even as I wrap myself in cozy quilts, the air is chilly and impacts my warm heart. It's like the whole world is coming in through the cracks and there isn't enough heat to warm us all. It is the blessing and curse of having a heart broken wide open. There is a crack in everything. That's how the pain gets in. Sometimes there is enough warmth and compassion. Other times the draft chills me to the bone.

*Active Meditation*

 Step outside and feel the air on your skin. Imagine each breath of air contains someone's pain and another's joy. Breathe deeply and experience the connection with the whole world. With your exhale, send a warm blanket of love, joy and compassion into the universe.

# December 2

# Drafty Window: Part 2

*"Someone touched me; I know that power
has gone out from me."*
*Luke 8:46*

Yesterday I wrote about my drafty window, and today the conversation continues. As I ponder the warm air seeping out my window, I'm reminded of Jesus's story when he felt his power leave him as the woman in need of healing touched his garment. He said, "Someone touched me." Is this how I feel when I'm aware of others' pain? Does compassionate power flow out to meet others' needs? Do I offer it willingly or is it sucked out unknowingly? Is warm air drawn out with the draft or does cold air come pouring through the window? How does another's hurt blow through the crack(s) in my heart?

Compassionate hearts are at risk of being drained of their own life. Sacrificial giving can end in death. So, today I ponder the balance between offering myself in service of others and protecting my warmth and health enough to have something left to give. It's like the leaky window. Do I want to plug the cracks so the cold can't get in? If I do, does this mean my warmth will no longer flow out?

*Action Invitation*

Position yourself by a door or window you can open and close. Open the portal a crack and notice the impact. Continue opening, little by little, until it feels like too much. Repeat the process in reverse, closing slowly. Finally, open the portal quickly and fully all at once, then close it just as hastily. Notice the difference between these two movements as you ponder the balance in opening and closing your heart to others.

## DECEMBER 3

# BECOMING FIRE

I am the fire of the world, burning with desire.

I am fire. Images dancing through my mind during the season of Advent. The flame. I am the fire of the world. I am flame. Light. Fire. To burn and not be consumed. Reaching toward the light. Becoming flame. Feeling this during centering prayer. Be fire. Be the flame.

I am the fire of the world burning with desire. Desire does not consume. It encompasses and spreads. With motives of fear, it can be destructive and destroy everything in its path. But desire and delight spreads . . . nourishes . . . overflows.

Today I am fire. Others warmed by my flame. Radiant, engaging. My truth shining through. Lovely. Kind. Free. Delightful. I am fire. My mantra for the coming year. Welcoming this into my life. Naming what is there. A spark. A light. The flame is coming into fruition. Ablaze. I am fire.

*Visualization*

Close your eyes and begin to imagine yourself as flame or fire. What are the gifts you bring to the world when you are aflame with passion? What does it look like to become fire? Imagine all fear being burned away. What then?

# HOW DO YOU DEFINE BUSY?

"Busy" is a word that evokes strong emotion in me and I find myself bucking up against it, particularly during the holiday season. The majority of the world seems to think we must all be frantic and operating on hyperspeed at this time of year. My hope and goal is to redefine what "busy" means—at least for me. Would you care to slow down and join me? What if instead of rushing from the next appointment or worrying about shopping for the perfect gift or doing any number of things that totally stress us out, busy looked something like this?

- Sleeping later than usual and tending to your dreams. Feeling your body awaken naturally and noticing the stretch of your limbs and spine while they loosen.

- Choosing to stay home in the evening and have soup and salad with your loved ones instead of rushing out the door for the next Christmas concert. Being busy with conversation and laughter rather than herding around with crowds.

- Pausing in the middle of the day to read a novel and take a nap. Busying yourself with restorative yoga and slowly sipped cups of tea.

- Instead of giving in to the huge to-do list by your side, opting for a few moments of silence and an Advent reading at noon, because you slept a little later in the morning.

What if busy looked like intentional movement and choice throughout the day? If we controlled busy rather than letting busy control us? What if we actually enjoyed this holiday season and took some time to wait as the Advent tradition suggests? What if busy looked like smiling at our neighbor, actually listening to the words of a holiday carol, or simply watching the lights twinkle on the Christmas tree?

*Pondering*

 How might you change if you redefined busy? How might the world feel different? What if you controlled busy instead of it controlling you?

# GRACIOUS TENDERS OF FIRE

Oh, I have a fire in my belly and sometimes it doesn't burn so pure. At those tenuous times, my spark threatens to hop out of its grate and scorch everything and everyone that gets in the way. Needless to say, those are not my proudest moments, and they are fabulous teachers of the complexity of our gifts and nature. I am grateful for the gracious care of those who love and tolerate my fiery temperament and lead me gently back to the place I long to be. It is a place where I am not attached to my thoughts, and thus they do not turn into judgments and I am at peace with the world and myself. It is a place where I recognize myself as fallible, broken, and wondrous and I can see others that way, too.

When my fire threatens to be one that consumes rather than warms, reaching out to steadfast friends is often the grace that saves me. These friends come around like gentle tenders of the flame, nurturing with word, musing, and metaphor to keep the fire a place of warmth and safety rather than danger and destruction. Peace to you, the fire tenders who show up in human form, books, nature, and the glorious Universe.

*Action Invitation*

 Take this time to light a candle or fireplace fire. Meditate on the beauty and wisdom of the flame. Notice the similarities and differences between your nature and the fire.

# DESERT AND DARKNESS

Is there a difference between being in desert times (the place associated with spiritual barrenness) and living in darkness? Both seem to include waiting. Are desert and darkness the same states of being? Is the difference between darkness and light defined simply by the attitude with which they are received? Where is light found during desolation? And, for what were the desert fathers and mothers searching? Were they barren and bereft of God's holy presence? Or were they closer to Spirit because of the barrenness?

Two books come to mind: Alan Jones's *Soul Making* and the devotional book *Streams in the Desert* by L. B. Cowman. Both of these are reminiscent of moving toward something. It may be painful in the midst of the experience, but the message is hope for something less painful—something more solid on which to stand. Does having hope mean we want to leave the desert or need to leave in order to find solace?

The seasons remind us that darkness ebbs and flows in our lives, just as days grow shorter toward winter solstice and then lengthen again when spring approaches. Darkness wraps around us like a cozy blanket and provides us with a time of rest and waiting. Thomas Moore in *Dark Nights of the Soul* says darkness is often associated with or labeled as depression. It is something we want to get out of or away from. I, however, have experienced profound times of solace in darkness that might have been missed had life been moving with ease and absolute comfort. After all, it's hard to see a twinkling star in the light of day.

So once again I return to the question: Are desert and darkness the same place? And, is it all about the attitude with which we view them? I do not believe either place to be void of God or Spirit even though at times we may feel bereft of a presence larger than ourselves. Maybe it all is about the attitude. Perhaps it's about unearthing our own rhythm in the darkness and finding our oasis in the desert. Maybe it's something I will ponder awhile longer.

*Active Meditation*

 Beginning with lights on, close your eyes and bring attention to the space at the bridge of your nose. Breathe into this area for a few moments. Next, either turn out the lights or cover your eyes with a blanket or towel. Continue breathing into the space at the bridge of your nose. Notice the qualities of moving from dark to light. Is one stance more comforting than the other? More distracting? Spend some time reflecting upon your attitude toward darkness and times of barrenness.

# THE RAINS CAME DOWN...

*...and the floods came up.*

One December night in 2007, I went to sleep with a breath prayer on my lips: "Breathe God in. Chaos goes out." It was a lovely way to drift into dreamland, and quite fortuitous since I knew things did not bode well when my husband woke me the next morning and said, "I could really use your help. There's water pouring into the basement."

Seattle was experiencing history-making rainfall—the second largest amount in any twenty-four-hour period ever. My family was quite fortunate compared to many throughout the city. Our basement (the largest livable square footage of our house) was soaked and all the furnishings had to be moved into the living and dining rooms. We spent more than twelve hours vacuuming and pumping water out of the house at the rate of about 120 gallons an hour. We were extremely grateful that the water came out of our house. Needless to say, it was quite a way to enter the holiday season.

My breath prayer seemed topsy-turvy as our living space turned chaotic. An interesting thing happened, however, because everyone I encountered the next day commented on my calm demeanor and positive attitude. The chaos had gone out even as the floods came up. It's amazing what a little breath can do.

*Active Meditation*

A breath prayer is a short sentence or two that can be said in one breath while breathing in and out. Close your eyes and focus on your inhale and exhale. Allow a prayer to arise on your breath. Consider carrying the words with you unceasingly throughout your day.

# A CHARLIE BROWN CHRISTMAS?

I can't seem to "do" Christmas anymore. The odd thing is that I love the holiday season and what it represents. I am not, however, excited about the commercial pressures and expectations of what the season "should" look like. Each year, I have felt myself pull away more from the hubbub and must do's of the season. I find myself enlivened by purchasing a modest unexpected gift rather than one given out of obligation. Or taking a walk in the winter rain and witnessing the world's splendor. Best of all, I love spending time with friends in intimate settings rather than attending obligatory holiday extravaganzas. Slowing down. Savoring the season instead of being consumed by it. Welcoming space to "do" it my way.

*Ponder and Apply*

What does savoring the season mean to you? Imagine it. Breathe it. Do it.

## DECEMBER 9

# SPOKEN WORDS.
# SEEN WORDS.

Several years ago, I encountered an Advent meditation written by the father of a deaf child. He was quite concerned that his daughter would never "hear" the Incarnational Christmas story in a language she could "understand." Because of this, he was worried she would miss the opportunity to embrace the "true light" offered. While I think I understand his compassion and desire for his daughter and other deaf children, I somehow felt this view dismissed the potential innate wisdom of his non-hearing child. Perhaps her other senses were more finely attuned to hear and know "true light" without the assistance of vocalized words.

Written and spoken language often gets top billing in the way we're supposed to learn. But what if we used all our senses to explore truth? Since that reading, I have been increasingly aware of the many ways I "hear." How about you? Do you believe you would know truth if you couldn't hear? Or read? Or smell? Or touch?

*Visualization and Action*

Consider which sense you rely upon most. For the next few moments take away that sense (i.e. cover your eyes, plug your ears, etc.) Now immerse yourself in knowing true light. Notice what you come to understand without your extra sense.

## December 10

# Vessels and Empty Space

H ave you ever taken the time to consider yourself as a vessel? If not, you might ponder what vessels or containers represent to you. Perhaps they demonstrate the mere act of holding, like a bowl. They can visually represent almost anything you can imagine. A womb. Cupped hands. A shell. A box. A gift. A decanter. The arms of God. Safety. Confinement. Crystal. Pottery. Earthenware.

Once you've named your vessel, ask yourself what you hold within in it. Is it overflowing? Does something need to be released? Is it noticeably empty? Now allow yourself to explore the connection between vessels and empty space. If you let go, will you feel empty, or will it allow more room for what needs to move in? Both? What if we as vessels, prepare the way for new adventures, life, experiences, and mystery by filling and emptying ourselves?

Ponder what it means to prepare the way for life. Smooth the vessel. Make room. Let go. What edges need to be sheared away? Rough places chipped off to make space for something new— forgiveness and holiness, grace and mercy. What if we are filled up only to be emptied again and again? Opening the door to our own dark places? Seeing the images that lie in shadow? What arises as you wait?

*Visualization and Meditation*

 Take a few moments to ponder the questions posed in today's meditation. Breathe deeply and allow yourself to be hollowed, filled, and emptied as you follow your breath. Feel your inward spaces being smoothed and becoming stronger with each inhale and exhale. Let all resistance fall away and listen for deeper grace.

# JOURNEY THROUGH THE NIGHT

Do you ever have those mornings when you wake up and feel like you have been on a prolonged journey throughout the night? One such morning, I realized I was lucid dreaming, so I lay quietly and tried to stay in the dream. It was neither a pleasant nor disturbing dream, but it was intriguing nonetheless.

In this exploration, I noticed my body felt like I had been on a long passage. There was a bus ride, a pick-up truck with its bed filled with loads of baggage, a parking lot with only handicapped spaces available. I pitched a tent next to the lot that was in a huge field of dry grass. My tent poles got twisted up and a depressed, sarcastic, and conflicted woman I know helped me realign the poles. There were two additional tents in the field, but no other occupants.

After pitching the tent, I rode along in my VW convertible, going through the fields of dry grass. I stood and tried to climb through the car while attached at the ankles to my husband. No one seemed to be driving the car.

There were lots of other unusual images and symbols throughout the dream. Most noticeable was a distinct feeling of being on a very long, foggy journey. Therefore, it was no surprise when I looked out my window this particular morning to see the neighborhood blanketed in white mist. Perhaps I was still dreaming?

*Action Invitation*

Keep an open journal next to your bed with a pen and small flashlight. When you awaken from a dream, jot down everything you can remember. In the light of day, spend some time exploring what you think each character and/or symbol may represent for you in your current life.

# JUDGMENT AND OBSERVATION

Have you ever found yourself wondering about the difference between judgment and observation? Can the two be separated? It is something to consider, both in terms of how we behave and how we respond when someone comments on our behavior.

In my lifetime, I've encountered people who begin many statements with, "I'm just making an observation. There's no judgment involved." While this can be true, the situation often crosses into judgment territory rapidly when a character assessment is included and there is no curiosity about the motivation behind the behavior.

Have you ever witnessed a driver wave a rude gesture at another person and thought to yourself, "How rude?" Judgment or observation? The gesture, I believe, is indeed rude. The driver? Having no idea what the motivation is behind the action, I cannot accurately assess the offender's character. Maybe, he's a real hothead or perhaps she just found out some bad news and needs to place the frustration somewhere.

So, what do you think? Is there a difference between judgment and observation? Do you hide your judgments behind words of observation? Would it make a difference in your world if you had curiosity about others' motivations?

*Pondering*

Consider a recent situation where you made a snap character assessment. Perhaps a grocery clerk was rude and you, therefore, deemed her unkind. Would it make a difference to know the clerk's grandmother had just died and she couldn't leave work because she's the sole supporter of her family? What if you were curious before making your judgment? Would it make a difference?

## DECEMBER 13

# FEAST DAY OF ST. LUCIA

Today is the feast day of my favorite saint, St. Lucia, or as I affectionately call her, St. Lucy—patron saint of blindness. Lucy means "light" and comes from the same Latin root as "lucid," which translates as "clear, radiant, and understandable." Stories declare Lucia consecrated her virginity to God and refused to marry a pagan suitor. Lucy was martyred, but when she miraculously could not be burned, her eyes were gouged out. Some renditions proclaim her executioners took them. Other tales say they were removed by her scorned would-be husband. In one version, Lucy was said to have torn her eyes out herself and handed them to her suitor who had denounced her as a Christian.

Regardless of the method of loss, Lucy wondrously was still able to see even without her eyes. While the stories announce this as miraculous, I wonder. Do we not all have this "miraculous" ability—to see without eyes, to hear without ears, to feel without touch? Is this not the handiwork of an extraordinary Creator? One who provides multiple pathways to unfolding, seeing, knowing, hearing, and seeking truth?

Let us join in the celebration of St. Lucia and the gift of sight.

*Active Meditation*

Today's invitation is to meditate on the gifts of light and vision. Begin by closing your eyes and then covering them with your hands or a blindfold. Notice what you can "see" from this vantage point. Remove your hands (while keeping your eyes closed) and observe the change in light quality. As you open your eyes, offer gratitude for sight and light.

# WIDE OPEN SPACE

Do you ever find yourself with so much wide-open space you don't know what to do? It's commonplace with over-commitments to become overwhelmed and paralyzed. But how ironic is the notion that not having anything scheduled can be as much of a distraction as having too much? When I have a full schedule, I crave free time and then—with wide-open days before me—I often search for structure. Author Julia Cameron says that artists actually need structure, and many times must devise it for themselves by creating schedules in lives that become too wide open to be productive.

In our overcommitted and super achieving culture, many of us consider ourselves worth less if we don't have a calendar filled with names and activities. A shift in this type thinking that works for me is to make a schedule out of the gift of solitude. I can relish the quiet. Choose my own music. Dance throughout the house or make mud pies. Anything goes because I have been given the gift of time. I get to decide what comes next without allowing others to dictate my way. Even the tiniest bit of movement (like shifting a thought) can add momentum to a stuck place. Taking the first step is the beginning of each amazing journey.

*Action Invitation*

Imagine you have all the time in the world before you. What would be your first small step? Can you do it now? If not, keep imagining steps until you land on the one you can do right now. Begin.

## December 15

## Shadows

By virtue of our existence in the form of matter, we have the potential to cast a shadow. This can be energetic, physical, or conceptual. Regardless, shadows exist in balance with light. Why is it, then, that humans choose to either avoid the shadow side or obsess as though we hold no goodness? It's easy to see the shadow and light in others, but in ourselves we often turn the other way.

We consider anger and grief unacceptable emotions and try to keep them stuffed in the shadows hoping they'll go away—a hope that often goes unanswered. My personal story conveys how my greatest joys have miraculously manifested through experiencing unfathomable pain. Onlookers have been shocked to see me laughing when my life "should" be solemn. Others quickly try to cheer me up and wipe away the necessary grief.

I don't know about you, but I need to be able to vent when I'm sad or angry and dance or play when I'm joyous without having to keep my feelings in the shadows. Emotions produce healing and wholeness from both sides. I don't believe that makes one better than the other. They're simply different, just as shadow complements light and vice versa.

*Visualization*

Look at your surroundings and bring your awareness to the interplay of shadow and light. Imagine how things would change with the absence of one or the other.

## DECEMBER 16

# WITHOUT WRITING

Without writing, it would be so easy to tell and retell the same old stories. To sit in a stagnant place and refuse to move. Without story, I would still believe I was alone. I would believe my parents didn't love me, instead of knowing they were broken just like me. Without writing, I would not know God as I do now. Without writing, I couldn't and wouldn't see the words sing on the page. I wouldn't know the depth of beauty and the power of silence. Without writing, I could not expand on the pages and into the world. Without writing, I just might die.

Little pieces of me drift away or chip off on the days I fail to put pen to paper. I must write from the desert places and the mountaintops—the times of sadness as well as the moments of joy. Miracles. Prophecies. Hurts and wonders. I've privately penned harsh words about others and myself only to continue writing and circle back to the center where we all meet and stand alone as unique and individual. Telling and retelling the stories brings us together. We can do it through written word, oral tradition, song, dance, music, art.

At the core, we are our stories. To write is to tell my story. It's what I do. It's who I am. How about you?

*Artistic Meditation*

 Set aside ten minutes in your day. Select your favorite medium of expression (writing, listening to music, art, cooking, etc.) Using this expression, focus on the center where we all meet—that place where we stand united, as unique and individual. Tell this story.

## December 17

# Wordless Sounds and Sighs

The theme of waiting often follows me into the busiest times of my life. When I have the least amount of time to slow down, I am reminded of the stillness and beauty that surrounds me everywhere if I allow myself to be present and listen.

Finding peace and serenity in unexpected places is almost as if God is stalking me. When I let go of expectations and wait without agenda, Spirit speaks for me in ways I cannot fathom. The whisper of trees. The joy of art's creation. Birds flying. Eagles soaring. A dog's warm nuzzle. Home's comfort. Words from out of nowhere.

Living an openhearted life leaves us vulnerable to synchronicities or what Carl Jung called meaningful coincidences. One such "coincidence" happened when the following Bible verse showed up not once or twice, but three times from three different sources in the matter of a few days. I think it says it all.

"The Spirit also helps us in our own weakness. For when we do not know what to say in prayer, the Spirit expresses what we mean in wordless sounds and sighs." Romans 8:26

*Meditation*

 Breathe deeply into your heart center while opening arms wide. Release all expectations and welcome the wordless sounds and sighs. Be open to synchronicity in the coming days.

# LAUGHTER. TEARS. HOPE. MAGIC.

Sometimes I cry for no reason at all. The same thing happens with laughter. I get caught up in the joy and simplicity of living this thing called life—the pathway that has all become one journey. It's hard to disentangle the inner world from the outer or the mundane from miracles. The lines of my story aren't straight like precise rows of wheat. They curve like a drunken toddler aiming her scooter toward a swimming pool. We know someone will get wet, but will they drown or giggle? The metaphors pour out of me like rain gushing inside a hurricane, but I need more than metaphor and simile. It can be exhausting, this making meaning out of everything, and so I turn to a few of my favorite things: hope and magic, laughter and tears.

To stir up hope and magic, let everything else go and allow yourself to laugh or cry from deep inside your belly. Welcome the kind of laughter or gut-wrenching tears that happens with safe and trusted friends. Sometimes these friends are the unseen kind, like ancestors who we only know through faded photographs. Or those whose names we hear whispered in the night just below our consciousness. Somehow I know they're near, and when I'm open to them, my emotions summon these ethereal friends like wind chimes blowing in a fairytale forest. Laughter is magic. It calls up ship captains from across the Scandinavian sea and dairy farmers from Irish pastures, dancing French girls, drumming Cherokee chieftains.

Laughter is contagious. It resonates through centuries, bringing all of time into one infinitesimal moment. Tears do the same thing when we allow them to flow unabashedly. Sometimes laughter turns to tears and other times, tears turn into laughter. The two play back and forth in a watery dance. It's all about releasing their potency.

*Active Meditation*

Stretch yourself today and practice laughing. Begin by saying *ha ha ha ha* out loud. Continue for at least one minute. Set a timer if necessary. It will likely feel awkward, but I invite you to try it. Observe with your non-judgmental witness.

# YES OR NO

Sacrifice becomes your unfulfilled religion. Caught between the place of yes and no. Hearing words like "Nice people don't quit" or "It's selfish to do what I really want." How often do we see yes as a way to be revered and admired? We convince ourselves others won't love us if we say no. Little by little, we shave off bits of ourselves until we are whittled down to a distorted vision of love and care. Our yes has become empty and so have we.

You see it happen in caregivers and martyrs who give and give until sacrifice becomes their religion and resentment sets in. We think by adding one more project, one more empty yes, we will feel better and receive more love. We give our hearts until there is no more to give. Our lights are hidden under a bushel where brilliance begins to fade. We forget light needs air to breathe.

*Body Practice*

 Focus on a place where you are saying yes when your heart longs to say no. With a deep inhale, pull the empty yes into your body and hold it there as long as you can while keeping in mind this feeling of burden. As you release your breath, allow your lungs to fill and imagine blood flowing freely through your body. Notice the difference. Repeat one or two times, feeling the contraction of a burdened no and the expansion of a live-giving yes.

## DECEMBER 20

# YIELD TO SIMPLICITY

The word simplicity speaks to me during this season. I believe simplicity draws us closer to our God center. Simplicity and humility. Not pomp and circumstance. God is not interested in a popularity contest. God does not need everyone to acknowledge Her or cheer Him on. Jesus did things in obscurity and subtlety, often striving to remove himself from the crowds and seeking quiet time with God.

The world seems to think that in order to be successful, everything must be bigger and better. Giant churches. Huge projects. Bestselling books. The list goes on. What is big enough? What would it look like to reach people simply—one by one? Heart by heart? Quietly and subtly coming alongside and joining fellow sojourners as they come to know God and themselves in big, quiet ways?

*Pondering*

What might it look like for you to yield to simplicity?

# BELLY OF THE WHALE

"When you are in the belly of the whale, let go, detach yourself, let the pain carry you where it needs to take you, don't resist, rather weep, wail, cry and put your mouth to the dust, and wait."

*Ron Rolheiser*

Inside the belly of the whale, it is dark. Today is winter solstice, the shortest day of the year in the Northern Hemisphere. For a season, this season, I am called to let the tears wash over me, to wail, to cry out and let the pain envelope and comfort me. Happiness will not suffice for now. Joy seems distant. Sorrow, its mirror image, hangs closely 'round my heart and soul.

I must learn a new way to comfort myself, and the way does not involve putting on a smile and taking care of everyone around me. How can I suffer, exist, and live in the dark night of the soul, when all around me are hollow words of "Merry Christmas" and "Happy Holidays?" "Cheer up," well-meaning friends say. "Get over it," I tell myself. Easy to say, but I don't even know what "it" is. I see fear in the eyes of my loved ones. They worry that I am not happy. "You're not yourself these days," they say. "I hope you come back soon." But I have not gone anywhere. This is me—all I am able to offer, right here and right now. Maybe it is not all of me, for it is more of the sorrowful side—some would say the dark side. And, just as I have been known to burst with joy, for now I am bursting with sorrow. I am learning that both are essential for the fullness I desire.

Give your burdens to the earth—the strength of the mountains, the vastness of the sea, the Great Unknown. Only these can carry the weight of my burdens. I am called to lay face down on the ground as the Muslims do, connecting my head with the earth. Feeling the solidity beneath me. It is holy ground.

Belly of the whale. It is dark inside here and even as I release myself to the darkness, I begin to feel lighter. A twinkling light. There must be great darkness for the tiniest light to shine. Wait. Just wait. It is the reminder I have heard throughout this Advent season. Wait.

*Visualization and Action*

Imagine for a moment the darkness inside the belly of a whale. Does panic arise or can you calm yourself? What tactics do you employ when darkness prevails? Notice your body's response to the word "wait."

# December 22

# Unfolding

Unfolding. Seeing. Knowing. Hearing. Seeking. Pursuing story. Questing for truth. Longing for connection to our inner soul. Where does it start? How do we begin?

Outside my window, Mt. Rainier stands grand and majestic as I pause to wonder, where did it begin? What is the depth of that resplendent giant? How high is the summit's peak? How many pilgrims have climbed its path? I wonder about our souls. Does the great mountain speak for you and me—growing and expanding—some days hiding behind the clouds, other days pure and visible for all to witness? Always there, yet at times forgotten.

*Artistic Meditation*

 Use a napkin or piece of paper and draw an image in the center. Fold the napkin in half and continue until you can fold no longer. Spend a moment looking at the napkin and consider the number of ways you could find the center (tearing, cutting, unfolding). Slowly unwrap the folds, imagining each turn as new awareness toward what is always there, yet not continuously seen. Watch the napkin grow and expand as you move toward the center. Consider what this might represent in your own life.

# WHO KNOWS YOU BEST?

I wonder if people I've just met sometimes "know" me better than those I've been around a long time. This thought entered my mind upon returning from a weeklong sojourn in the heart of Texas. My main intent for the trip was to attend a spiritual directors' conference. Along the way, I added time to spend with a range of family and friends, including those who have known me my whole life, a college roommate, and friends I met more than twenty years ago.

The week was filled with wonderful conversations and reminiscences. The most memorable experience, however, occurred with a woman I met at the conference, spent no more than two hours with, and likely will not encounter again in this life. We shared one of those moments where I absolutely knew without a shadow of a doubt that I had looked into another's soul and she into mine. Words cannot adequately describe, but my life was indelibly marked by that encounter.

This intimate meeting left me knowing there is a Presence greater than I—One who delivers surprises when we least expect. I also wonder about the loneliness that can be felt when those who are supposed to "know" us seem to not really see. I ponder how I might, too, be blind.

*Journal Meditation*

Make a list of the people you've interacted with over the past few days. Without judgment, rate each experience between 1 and 5 (one being least meaningful). Spend a few moments being curious and consider what, if anything, you might change.

# REACHING FOR SOLITUDE

Garbage trucks rumbling. Therapy fan humming. Utensils clinking. Sigor Rós strumming. Where is the quiet? I'm starting the day at a run. Restless nights. Tylenol PM offering me sleep and then carrying me into mid-morning. Phone ringing. Husband puttering. Cleaning people coming. I need to go. Bath running. Meeting waiting. Candle burning. Solitude calling.

This is not how I want to begin a day . . . or end a year. But this is what I have. This moment right now. Music climaxing. Gentle now. God is here. Here with me in my little corner. My old blue chair. Breathe. Have this moment. Carry it into the day. Be still and know that I am God. Ahhh. Awe. Beautiful. Blessed.

It only takes a moment to breathe. To be quiet. To be still. My bath beckons. The day awaits. Christmas will be here soon.

*Meditation*

Whether you feel rushed or content in this moment, I invite you to simply breathe deeply. Offer this moment to stillness and the day that lies ahead.

## December 25

# A Mother's Offering

Today I release you into the world.

May you find peace, joy, and comfort in the life that lies ahead.

May stillness be your friend and happiness your constant companion.

May you always know you are loved and cared for by me, by others, and by the Universe.

May you learn to love yourself deeply and know that as you follow your heart, truth and love will guide your path.

May fear steer you forward and never hold you back.

May you be safe and steady, knowing what it means to feel the ground solidly beneath your feet and the heavens high over your head.

May you know you are a gift to the world, unimaginable and indescribable.

May you know peace and contentment all the days of your life.

*Meditation*

Allow yourself to pause in peace this day.

# DID YOU CELEBRATE WELL?

December 25 has come and gone, and today I sit pondering . . . what is this thing called Christmas and can we celebrate it well? The world tells us we are to be filled with joy, wonder, and goodwill toward humankind. Christians are called to celebrate the birth of a Savior, One who for many has been lost amidst shopping bags and eggnog.

We seek impossible perfection during the holidays. We say, put on a happy face. Go to church. Celebrate—even if it hurts. So, I ask again . . . what is this thing called Christmas and can we celebrate it well? Those with families often find Christmas to be fabulously messy with tears and gales of laughter. And those without families experience their own messiness. Regardless, emotions run high and meltdowns abound. I have found, however, when we risk opening our hearts to the mess of life, we see and know we're all human and understand that no one is exempt from life's hard times.

Christmas Eve found me oohing and ahhhing over the sweetness of a Christmas pageant, and moments later gulping for air through sobbing tears because it was too much to bear. Then almost as quickly, I was bursting with gratitude and joy for the gathering around my table. My heart was filled to the brim and broken wide open all at the same time.

Obviously, Christmas has the capacity to bring up *lots* of emotions. It is a great metaphor for life. The mess and the beauty. I love it and I hate it. I overflow with joy one moment and I burst into tears the next. Bottom line—Christmas is hard and Christmas is wonderful. I think I feel every emotion possible during this season. It's no wonder I can come away feeling exhausted and a bit weepy with no solid answer to my own question . . . what is this thing called Christmas and can we celebrate it well?

*Ponder and Apply*

Pause and ponder how you celebrate anything well. Do you cry until you laugh? Laugh until you cry? Dance, sing, or sit in silence? Close your eyes and remember the great celebrations of your life.

# MUSINGS ON A WINTER DAY

A white cloak of peace and contentment has settled over my neighborhood as I sit snuggled inside my cozy house. Looking out the window at snow-covered branches, I think of the new birth that awaits within—the bud of spring wrapped inside thick branches. How does new life form? I ask the same of myself.

I wonder about birth—about resurrection. What of the centuries of civilizations and ancient myths that are wrapped around life . . . death . . . rebirth? What of the winter of our souls? Wrapped in darkness and often cold? How many will not make it to spring? Brittle branches that will break off in the storm of life never to sprout fresh again?

Today, I sit wrapped in winter. It is dark and white. It brings me warmth with lit candles and the coziness of handmade quilts. Today I think of Mary, mother of Jesus, saying yes to God. I am reminded of my own moments with God-radiance when I have said yes, overpowered by the brilliance of the Universe, like the winter landscape wrapped in effervescent splendor. My heart longs for luminosity and new birth and my heart is content. Today I am grateful to be alive with awareness of each moment—each season of life.

*Action Invitation*

 Find a warm, cozy blanket and wrap yourself up snuggly. Consider this season of your life. Do peace and contentment envelop you? Or are you harried and worn out, waiting for the season to come to an end? Let the warmth of the blanket be a cloak of peace and contentment. Express gratitude for these moments of the day.

## December 28

# Four Calling Birds

In the Pacific Northwest, a rare blanket of snow covered our city one winter week. It proved to be a beautiful and wonderful gift as it allowed for much needed slowing down. A peacefulness settled over my soul, and now, even though the snow has melted, I am allowing the quiet to continue to envelop me as I luxuriate in the blessings of the twelve days of Christmas which fall between December 25 and January 6. This is a new experience for me to not sit down on December 26, collapse with exhaustion and say, "Phew! I'm so glad Christmas is over!" I still feel in the thick of it, so to speak, and have truly relished the whole season, mainly by keeping it incredibly simple.

Today, this fourth day of Christmas, my mind goes to the traditional song and I think of the four calling birds that were gifted on this day. During my quiet time, I began to synthesize some of the bubblings of the last days, weeks, and months in anticipation of what I see ahead in the New Year. The "calling birds" seem to be speaking of new horizons for the coming year. They are whispering for me to develop my own unique way of being in the world through the gifts I have gathered along the way. They are gifts only I can offer in my special way, just as your uniqueness sings its own song.

*Visualization and Meditation*

Gently close your eyes and imagine a landscape covered with pure white snow. Allow yourself to drift into the silence of this beauty. Breathe deeply as you gently begin to focus on the gifts you bring to the world. Listen closely. What are the "birds" that may be calling to you as we enter a new year?

# MIRACLE? YES, PLEASE.

I read a story about miracles one day and was so touched that I sat alone in my car and cried. Later when I tried to remember the specifics of the story, my mind went blank. It's almost like the miracle disappeared.

Maybe that's what miracles are—small moments that reach out through the unexpected ordinary in our day. They grab us and squeeze so tightly that tears stream down our cheeks and we can't say why or how, but we know we've been moved and changed.

The only miracles I heard about while growing up were humongous heroic gestures like David slaying the giant and Moses parting the Red Sea. Miracles were the unattainable stuff of storybooks. Today, I think they may be something different, a quality attainable and available in any given moment.

What if a miracle meant simply changing your attitude about something you thought you'd be stuck with forever? What if it meant opening your eyes to what's right in front of you? What if you saw miracles in sunbeams and freckles? In squirrels and eagles? In here and now? In this past year and next?

*Visualization and Meditation*

 Sit quietly and follow your breath. Softly hold an intention of noticing what miracles look like to you. Allow those impressions to float through your mind on the whisper of your inhale and exhale.

## December 30

## Tides

Events rise and fall in our lives like the tide flowing in and out from the shore. While the experience may be far from us in linear time, the moments are there like droplets absorbed in the sand. Ritual and recollection allow me to wrap these tender memories inside my heart. How shall I remember? What will I name and receive from the time?

Faces. Applause. Asking for what I want—honoring and receiving it. The beauty of newfound friends. Complexity and simplicity. Uniqueness and disparity. Setting aside time to be filled and emptied again and again. Laughter and loneliness. Confirmation and serendipity. Mountain peak and murky pond. Presence to now. Fluid and free. Listening moment by moment. Honoring. Loving.

Living. Lusciousness. Dancing in the morning. Composing in the afternoon. Strolling under the starlit sky. Universe responding without pause, like the tide flowing in and out from the shore.

*Journal Meditation*

As the year draws to a close, make a list of remembrance from the past twelve months.? What would be best left behind? Write these on another list, then dispose of them with your own ritual. What do you choose to carry forward? Set an intention to take these into the new year.

## December 31

# Diamonds in the Sky

Our lives are filled with indescribable beauty, joy, and sorrow. I cherish fresh and weathered faces in the heartache of my day. The memory of jubilant voices lifted in song carries me to the sky, mixed tears and laughter filling me with love.

The chains of sadness have broken and no longer ensnare me. Their hold is like pesky yarn that occasionally entangles me. The fear of darkness has faded and the light is glorious. I see a new glow reflecting on the water and gleaming upon the sand. The waves of life continue to ebb and flow as our lives sparkle on the surface like diamonds.

We are forever entwined, indivisible as drops of water filling the ocean.
Where does one life begin and another end?
They cannot be separated. I am in you and you in me. Our tears may fill the ocean, but our joy will lift the sails of a million parachutes.

Let us remember we can fly and we need not—must not—drown in sorrow.
Sorrow is sweet because it reminds us from where we have come. Let it remain sweet and not turn bitter.
Let us drink pure fresh water each day all the while knowing . . . the bile may rise again in our throats and need to be expelled from our bodies.

We have come full circle . . . experienced the richness of life.
Let us live life to the fullest, never being afraid to take risks or
embrace sorrow.
Without the depths of sorrow, we can never experience the height
of joy. We cannot soar like eagles.
There is no chance to defy gravity if we remain inert on the
ground.

Life is a trajectory—it must be—otherwise we slowly, sadly melt
into the landscape and disappear.
Our beauty goes unnoticed when we live in fear. Therefore,
embrace sorrow and joy.
Let the emotions have their way and,
Together, let us sparkle like diamonds in the sky.

*Poetry Ponder*
> What are your diamonds in the sky?

# WITH GRATITUDE...

The list of gratitude and acknowledgements reads like an epic journey for my soul. If every story has a beginning, middle and end, then I choose to begin this one with gratitude and love for my immediate family—Bill, who faithfully supports me in following my heart's desires; Jonathon with his giant two-by-four of awakening; and Maryjane with her mercurial mirror and wise ways.

In the middle of this journey lay the countless mentors I've encountered along the way—friends, foes, family, clients, students, strangers, and teachers from every realm. They have seeded the fruits of this dream and made its pages come alive.

And at the end are those who nudged and pushed me through the final stages of manifestation. They held my hand, proofread and designed, supported and encouraged—like tender midwives assisting the birth of a precious child.

Everyone showed up at exactly the right moment for his or her perfect role. My gratitude is immense. My memory, somewhat faulty. Therefore, I've chosen not to be overly specific, lest I omit anyone at press time. If you are reading this: Thank you.

Please take a moment right now to pause and breathe deeply. Allow the depth of my gratitude to wash over you like fresh rain in a parched land. May each drop enliven you and touch your heart deeply—today and always.

My heart is filled with joy and my cup runneth over. I choose to give away me every day. I am eternally grateful for everyone's sharing in this gift. Namaste.

**Kayce Stevens Hughlett** is a tender, a healer, and an artist of being alive who believes in everyday magic and that complex issues often call for simple practices. She holds a master's in counseling psychology from the Seattle School of Theology and Psychology and she is a certified Martha Beck Life Coach.

Her 2019 memoir, *SoulStroller: experiencing the weight, whispers, & wings of the world* won the prestigious Nautilus Book award and Chanticleer's Journey award. Her 2015 novel *Blue* won the CIBA Somerset Award for best women's fiction. She is co-creator of SoulStrolling® ~ a movement for mindfulness in motion, and creator of the magical SoulStrolling Inspiration Deck. Raised in the heartland of Oklahoma, she now resides in Seattle, Washington with her family and muse, Aslan the Cat. More at **www.kaycehughlett.com**.

# OTHER BOOKS BY
# KAYCE STEVENS HUGHLETT

*Blue, a novel*

One insecure perfectionist. One guilt-ridden artist. One child-woman who talks to peacocks. A trio of complex heroines on separate journeys toward a single intertwined truth.

A subtle psychological mind-bender where each heroine is her own worst enemy. Eccentric. Lovable. Unforgettable.

*SoulStroller:*
*experiencing the weight, whispers, & wings of the world*

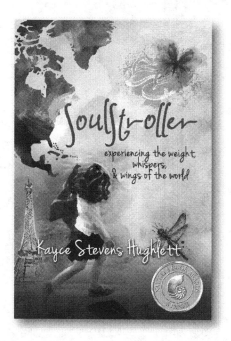

Seductive, sincere, and at times hysterical and heartbreaking, this memoir follows author and good girl, Kayce Stevens Hughlett out of her carefully constructed comfort zone into the world of international travel, healers, wise winged mentors, and inspiring versions of humankind.

Labeled shy and rendered virtually silent by age six, Kayce had been raised to fit the role of perfect wife, doting mom, and accomplished woman. She fulfilled her mission by her mid-forties when society said she had it all. Society was wrong. When her eldest child disappears into the haze of addiction, her perfect world changes faster than you can say, Get it right!

Ethereal, gritty, and relatable, *SoulStroller* is the evolution of a woman too timid to speak her mind into someone who writes her own rules and redefines what it means to live with silence, compassion, and joie de vivre.